Chicago
day BY day™

2nd Edition

By Laura Tiebert

WILEY
Wiley Publishing, Inc.

Contents

Published by:

Wiley Publishing, Inc.

111 River St.
Hoboken, NJ 07030-5774

ISBN 978-0-470-42208-3
Editor: Anuja Madar
Production Editor: Jonathan Scott
Photo Editor: Richard Fox
Cartographer: Roberta Stockwell
Production by Wiley Indianapolis Composition Services

For information on our other products and services or to obtain technical support, please contact our Customer Care Department within the U.S. at 800/762-2974, outside the U.S. at 317/572-3993 or fax 317/572-4002.

Wiley also publishes its books in a variety of electronic formats. Some content that appears in print may not be available in electronic formats.

Manufactured in China

5   4   3   2   1

A Note from the Editorial Director

Organizing your time. That's what this guide is all about.

Other guides give you long lists of things to see and do and then expect you to fit the pieces together. The Day by Day guides are different. These guides tell you the best of everything, and then they show you how to see it *in the smartest, most time-efficient way*. Our authors have designed detailed itineraries organized by time, neighborhood, or special interest. And each tour comes with a bulleted map that takes you from stop to stop.

Hoping to see the magnificent architecture of the Windy City, or to tour the highlights of the Museum of Science and Industry? Planning a walk through the Gold Coast, or a whirlwind tour of the very best that Chicago has to offer? Whatever your interest or schedule, the Day by Days give you the smartest routes to follow. Not only do we take you to the top attractions, hotels, and restaurants, but we also help you access those special moments that locals get to experience—those "finds" that turn tourists into travelers.

The Day by Days are also your top choice if you're looking for one complete guide for all your travel needs. The best hotels and restaurants for every budget, the greatest shopping values, the wildest nightlife—it's all here.

Why should you trust our judgment? Because our authors personally visit each place they write about. They say what they think and would never include places they wouldn't recommend to their best friends. They're also open to suggestions from readers. If you'd like to contact them, please send your comments our way at feedback@frommers.com, and we'll pass them on.

Enjoy your Day by Day guide—the most helpful travel companion you can buy. And have the trip of a lifetime.

Warm regards,

Kelly Regan

Kelly Regan
Editorial Director
Frommer's Travel Guides

About the Author

Laura Tiebert is a freelance writer whose travels have taken her from the frozen tundra of Dawson City in Yukon Territory to the wide sand beaches of Muscat, Oman. Today, she stays a bit closer to home in Wilmette, Illinois, where she lives with her husband and two sons. She is the author of *Frommer's Chicago with Kids* and *Chicago For Dummies*.

Acknowledgments

This book is better because of the insightful editing of Anuja Madar and Naomi Kraus. Thank you!

An Additional Note

Please be advised that travel information is subject to change at any time—and this is especially true of prices. We therefore suggest that you write or call ahead for confirmation when making your travel plans. The authors, editors, and publisher cannot be held responsible for the experiences of readers while traveling. Your safety is important to us, however, so we encourage you to stay alert and be aware of your surroundings.

Star Ratings, Icons & Abbreviations

Every hotel, restaurant, and attraction listing in this guide has been ranked for quality, value, service, amenities, and special features using a **star-rating system**. Hotels, restaurants, attractions, shopping, and nightlife are rated on a scale of zero stars (recommended) to three stars (exceptional). In addition to the star-rating system, we also use a **kids icon** to point out the best bets for families. Within each tour, we recommend cafes, bars, or restaurants where you can take a break. Each of these stops appears in a shaded box marked with a coffee-cup-shaped bullet ☕.

The following **abbreviations** are used for credit cards:

AE	American Express	DISC	Discover	V	Visa
DC	Diners Club	MC	MasterCard		

Frommers.com

Now that you have this guidebook to help you plan a great trip, visit our web-site at **www.frommers.com** for additional travel information on more than 4,000 destinations. We update features regularly to give you instant access to the most current trip-planning information available. At Frommers.com, you'll find scoops on the best airfares, lodging rates, and car rental bargains. You can even book your travel online through our reliable travel booking partners. Other popular features include:

A Note on Prices

In the "Take a Break" and "Best Bets" sections of this book, we have used a system of dollar signs to show a range of costs for 1 night in a hotel (the price of a double-occupancy room) or the cost of an entree at a restaurant. Use the following table to decipher the dollar signs:

Cost	Hotels	Restaurants
$	under $125	under $15
$$	$125–$300	$15–$30
$$$	$300–$450	$30–$45
$$$$	$450–$600	$45–$60
$$$$$	over $600	over $60

An Invitation to the Reader

In researching this book, we discovered many wonderful places—hotels, restaurants, shops, and more. We're sure you'll find others. Please tell us about them, so we can share the information with your fellow travelers in upcoming editions. If you were disappointed with a recommendation, we'd love to know that, too. Please write to:

Frommer's Chicago Day by Day, 2nd Edition
Wiley Publishing, Inc. • 111 River St. • Hoboken, NJ 07030-5774

16 Favorite
Moments

16 Favorite Moments

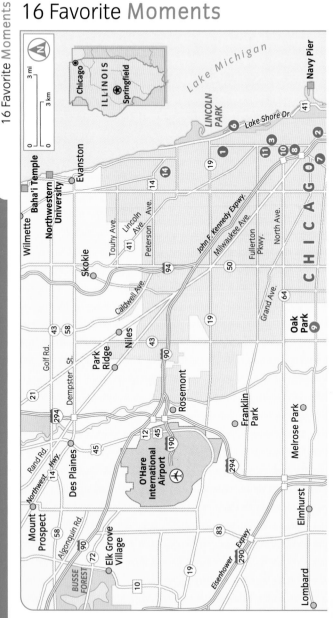

Previous page: The Chicago skyline.

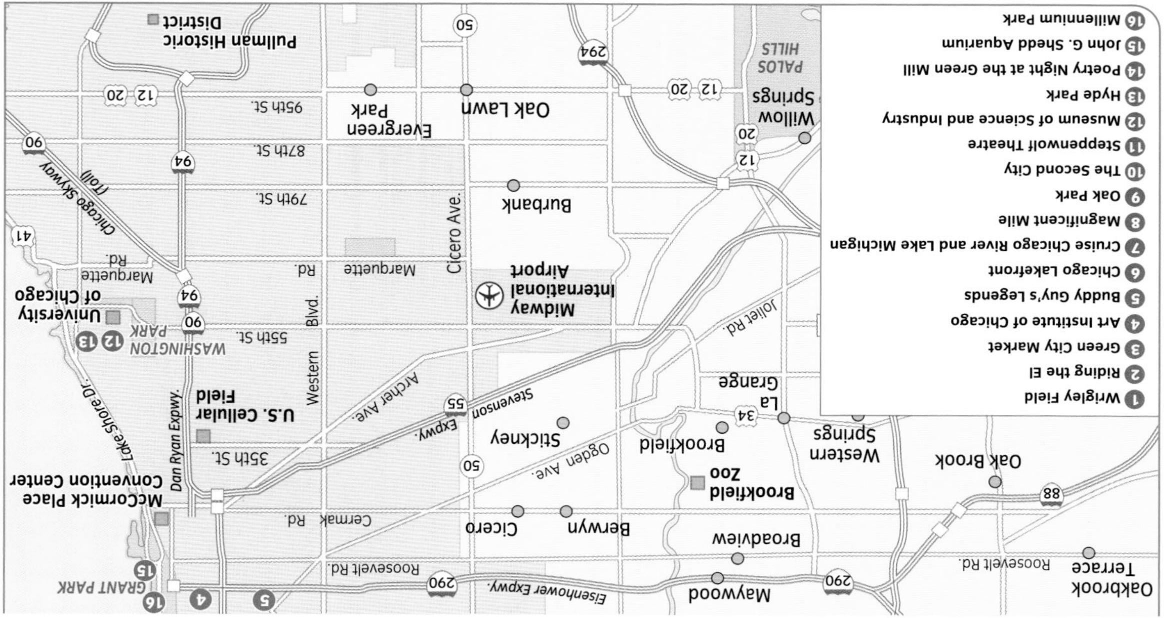
1 Wrigley Field
2 Riding the El
3 Green City Market
4 Art Institute of Chicago
5 Buddy Guy's Legends
6 Chicago Lakefront
7 Cruise Chicago River and Lake Michigan
8 Magnificent Mile
9 Oak Park
10 The Second City
11 Steppenwolf Theatre
12 Museum of Science and Industry
13 Hyde Park
14 Poetry Night at the Green Mill
15 John G. Shedd Aquarium
16 Millennium Park
GRANT PARK
McCormick Place Convention Center
Lake Shore Dr.
WASHINGTON PARK
University of Chicago
Marquette Rd.
Chicago Skyway (Toll)
Dan Ryan Expwy.
U.S. Cellular Field
35th St.
55th St.
79th St.
87th St.
95th St.
Pullman Historic District
Western Blvd.
Cermak Rd.
Roosevelt Rd.
Archer Ave.
Marquette Rd.
Evergreen Park
Cicero Ave.
Stevenson Expwy.
Eisenhower Expwy.
Cicero
Berwyn
Stickney
Ogden Ave.
Midway International Airport
Burbank
Oak Lawn
Maywood
Broadview
Brookfield Zoo
Brookfield
La Grange
Joliet Rd.
Willow Springs
PALOS HILLS
Western Springs
Oak Brook
Oakbrook Terrace
Roosevelt Rd.
290
88
50
55
34
12
20
294
90
94
41

Frank Sinatra once proclaimed Chicago his kind of town. It's mine, as well. Awaiting you in the Windy City are new discoveries and favorite places you'll want to visit again and again, from riding the "El" to singing along with the crowds at Wrigley Field's seventh-inning stretch. In this section, I describe some quintessential Chicago experiences that just might become part of your family's vacation lore. They may make Chicago your kind of town, too.

1 Take yourself out to the ball-game at Wrigley Field. Our historic ballpark approaches perfection with its ivy-covered walls, hand-operated scoreboard, and view of the jade-colored, glassy waters of Lake Michigan from the upper decks. Now that lights have been installed, the Cubs play night games, but Wrigley is still best experienced on a summer afternoon, when you'll be surrounded by plenty of natives playing hooky from work—a Windy City tradition. *See p 17,* ⑬

Historic Wrigley Field, home of the Chicago Cubs and the best seventh-inning stretch in baseball.

2 Take a ride on our famous "El" train. Our elevated train is not only the least expensive ride in town, it's an experience that can be had only in Chicago. For the best views, board the Brown Line at Washington/Wells, and ride it around the Loop through the canyons of office buildings (you'll be close enough to peer into some of them). It'll take less than 30 minutes of your touring time, and kids love it. *See p 9,* ①

3 Sample the Midwest's best farm-grown foods at the Chicago Green City Market. Founded by prominent Chicago chefs, this Lincoln Park market allows regular folks to buy the same organic and sustainably grown foods that will appear on plates in the best restaurants in town. There's music, live cooking demonstrations, and a chance to sample French-style crepes made to order with market ingredients. *See p 17,* ⑩

4 Marvel at the intricate pointillism of Seurat's *A Sunday on La Grande Jatte* and other masterpieces at Chicago's grande dame of museums, the Art Institute. You'll find Seurat's work in the renowned Impressionist collection, which also features one of the world's largest collections of Monet paintings. Your second stop should be the collections of European and American contemporary art, home to works by Picasso, Matisse, Dalí, Pollock, and Warhol. *See p 38.*

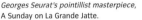

Georges Seurat's pointillist masterpiece, A Sunday on La Grande Jatte.

5 **Get the blues at one of the city's many great music joints.** At B.L.U.E.S., stellar female performers are the draw. At Buddy Guy's Legends, the Louisiana-style soul food and barbecue makes it worth arriving early and settling in for the evening. If you visit Chicago in January, don't miss out on a performance by the legendary guitarist who owns this place; but book ahead— the shows sell out well in advance. *See p 116.*

6 **Stroll the lakefront and ogle our inland ocean.** Chicago's forefathers had the foresight to keep the city's 29 miles (47km) of lakefront free and clear of development. As a result, you can bike, rollerblade, jog, or walk along Lake Michigan and enjoy a chain of parks that includes Chicago's signature Lincoln Park and Grant Park. *See p 90.*

7 **Admire our renowned skyline on a boat cruise along the Chicago River and Lake Michigan.** The best way to get a perspective on Chicago's history and learn about the dramatic buildings that form the city's skyline is to take an architecture boat tour. Some of the best are run by the Chicago Architecture Foundation, covering some 40 buildings with entertaining and enlightening narrative from an army of well-versed docents. *See p 14,* **1***.*

8 **Check out the wares on the Magnificent Mile.** Shopping is the thing on Michigan Avenue, and you can easily while away a day browsing and buying your way up the avenue. Other areas of the city offer chic boutiques and hard-to-find antiques and vintage clothing, but for a huge selection offering something for everyone, the Magnificent Mile is your best bet. *See p 71.*

9 **Explore the outdoor architectural museum that is Oak Park.** If you have a passion for architecture or literature, you'll find plenty of sights to see in this suburb on the western border of the city. Ernest Hemingway was born here, and his home and a museum offer insight into Oak Park's most famous native son. But most visitors are drawn to the Frank Lloyd Wright Home & Studio, and to the homes lining Oak Park's well-maintained streets that the famous architect designed. *See p 148.*

10 **Share a laugh at The Second City.** Training ground for the country's best comedians, The Second City excels in long-form improvisational comedy. Ensembles change frequently, so check the local newspapers for reviews of the latest offering. And, if you like your history mixed with humor (and who doesn't?), don't miss The Second City's Neighborhood Tours, guided by actors, in cooperation with the Chicago Historical Society. *See p 126.*

11 **Grip the edge of your seat at a Chicago theater company performance.** Whether you choose a production by the Steppenwolf Theatre Company, Goodman Theatre, or a smaller venue such as Victory Gardens Theatre, don't miss a chance to see what might be the

Frank Lloyd Wright's Unity Temple in Oak Park, noted for its Prairie School design.

next big hit to move to Broadway. *See p 127.*

⑫ **Climb aboard a captured U-boat at the Museum of Science and Industry,** the granddaddy of interactive museums. The U-505, captured in 1944 and brought to the museum 10 years later, is only one of 2,000 exhibits. It's easy to spend a day here, especially if you take in an Omnimax movie, located in the Henry Crown Space Center, where you can also hop aboard a simulator to experience a space shuttle flight. *See p 42.*

⑬ **Explore Hyde Park's Gothic quadrangle and magnificent mansions.** Home to the University of Chicago, with its 73 Nobel laureates, intimidating buildings with Gothic spires, and hallowed academic halls, Hyde Park is sure to impress. Off-campus, Hyde Park is an integrated, cosmopolitan neighborhood that's home to one of Frank Lloyd Wright's finest works, the Robie House. *See p 64.*

⑭ **Take in jazz or a poetry slam at Green Mill.** This popular watering hole of the 1920s and 1930s still retains its speak-easy flavor. On

Check out your reflection in Millennium Park's Cloud Gate *sculpture.*

A WWII U-boat, on display at the Museum of Science and Industry.

Sunday night, Green Mill hosts the Uptown Poetry Slam, where poets vie for the open mic. Most nights, though, jazz is on the menu from about 9pm 'til the wee hours, so sink into a plush velvet booth and enjoy. *See p 129.*

⑮ **Get snout-to-nose with the baby belugas at John G. Shedd Aquarium.** The world's largest indoor aquarium is a city treasure. Don't miss the Oceanarium, which re-creates a Pacific Northwest coastal environment and features a wall of windows that reveals the lake outside and creates the illusion of one uninterrupted expanse of sea (that's where you'll find those baby belugas). *See p 21,* ⑧.

⑯ **Interact with the sculpture at Millennium Park,** the city's newest urban showpiece. One of the most popular attractions is *Cloud Gate,* the huge elliptical sculpture by British artist Anish Kapoor, in which you can examine your reflection in funhouse-like distortions. While you're here, don't miss the stunning Frank Gehry–designed Pritzker Music Pavilion, home to free summer concerts performed by the Grant Park Symphony Orchestra. *See p 10,* ⑧. ●

The Best in One Day

W. Ohio St.

W. Grand Ave.

W. Illinois St.

W. Hubbard St.

N. Kingsbury

N. Orleans St.

N. Franklin St.

N. Clark St.

N. Dearborn St.

N. State St.

RIVER NORTH

W. Kinzie St.

North Branch Chicago River

Merchandise Mart

Chicago River

E. Wacker Dr.

Columbus Dr.

W. Wacker Dr.

E. Wacker Pl.

E. So. Water St.

N. Wells St.

N. LaSalle St.

W. Lake St.

E. Lake St.

N. Wabash Ave.

N. Stetson Ave.

N. Michigan Ave.

W. Randolph St.

E. Randolph Dr.

N. Canal St.

N. Clark St.

N. Dearborn St.

N. State St.

5 **2** **3**

W. Washington **1** St.

MILLENNIUM

8

PARK

Columbus Dr.

4

W. Madison St.

THE

W. Monroe St.

LOOP

S. Wacker Dr.

South Branch Chicago River

E. Monroe Dr.

W. Adams St.

E. Adams St.

7 **Art Institute of Chicago**

Union Station

Sears Tower

S. Franklin St.

W. Jackson Blvd.

E. Jackson Dr.

W. Van Buren St.

6

S. Wabash Ave.

GRANT

PARK

Eisenhower Expwy.

W. Congress Pkwy.

E. Congress Pkwy.

E. Michigan Ave.

Columbus Dr.

✉ **Post Office**

W. Harrison St.

S. Sherman St.

S. LaSalle St.

S. Clark St.

S. Federal St.

S. Dearborn St.

S. Plymouth Ct.

S. State St.

E. Balbo Ave.

E. Balbo Dr.

SOUTH LOOP

E. 8th St.

0 ———— 1/4 mi
0 ———— 0.25 km

94
41
90
Wrigley Field
CHICAGO
Map area
290
Lake Michigan
U.S. Cellular Field
55
90
41
94
⊕ **Midway**

0 ———— 3 mi

- **1** Brown Line "El" Washington/ Wells Station
- **2** Macy's
- **3** Soda Fountain
- **4** Miro's *Chicago*
- **5** Reliance Building
- **6** Chicago Public Library/ Harold Washington Library Center
- **7** Art Institute of Chicago
- **8** Millennium Park

Previous page: The Crown Fountain in Millennium Park.

With 1 day to spend in Chicago, focus on the heart of the city. The Loop is a collection of commercial, governmental, and cultural buildings contained within a corral of elevated train tracks. Here you'll find classic Chicago experiences, plus the chance to glimpse the city's future in its newest urban showcase, Millennium Park. START: **Washington/Wells El Station.**

1 ★★★ kids Ride the Brown Line "El" (Elevated Train) around the Loop. Board the Brown Line at Washington/Wells, and ride it around the Loop through the canyons of office buildings (you'll be close enough to peer into some of them). Stop off at Randolph/Wabash (or, if you don't mind a longer walk, ride to Clark/Lake). ⏱ *30 min. Avoid rush-hour boarding before 9am and from 3:30–6:30pm.* ☎ *888/YOURCTA. www.transit chicago.com. Tickets $1.75 per ride, 85¢ for kids 7–11 and seniors, free for kids under 7. El: Brown Line to Washington/Wells.*

A ride on the city's famous "El" train is a quintessential Chicago experience.

2 Macy's. In 2006, the former Marshall Field's became Macy's, much to locals' chagrin. This department store's clock is one of the city's most-recognized icons. Browse the store's famous windows, or stop in for Frango Mints, a favorite Chicago souvenir. Head inside to check out

Joan Miro's Chicago *is just one of many world-class sculptures found in the Loop.*

the largest Tiffany glass mosaic dome in the United States. ⏱ *5 min.– 2 hr. (if you want to shop). 111 N. State St. at Randolph St.* ☎ *312/781-1000. Hours vary seasonally; call ahead. El: Red Line to Washington.*

Quench your thirst at the **3 classic soda fountain** in Macy's, and add a twist of lemon, cherry, or vanilla flavor to your soft drink. *111 N. State St.* ☎ *312/781-1000. $.*

4 Miro's *Chicago.* Originally called *The Sun, the Moon and One Star,* Joan Miro's *Chicago* was unveiled in 1981. This 40-foot-tall sculptural representation of a woman with outstretched arms sits in the Brunswick Plaza on Washington Street, and overlooks the Picasso sculpture at the Daley Center. ⏱ *5 min. On the plaza of 69 W. Washington St. El: Red Line to Washington.*

⑤ Reliance Building. Now the Hotel Burnham, this building, with a terra cotta and glass exterior, was one of the world's first skyscrapers. Stop inside to admire the terrazzo tile floors, white marble wainscoting, and mahogany door and window frames. Room numbers painted on the translucent doors recall the structure's days as an office building. Today, the Hotel Burnham features eclectic decor and an excellent ground-floor restaurant with a view onto State Street (p 100). ⏲ *15 min. 1 W. Washington St.* ☎ *312/782-1111. El: Red Line to Washington.*

⑥ kids Chicago Public Library/ Harold Washington Library Center. This hulking Italian Renaissance building is the world's largest public library. Named for the city's first and only African-American mayor, who died of a heart attack in 1987 while still in office, the building fills an entire city block. On the second floor, the Thomas Hughes Children's Library makes an excellent resting spot for families traveling with kids. ⏲ *30 min. 400 S. State St.* ☎ *312/747-4300. www.chipublib.org. Free admission. Mon–Thurs*

The Chicago Public Library is the largest public library in the world.

Built in 1890, the Reliance Building features a landmark Gothic exterior.

9am–7pm; Fri–Sat 9am–5pm; Sun 1–5pm. Closed holidays. El: Brown or Purple line to Library.

⑦ ★★★ Art Institute of Chicago. Stop in to view the Impressionist collection on the second floor, a highlight of this, Chicago's grande dame of museums. With 33 paintings by Claude Monet, dancers by Degas, and Seurat's legendary masterpiece, *A Sunday Afternoon on La Grande Jatte,* this museum is a must for any art lover. ⏲ *1 hr. See p 38.*

⑧ ★★★ kids Millennium Park. When Chicago's newest showpiece debuted in summer 2004, it won raves for its winning combination of beautiful landscaping, elegant classically inspired architecture, and public entertainment spaces. Today, it's become a favorite tourist destination, second only to Navy Pier. A tourist rite of passage is having a photo taken in the reflection of "The Bean," which has become Chicagoans' unofficial favorite sculpture. And, the spectacular Frank Gehry–designed Jay Pritzker Pavilion is host to the nation's only free, outdoor, municipally-supported classical music series, the Grant Park Music Festival.

Millennium Park

Columbus Dr.

GREAT LAWN

D Jay Pritzker Pavilion

F Lurie Garden

Monroe St.

Art Institute of Chicago

Millennium Park Welcome Center

Randolph St.

Chase Promenade North

Chase Promenade Central

Chase Promenade South

SBC Plaza

C

Boeing Gallery North

Boeing Gallery South

Wrigley Square and Millennium Park Monument

A

B

Ice Rink

Michigan Ave.

Washington St.

Madison St.

Visitor Information Center

◀)) Audio Tour

🍴 Dining

ⓘ Information

P Parking

🚻 Restrooms

♿ Wheelchair accessible

If the weather is fine, you can make a picnic out of the sandwiches and salads served at the **8A Park Grill & Cafe** (11 N. Michigan Ave.; ☎ 312/521-7275; $). **8B** The **Crown Fountain,** and its two towers of glass blocks with a shallow reflecting pool between them, is perfect for kids to splash around in warm weather (late at night, you'll find revelers doing the same). Faces of Chicagoans are projected through the glass—and their mouths spew water when you least expect it. **8C** The *Cloud Gate* is an elliptical sculpture made of highly polished steel that reflects the nearby skyline, landscape, and lights. For the most mind-bending funhouse view, stand underneath the sculpture. The park's centerpiece is the

8D Jay Pritzker Pavilion, an outdoor music venue designed by Frank Gehry; massive stainless steel ribbons top the stage. Another Gehry-designed standout, **8E BP Pedestrian Bridge,** curves and winds its way over Columbus Drive, providing changing views of the cityscape as you walk. Finally, stroll **8F The Lurie Garden,** where 250 varieties of native perennial plants re-create a Midwestern prairie. ⏱ *2 hr. Michigan Ave. from Randolph St. on the north end to Monroe St. on the south, and west to Columbus Dr.* ☎ *312/752-1168. www.millenniumpark.org. Free admission. Daily 6am–11pm. El: Blue Line to Washington, Red Line to Lake and Brown, Green, Orange, or Purple line to Randolph.*

The Best in Two Days

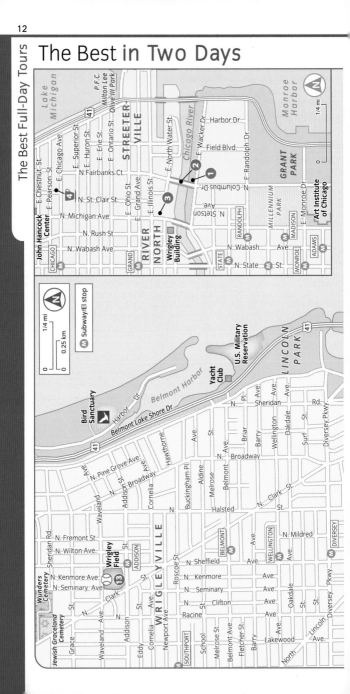

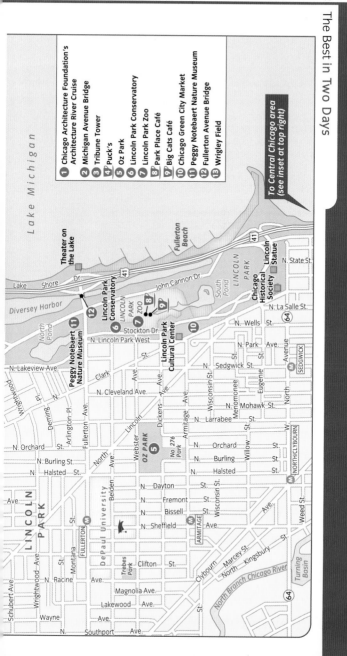

1 Chicago Architecture Foundation's Architecture River Cruise
2 Michigan Avenue Bridge
3 Tribune Tower
4 Puck's
5 Oz Park
6 Lincoln Park Conservatory
7 Lincoln Park Zoo
8 Park Place Café
9 Big Cats Café
10 Chicago Green City Market
11 Peggy Notebaert Nature Museum
12 Fullerton Avenue Bridge
13 Wrigley Field

To Central Chicago area (see inset at top right)

Lake Michigan

Theater on the Lake

Lincoln Park Conservatory

Fullerton Beach

Lincoln Statue

Chicago Historical Society

Diversey Harbor

North Pond

Peggy Notebaert Nature Museum

Lincoln Park Cultural Center

South Pond

John Cannon Dr.

Lake Shore Dr.

Stockton Dr.

LINCOLN PARK

N. State St.

N. La Salle St.

N. Wells St.

N. Park Ave.

N. Sedgwick St.

N. Lincoln Park West

N. Lakeview Ave.

N. Cleveland Ave.

Wisconsin St.

Menomonee St.

Mohawk St.

N. Larrabee St.

SEDGWICK

North Ave.

Wrightwood

Deming Pl.

Arlington Pl.

Fullerton Ave.

Clark Ave.

Lincoln Ave.

Dickens Ave.

Armitage Ave.

Webster Ave.

Oz Park

No. 276 Park

Eugenie St.

N. Orchard St.

N. Burling St.

N. Halsted St.

N. Dayton St.

N. Fremont St.

N. Bissell St.

N. Sheffield Ave.

N. Orchard St.

N. Burling St.

N. Halsted St.

Willow St.

NORTH/CLYBOURN

Weed St.

Belden

North Ave.

ARMITAGE

LINCOLN PARK

FULLERTON

Montana St.

DePaul University

Trebes Park

Clifton St.

Clybourn

Marcey St.

North Kingsbury St.

North Branch Chicago River

Turning Basin

Schubert Ave.

Wrightwood Ave.

N. Racine Ave.

Magnolia Ave.

Lakewood Ave.

Wayne Ave.

N. Southport Ave.

41

64

On your second day in Chicago, take to the water for a boat cruise, and gain insight into the people and events that shaped the city's famous skyline. Stroll the Magnificent Mile, with its glittering array of shops, and finish your day in scenic Lincoln Park, with its charming centerpiece, Lincoln Park Zoo. START: Southeast corner of the Michigan Avenue Bridge. Bus: 151 (Michigan Ave.) to Illinois Street.

① ★★★ Chicago Architecture Foundation's Architecture River Cruise. You'll see more than 50 buildings from a unique perspective as you glide along the north and south branches of the Chicago River. Narration is provided by docents, who do a good job of making the cruise enjoyable for all visitors, no matter what their level of architectural knowledge. In addition to pointing out famous buildings—Marina City, the Civic Opera house, the Sears Tower, and Merchandise Mart, to name a few—they approach the sites thematically, explaining, for example, how Chicagoans' use of the river has changed in the past 2 centuries. If you have very young kids, you may prefer the shorter (and less expensive) tours by Wendella Sightseeing Boats. Kids' tickets cost $12, and the tours last 1 hour. ⏱ 1½ hr. Southeast corner of Michigan Ave. bridge. Tickets $28 per person weekdays, $30 on weekends and holidays. Daily June–Oct 11am–3pm (weekends only May and Nov). Purchase tickets in advance through Ticketmaster (☎ 312/902-

The Michigan Avenue Bridge offers some of the city's best photo ops.

A cruise along the Chicago River is one of the best ways to see the city's fabulous architecture.

1500), or avoid the service charge and buy your tickets at the ArchiCenter, 224 S. Michigan Ave. (www.architecture.org), or at the boat launch. Wendella Sightseeing Boats depart from Michigan Ave. bridge (on the northwest side, at the Wrigley Building). ☎ 312/337-1446. www.wendellaboats.com. Tickets $23 adults, $21 seniors, $12 children under 12. Daily Apr–Oct. Bus: 151.

② ★ Michigan Avenue Bridge. Gaze up at the Gothic splendor of the Tribune Tower and the white brilliance of the William J. Wrigley Jr. Building from Chicago's most famous bridge, one of many that span the Chicago River. Designed to improve transportation and enhance the riverfront, the bridge was completed in 1920, followed by the Wacker Drive

esplanade (1926). Together, they provided an impressive gateway to North Michigan Avenue and led to its development as one of the city's premier thoroughfares. Views from every direction are stunning, but for one of the city's best photo ops, look west down the Chicago River. ⏱ *15 min. El: Green, Purple, Brown, or Orange line to State.*

3 Tribune Tower. This Gothic design was the result of an international competition to create "the most beautiful office building in the world," held in 1922 by the *Chicago Tribune* newspaper. The winning entry, with a crowning tower and flying buttresses, was based on the design of the French cathedral at Rouen. The base of the building is studded with more than 120 stones from famous sites and structures in all 50 states and dozens of foreign countries—from the Parthenon to Bunker Hill. The lobby and gift shop of the Tribune Tower are worthy stops for Cubs fans (the baseball team is owned by the Tribune Company). ⏱ *15 min. 435 N. Michigan Ave. ☎ 312/222-3232. Bus: 151.*

The Tin Man, one of many Wizard of Oz sculptures inside Oz Park.

The eye-catching Tribune Tower combines Gothic elements with traditional sky-scraper design.

4 ☕ Puck's, a cafe operated by Wolfgang Puck of Spago restaurant fame, has seating overlooking the Museum of Contemporary Art's 1-acre terraced sculpture garden. Mediterranean and Asian influences enliven classic dishes, as exemplified by the three-bean salad with shrimp, lime, and cilantro, and the smoked shrimp pizza with sun-dried tomatoes and leeks. *Inside the Museum of Contemporary Art, 220 E. Chicago Ave. (1 block east of Michigan Ave.). ☎ 312/280-2660. www.mcachicago. org. $$. El: Red Line to Chicago.*

5 kids Oz Park. One of Lincoln Park's most famous residents was L. Frank Baum (1856–1919), the author of *The Wonderful Wizard of Oz,* who settled in Chicago in 1891. Take a quick stroll through this 13-acre park, created in 1967 in his honor. You'll find larger-than-life statues of many *Wizard*-related characters, including, most prominently, *The Tin Man,* designed by metal sculptor John Kearney. The paths are perfect for walking off your meal. There's an "Emerald Garden" for strolling, and

"Dorothy's Playlot," a shady, sprawling playground with wooden climbing structures. ⏱ *30 min. 2021 N. Burling St. (at Lincoln Ave.)* ☎ *312/ 747-2200. Free admission. Open daily until dusk. El: Brown Line to Armitage.*

⑥ **Lincoln Park Conservatory.** If the weather's uncooperative, a visit to this conservatory's climate-controlled environs can be a real mood-lifter. It's comprised of four greenhouses—the Palm house, the Fernery, the Tropical house, and the Show house—that offer seasonal displays. Even on the coldest day of winter, the Azalea and Camellia show that begins in late January is sure to put a spring in your step. Outside the front doors of the conservatory is an expansive lawn with a French garden: Photo opportunity! Don't miss the lovely Bates Fountain on the conservatory's south side, designed by famous sculptor Augustus Saint-Gaudens. ⏱ *30 min. Fullerton Ave. (at Stockton Dr.).* ☎ *312/742-7736. The best way to get to Lincoln Park from the Miracle Mile is to stroll the lakefront from Oak St. Beach to North Ave. Beach, then cross the pedestrian bridge over Lake Shore Dr. and into the park. Free admission. Daily 9am–5pm. Bus: 73, 151, or 156.*

⑦ ★★★ **kids** **Lincoln Park Zoo.** The nation's oldest zoo, founded in 1868, is also one of the last free zoos in the country. You'll want to

The Lincoln Park Conservatory's indoor gardens are lush even in winter.

meander a while among the landmark Georgian revival buildings and modern structures set amid gently rolling pathways, verdant lawns, and a profusion of flower gardens. The star attraction is the **Great Ape house,** where you can watch ape families interact. Also worth a stop is the **Regenstein African Journey,** home to elephants, giraffes, rhinos, and other large mammals. Kids flock to the ever-popular **Sea Lion Pool,** and there's a **Pritzker Children's Zoo** and **Farm-in-the-Zoo,** where children are encouraged to touch a variety of small animals under the supervision of zookeepers. **The Farm** is a working reproduction of a Midwestern farm, complete with chicken coops and demonstrations of butter churning. Finish off your visit with a ride on the truly lovely **Endangered Species Carousel.** ⏱ *2–3 hr. 2200 N. Cannon Dr. (at Fullerton Pkwy.).* ☎ *312/742-2000. www.lpzoo.com. Free admission. Buildings daily 10am–5pm (until 6:30pm Sat–Sun Memorial Day to Labor Day); grounds 9am–6pm (until 7pm Memorial Day to Labor Day and until 5pm Nov 1–May 31). Bus: 151.*

A Siberian tiger; one of the many big cats found at the Lincoln Park Zoo.

Inside the Lincoln Park Zoo, the ⑧ **Park Place Café** food court (near the Lion house; $) is a good option for some quick refreshment.

For a snack with a view, try the rooftop eatery, **9** **Big Cats Café** (near the Birds of Prey exhibit; $), which offers muffins, scones, focaccia sandwiches, salads, and flatbreads.

10 **Chicago Green City Market.** Chefs from Chicago's best restaurants load up their trucks with organic foods sold at this outdoor market, which takes place Wednesday and Saturday mornings along the path between 1750 North Clark St. and Stockton Drive. You can browse the stalls right along with the pros. You might find fresh goat cheese or (in season) freshly picked blueberries; if you're hungry, you can get a made-to-order French-style crepe. Live music is also featured. ⏱ *30 min.–1 hr. In Lincoln Park, between 1750 N. Clark St. and Stockton Dr. www.chicagogreencity market.org. May–Oct Wed and Sat 7am–1:30pm. Bus: 151.*

11 kids **Peggy Notebaert Nature Museum.** This environmental museum, built into the rise of an ancient sand dune that was once the shore of Lake Michigan, features rooftop-level walkways offering a view of birds and other urban wildlife below. Paths wind through gardens planted with native Midwestern wildflowers and grasses, and trace the shoreline of Lincoln Park's newly restored North Pond. The best exhibit is the **Butterfly Haven,** a greenhouse habitat that's home to about 25 Midwestern species of butterflies and moths. Another exhibit, **City Science,** displays the inner workings of a 3,000-square-foot, two-story "house," where visitors can view the pipes and ducts that connect

The butterfly haven at the Peggy Notebaert Nature Museum is home to many colorful species.

Chicagoans flock to the Green City Market in summer for fresh produce.

homes with power sources miles away. ⏱ *1 hr. Fullerton Ave. and Cannon Dr. ☎ 773/755-5100. www.chias. org. Admission $9 adults, $7 seniors and students, $6 kids 3–12, free for kids under 3; free admission Thurs. Mon–Fri 9am–4:30pm; Sat–Sun 10am–5pm. Closed Thanksgiving, Dec 25, and Jan 1. Bus: 151.*

12 **Fullerton Avenue Bridge.** Take advantage of a wonderful photo opportunity at the bridge that runs over the lagoon, just before you get to Lake Shore Drive. Standing on the south side of Fullerton, you'll have a great view of the skyline and Lincoln Park (especially at sunset)—it's the perfect place to take a final snapshot to commemorate your day. ⏱ *5 min. Bus: 151 or 156.*

13 ★★★ kids **Wrigley Field.** There's no better way to create family lore than a game at Wrigley, where your kids (or you) can stuff themselves with hot dogs, licorice whips, and peanuts and begin their careers as future Cubs fans. If you are bringing kids, due to the noise levels and general commotion of getting in and out of the stadium, I'd recommend this only for children ages 5 and older. *For more on Wrigley Field, see p 24 and p 130.*

The Best in Three Days

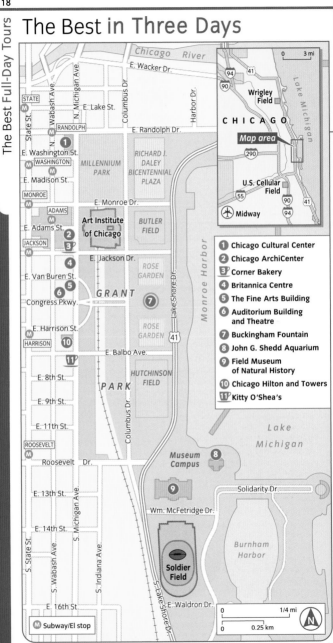

0   3 mi

94
90   41

Wrigley
Field

CHICAGO

Map area

290

U.S. Cellular
Field

55

90
41

✈ Midway

1 Chicago Cultural Center
2 Chicago ArchiCenter
3 Corner Bakery
4 Britannica Centre
5 The Fine Arts Building
6 Auditorium Building
   and Theatre
7 Buckingham Fountain
8 John G. Shedd Aquarium
9 Field Museum
   of Natural History
10 Chicago Hilton and Towers
11 Kitty O'Shea's

Chicago River
E. Wacker Dr.

N. Michigan Ave.
N. Wabash Ave.
State St.

E. Lake St.

Columbus Dr.

Harbor Dr.

STATE

RANDOLPH

E. Randolph Dr.

1

E. Washington St.

WASHINGTON

MILLENNIUM
PARK

RICHARD J.
DALEY
BICENTENNIAL
PLAZA

E. Madison St.

MONROE

ADAMS

E. Monroe Dr.

E. Adams St.

Art Institute
of Chicago

BUTLER
FIELD

2
3

JACKSON

E. Jackson Dr.

ROSE
GARDEN

4

E. Van Buren St.

5

GRANT

7

6

Congress Pkwy.

Monroe Harbor

E. Harrison St.

HARRISON

10

ROSE
GARDEN

41

E. Balbo Ave.

11

E. 8th St.

HUTCHINSON
FIELD

PARK

E. 9th St.

E. 11th St.

Columbus Dr.

Lake
Michigan

ROOSEVELT

Roosevelt   Dr.

Museum
Campus

8

E. 13th St.

9

Solidarity Dr.

S. State St.
S. Wabash Ave.
S. Michigan Ave.
S. Indiana Ave.

E. 14th St.

Wm. McFetridge Dr.

Burnham
Harbor

Soldier
Field

E. 16th St.

S. Lake Shore Dr.

E. Waldron Dr.

M Subway/El stop

0   1/4 mi
0   0.25 km

N

On your third day in Chicago, stroll the "Michigan Avenue Cliff," known for its imposing wall of grand buildings. In warmer months, stop in Grant Park and stand in the refreshing spray of Buckingham Fountain, then head to Museum Campus, a green expanse that comprises one of the most impressive collections of museums in the country. START: **Chicago Cultural Center, corner of South Michigan Avenue and Washington Street. El: Randolph or Washington/State El station.**

1 ★★ Chicago Cultural Center. Built in 1897 as the city's library, this National Historic Landmark's basic Beaux Arts exterior doesn't begin to hint at the building's sumptuous interior. Inside you'll find rare marble; fine hardwoods; stained glass; polished brass; and mosaics of Favrile glass, colored stone, and mother-of-pearl inlaid in white marble. The crowning centerpiece is the world's largest Louis Comfort Tiffany art glass dome, newly renovated in 2008, in Preston Bradley Hall—it's dazzling. The Cultural Center houses one of the Chicago Office of Tourism's main visitor centers, which makes it an ideal place to start your day. ⏱ *30 min. 78 E. Washington St.* ☎ *312/744-6630. www.cityofchicago. org/exploringchicago. Free admission. Mon–Thurs 10am–7pm; Fri 10am–6pm; Sat 10am–5pm; Sun 11am–5pm. Closed holidays. El: Brown, Green, Orange, or Purple*

Stop off at the Chicago ArchiCenter for information on guided tours and the city's architecture.

The exquisite interior and Tiffany Dome of the Chicago Cultural Center.

line to Randolph, or Red Line to Washington/State.

2 ★★★ Chicago ArchiCenter. The Chicago Architecture Foundation's shop and tour center is intended to help everyone appreciate the city's main claim to fame. Exhibits include a scale model of downtown Chicago, profiles of the people and buildings that shaped the city's look, and a searchable database with pictures and information on many of Chicago's best-known skyscrapers. The best gift shop in the city offers architecture-focused books, decorative accessories, and gifts. "Architecture ambassadors" provide information on a wide range of available tours. ⏱ *30 min. 224 S. Michigan Ave.* ☎ *312/922-3432. www. architecture.org. Free admission. Exhibits daily 9:30am–4pm; shop and tour desk Mon–Sat 9am–6:30pm, Sun 9am–6pm. El: Red Line to Jackson.*

The distinctive Britannica Centre is best known for its pyramidal peak.

3 **Corner Bakery,** a casual restaurant and bakery, offers sweet treats (don't miss the tart lemon bars dusted with powdered sugar), plus a range of substantial salads and sandwiches (try the ham and Swiss on pretzel bread). *224 S. Michigan Ave. (at Jackson).* ☎ *312/ 431-7600. $.*

4 Britannica Centre. To view this building's highlight, look up. A part of Michigan Avenue's distinctive wall of buildings since 1924, Britannica Centre, originally known as the Straus Building and then as the Continental National Insurance Company building, is known for the glass, blue-lighted "beehive" ornament atop its pyramidal peak. The venerable *Encyclopaedia Britannica*, the oldest continuously published reference work in the English language, has been headquartered in Chicago since the mid-1930s. ⏱ *5 min. 310 S. Michigan Ave.* ☎ *312/347-7159. El: Red Line to Jackson.*

5 The Fine Arts Building. This 1885 building was originally a showroom for Studebaker carriages. Converted into an arts center in 1898, the building provided offices and studios for the likes of *Wizard of Oz* author L. Frank Baum and Frank Lloyd Wright. Take a quick walk through the marble-and-wood lobby, and, if you like, ride the vintage elevators to the top floor to view walls of spectacular murals that date from the building's conversion. ⏱ *30 min. 410 S. Michigan Ave.* ☎ *312/427-7602. Free admission. Daily 7am–10pm. El: Brown Line to Library.*

6 ★ Auditorium Building and Theatre. Designed and built in 1889 by Louis Sullivan and Dankmar Adler, the Auditorium was an architectural wonder of its time: the heaviest and most massive edifice on earth, the most fireproof building ever constructed, and the tallest

Scenic Lake Shore Drive offers marvelous views of Lake Michigan (see p 90).

The Auditorium Building and Theatre features exquisite interior ornamentation.

building in Chicago. Today, the 4,000-seat theater hosts touring Broadway productions. One-hour tours on Mondays allow visitors time to marvel at the gorgeous arched design (lit by thousands of bulbs) that Sullivan created using his trademark ornamentation—in this case, elaborate golden stenciling and gold plaster medallions. ⏲ *30 min. (1 hr. if you take a tour). 50 E. Congress Pkwy. ☎ 312/922-2110. www.auditoriumtheatre.org. 1-hr. guided tour Mon 10am and noon (call ☎ 312/431-2389 ext. 0 to make reservations) for $8 per person. El: Brown Line to Library.*

7 Buckingham Fountain. Grant Park's immense baroque centerpiece—the starting point for the famous Route 66 to Los Angeles—is constructed of pink Georgia marble and patterned after the Latona Fountain at Versailles (although Buckingham is twice its size). The fountain, donated to the city of Chicago by philanthropist Kate Buckingham, first opened in 1927. From April through October, the fountain spurts columns of water

up to 150 feet in the air every hour on the hour; beginning at 4pm, a whirl of colored lights and music makes for quite a show (the fountain shuts down at 11pm). If you visit in spring, be sure to stroll the adjacent esplanades and their lovely rose gardens. ⏲ *10 min. Inside Grant Park, at Columbus Dr. and Congress Pkwy. www.chicagoparkdistrict.com. Apr–Oct daily 10am–11pm. Bus: 6 or 146.*

8 ★★★ kids John G. Shedd Aquarium. The first thing you'll see as you enter the world's largest indoor aquarium is the 90,000-gallon tank occupying the Beaux Arts–style central rotunda. The Caribbean Coral Reef exhibit features nurse sharks, barracudas, stingrays, and a hawksbill sea turtle. The next don't-miss exhibit is Amazon Rising: Seasons of the River, displaying piranhas, birds, sloths, insects, spiders, snakes, caiman lizards, and monkeys. Wild Reef–Sharks at Shedd features 26 interconnected habitats (more than 750,000 gallons of water) that encompass a Philippine coral reef patrolled by sharks and other predators. Another highlight is the 3-million-gallon saltwater **Oceanarium,** a stunning indoor marine mammal pavilion that re-creates a Pacific Northwest coastal environment. Here, a crew of friendly trainers puts dolphins through their paces during daily scheduled performances. ⏲ *1 hr. 1200 S. Lake Shore Dr. ☎ 312/939-2438.*

Catch the nightly sound and light show at Buckingham Fountain in summer.

Walker's Warning

Though Chicago is a great city to explore on foot, Lake Shore Drive is no place for pedestrians. People have been seriously injured and even killed attempting to dodge the traffic on this busy road. Near Grant Park, cross only in crosswalks at Jackson Boulevard or Randolph, East Monroe, or East Balbo drives, or by using the underpass on the Museum Campus. North of the river, utilize underpasses or bridges at East Ohio Street, Chicago Avenue, Oak Street, and North Avenue.

The Oceanarium's Beluga whales at the John G. Shedd Aquarium.

www.sheddaquarium.org. Oceanarium is closed at press time; call or visit the website for updated information. The Total Experience Pass (to the Wild Reef, Amazon Rising, Caribbean Reef, Waters of the World, a pet show and a choice of the 4-D experience) is $18 for adults, $14 seniors and kids 3–11. Free admission to aquarium Mon–Tues Sept–Nov, 1 week in June and 1 week in Oct. See website for more info. Mon–Fri 9am–5pm (until 6pm Memorial Day to Labor Day); Sat–Sun 9am–6pm. Bus: 6 or 146.

⑨ ★ kids Field Museum of Natural History. Indulge your inner Indiana Jones while exploring this renowned museum's 9 acres of exhibits. The museum was founded in 1893 to house natural history collections brought to Chicago for the World's Columbian Exposition. A wonderful new addition, the **Crown Family Playlab,** caters to the young set with hands-on digs for dinosaur bones, a dress-up station where kids can don a coyote costume to trot through a mock-up of the Illinois woodlands, and a science lab, where kids can examine insects in amber, fossils, and animal skulls.

"Sue," the famous Tyrannosaurus rex fossil at the Field Museum of Natural History.

Field Museum of Natural History

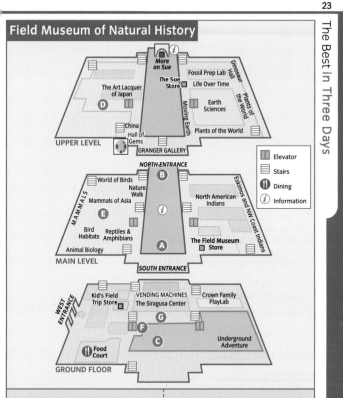

Standing proudly at the north side of the grand **9A Stanley Field Hall** is the largest, most complete *Tyrannosaurus rex* fossil ever unearthed. The $8.4-million specimen is named **9B ★★ "Sue"** for the paleontologist who found it in South Dakota in 1990. Head downstairs to **9C ★ Inside Ancient Egypt,** a spellbinding exhibit that realistically depicts scenes from Egyptian funeral, religious, and other social practices. **9D Traveling the Pacific** re-creates scenes of island life in the South Pacific; there's even a full-scale model of a Maori meeting house. **9E Africa** is an assemblage of African artifacts and provocative, interactive multimedia presentations. Two other signature highlights: the taxidermied bodies of **9F Bushman** (a legendary lowland gorilla from the city's Lincoln Park Zoo) and the **9G Man-Eating Lions of Tsavo** (the pair of male lions who munched nearly 140 British railway workers constructing a bridge in East Africa in 1898). ⏱ *2–3 hr. Roosevelt Rd. and Lake Shore Dr.* ☎ *312/922-9410. www.fieldmuseum.org. Admission $14 adults, $11 seniors and students with ID, $9 kids 4–11; free for teachers, armed forces personnel in uniform, and kids 2 and under. Free admission in Feb, plus second Mon in Mar–Dec and a week each in Sept and Oct (see website for info). Daily 9am–5pm; last admission 4pm. Closed Dec 25 and Jan 1. Bus: 6, 10, 12, 130, or 146.*

The massive Chicago Hilton and Towers has been a fixture in Chicago since 1927.

⑩ Chicago Hilton and Towers. This massive brick and stone building was the largest hotel in the world when it opened in 1927. It's worth a stop to gaze at the Grand Stair lobby, done in a classical-rococo style, which is the most magnificent in the city. ⏱ *15 min. 720 S. Michigan Ave. (at Balbo Dr.).* ☎ *312/ 922-4400. www.hilton.com. El: Red Line to Harrison/State.*

⑪ Kitty O'Shea's is one of the most authentic Irish pubs in town (even though it's a hotel bar), with imported Irish bartenders and traditional Irish music. Pick up an Irish/American newspaper at the entrance, then relax with a pint in a cozy booth. If you've worked up an appetite, the lamb stew, shepherd's pie, or fish and chips will keep you feeling as if you've landed on the Emerald Isle. *720 S. Michigan Ave.* ☎ *312/294-6860. $.* ●

Taking Yourself Out to a Ballgame

It's been a long dry spell: The Cubbies haven't made a World Series since 1945, and haven't been World Champs since 1908, but that never deters die-hard Cubs fans, who are perennial optimists. Each April, they show up for opening day at Wrigley Field in what is almost certainly inclement weather, sure that their team's year has arrived. (Wrigley Field, 1060 W. Addison St.; ☎ 773/404-CUBS; www. cubs.mlb.com; see p 130.)

Win or lose, a day at Wrigley is a don't-miss Chicago experience (and tickets tend to sell out accordingly). From the ivy-covered outfield walls to the hand-operated scoreboard and "W" or "L" flag announcing the outcome of the game to the unfortunates who couldn't attend, Wrigley Field is a pure slice of Americana. Buy a hot dog and some Cracker Jack, and join in the chorus of "Take Me Out to the Ballgame" during the seventh-inning stretch (since the death of long-time announcer Harry Caray, the crowd is led by a guest singer, often a visiting celebrity). Because Wrigley Field is small, just about every seat is decent. Families, however, might want to avoid the bleacher seats, because fans there can get a little overzealous in their rooting for the home team (and drinking).

The Loop: An Architectural Tour

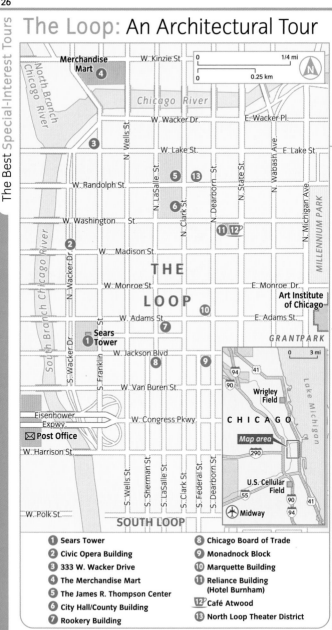

1 Sears Tower
2 Civic Opera Building
3 333 W. Wacker Drive
4 The Merchandise Mart
5 The James R. Thompson Center
6 City Hall/County Building
7 Rookery Building
8 Chicago Board of Trade
9 Monadnock Block
10 Marquette Building
11 Reliance Building (Hotel Burnham)
12 Café Atwood
13 North Loop Theater District

Previous page: A walk around The Loop is a must for architecture fans.

Architecture buffs and laypeople alike will revel in the Loop's array of outstanding landmark buildings. The structures found in this area represent a variety of important and influential historical styles, from the rounded arches and thick walls of Richardsonian Romanesque (1870–1900) to the stark simplicity and functionalism of International Style (1932–45). These buildings were the blueprints for many similar structures in North America. START: **Wacker Drive in front of the Civic Opera House. El: Brown Line to Washington Station.**

❶ Sears Tower. This 110-story building was the tallest building in the world when it opened in 1973, but has since been eclipsed by the Burj Dubai in Dubai. For what it's worth, the Sears Tower still holds the record in the category of "tallest skyscraper measured to the top of the antenna." It's still a marvel of engineering, but nowadays it's just a really, really tall office building that isn't even home to Sears, Roebuck & Company anymore (they moved out in 1992). The Skydeck on the 103rd floor does offer exceptional views (on a clear day, visibility extends up to 50 miles/80.5km), but the expensive elevator ride to the top is a

The Sears Tower, the tallest building in North America.

horror for anyone with claustrophobic tendencies, and the amount of time you have to wait in the sluggish lines to get to the top is better spent elsewhere. My recommendation for this overrated tourist magnet: Take a quick look at the building and move on. ⏱ *5 min. 233 S. Wacker Dr. (enter on Jackson Blvd.).* ☎ *312/875-9696. www.the-skydeck.com. Admission $13 adults, $9.50 kids 3–11. May–Sept daily 10am–10pm; Oct–Apr daily 10am–8pm. El: Brown, Purple, or Orange line to Quincy.*

❷ ★ Civic Opera Building. Fronting the broad roadway of Wacker Drive (named after Charles Wacker, a civic-minded brewer and a director of the World's Columbian Exposition of 1893), this Art Deco/ French Renaissance building was completed in 1929. Utility magnate Samuel Insull, the president of the

The immense Civic Opera Building, home to the Lyric Opera of Chicago.

Chicago Civic Opera Association in the '20s, installed a 3,500-seat opera house and a 900-seat theater in this 45-story office building so the property's commercial rents would subsidize the arts. The Grand Foyer of the opera house, with its 40-foot-high (12m) ceiling and gold leaf–topped marble columns, is worth a peek when the building is open. The building is home to the Lyric Opera of Chicago (p 127); the season runs from late September to March. 🕐 *5 min. 20 N. Wacker Dr.* ☎ *312/ 332-2244. www.lyricopera.org. El: Brown Line to Washington.*

③ 333 W. Wacker Drive. The green-hued facade of this 36-story building reflects the Chicago River like a massive looking glass. The post-modern structure was designed to blend with its surroundings, and the curved exterior artfully echoes the curve in the river. Indeed, the best way to view this building is from the river (you'll be able to experience this on an architectural river tour—see p 14, ①). Designed by Kohn Pedersen Fox in 1983, the building was squeezed onto a triangular lot that was previously thought suitable only for a parking lot. Another good vantage point for viewing the edifice is from the Franklin Street Bridge. 🕐 *5 min.*

The Merchandise Mart is the world's largest commercial building.

The reflective facade of 333 W. Wacker Dr.

333 W. Wacker Dr. (at Lake St.). El: Brown, Purple, or Orange line to Washington.

④ The Merchandise Mart. The world's largest commercial building (it's second in size only to the Pentagon) was built by Marshall Field as a wholesale emporium and completed in 1931. The design elements are discreetly Art Deco. If you view the building from across the river, you'll see a line of pillars upon which rest oversize busts of the icons of American merchandising, including Marshall Field, Edward A. Filene, Frank Winfield Woolworth, Julius Rosenwald (Sears), and Aaron Montgomery Ward. Today the Mart serves as a showcase for dealers in furnishings, and most of the interior is open to dealers only. The public, however, can explore the lobby and ground floor, which features Luxe Home, an eye-popping array of high-end home decorating shops, including Christopher Peacock's kitchen design showroom. 🕐 *15 min. Wells and Kinzie sts. www.merchandisemart.com. El: Brown Line to Merchandise Mart.*

⑤ The James R. Thompson Center. Chicagoans still refer to this cascading glass-and-steel building— the work of celebrated contemporary architect Helmut Jahn—by its original name, the State of Illinois Building. That's fitting, as the 16-story structure houses the Chicago branches of the state government. The glass walls that enclose the

offices are said to be a symbolic reference to "open government." For spectacular views, ride the glass elevator to the top—not a pleasant experience for anyone with a fear of heights. The Illinois Bureau of Tourism operates an information desk near the main entrance. 🕐 10 min. 100 W. Randolph St. (at LaSalle St.). ☎ 312/814-9600. Tourism Information Desk open Mon–Fri 8:30am– 4:30pm. El: Brown Line to Clark/Lake.

6 City Hall/County Building. This landmark Classical Revival building, dating back to 1911, is composed of two sections: City Hall fronts LaSalle Street on the western side, and The County Building, the older and more classically inspired edifice, faces Clark Street on the east. The county section's exterior, with its 75-foot (23m) Corinthian columns, is the more notable of the two, designed in part by one of Chicago's legendary architectural firms, Holabird & Roche. The public meetings of the volatile Chicago City Council, held in the council chambers of City Hall, are worth a visit. Call ahead to find out when the council is in session. 🕐 10 min. Washington, LaSalle, Randolph, and Clark sts.

The Rookery Building's ornate spiral staircase was designed by Frank Lloyd Wright.

Decorative exterior detail on the edifice of the City Hall/County Building.

☎ 312/744-6871. Free admission; open when City Council is in session. El: Brown Line to Washington.

7 ★★★ Rookery Building. This relic of Old Chicago, completed in 1888, was named for a demolished city hall building that once stood on this site—the roost of many pigeons and politicians. The rough granite base and turrets show the influence of the heavy Romanesque style of H. H. Richardson. Venetian and Moorish influences are evident on the exterior. I wholly recommend seeing the open interior court (designed by Frank Lloyd Wright) that rises the full height of the landmark building's 11 stories. The ornately decorated space was constructed from iron, copper, marble, glass, and terra cotta. 🕐 15 min. 209 S. LaSalle St. El: Brown Line to Quincy.

8 ★ Chicago Board of Trade. This streamlined Art Deco building, one of the best examples of that style in the city, opened in 1930. It houses the raucous economic free-for-all that is the world's largest commodities exchange, where corn, wheat, and other futures contracts are traded. Along the landmark building's rear wall, a postmodern addition by Helmut Jahn offers a repetition of the pyramid-shaped roof. The statue of the Roman

The Monadnock Block is notable for its continuity of style, even though its buildings were constructed using two very different methods.

goddess Ceres on the top of the 45-floor structure strikes a quirky architectural note—she was left faceless because the designers figured nobody would get close enough to see her features. Due to security restrictions, the public is not permitted inside the building.
🕐 *5 min. 141 W. Jackson Blvd.* ☎ *312/435-3590. www.cbot.com. El: Blue Line to Jackson/Dearborn.*

⑨ ★ Monadnock Block. This significant block actually consists of two buildings, built 2 years apart using two very different construction methods. **Monadnock I,** on the northern end, was built by Burnham and Root between 1889 and 1891, with deeply recessed windows at street level, encased by walls up to 8 feet (2.5m) thick. It was the last skyscraper in the United States to use this method of construction. **Monadnock II,** built by Holabird & Roche in 1893, is one of the country's first steel-framed buildings, but is noteworthy in that it maintains a continuity of style with Monadnock I.
🕐 *10 min. 53 W. Jackson Blvd. El: Blue Line to Jackson/Dearborn.*

⑩ ★ Marquette Building. Named for Jacques Marquette, a French Jesuit explorer who was one of the first Europeans to record the existence of the area now known as Chicago, this 1895 building was one of the country's first commercial skyscrapers. The marble lobby, which is worth seeing, commemorates the spirit of exploration with a series of explorer-themed relief sculptures and Tiffany windows.
🕐 *10 min. 140 S. Dearborn St. El: Blue Line to Jackson/Dearborn.*

⑪ ★★★ Reliance Building (Hotel Burnham). This prototype of the modern skyscraper was made possible by the development of high-speed elevators and steel framing. The terra cotta and glass facade gives the 1895 building a modern appearance. Its window design—a large central pane of glass flanked by two smaller, double-hung windows for ventilation—eventually became known as the Chicago Window. It's now home to the Hotel Burnham (named for the building's famous architect, Daniel Burnham). Fans of architectural design should take the elevator to the splendid upper floors (those above the eighth floor are original).
🕐 *20 min. 1 W. Washington St. (at State St.).* ☎ *312/782-1111. www. burnhamhotel.com. El: Red Line to Washington.*

Ideal for a pick-me-up, the eclectic **⑫ ★★★ Café Atwood** serves American comfort food. The grilled flatbread with caramelized onions and wild mushrooms is a standout. When the weather is fine, eat in the sidewalk seating area and watch the parade of passers-by. *In the Hotel Burnham (p 100).* ☎ *312/368-1900. www.atwoodcafe.com. $$.*

⑬ ★ North Loop Theater District. This row of renovated historic theaters along Randolph Street was a long-time dream of city planners, and on this short tour, you'll see why: Their colorful, glitzy facades and over-the-top decor give each a unique character.

North Loop Theater District

Chicago River

W. Upper Wacker Dr. — W. Lower Wacker Dr.

E. Lower Wacker Dr.

N. Upper Michigan Ave.

W. Haddock Pl. — E. Haddock Pl.

W. Lake St. — E. Lake St.

N. Garvey Ct.

N. Clark St.

James R. Thompson Center

Chicago Title

W. Couch Pl. — E. Benton Pl.

Ⓓ Ⓔ Ⓑ Ⓒ

W. Randolph St. — E. Randolph St.

N. La Salle St.

Ⓐ

Chicago City Hall

Daley Civic Center

N. State St.

Macy's

N. Wabash Ave.

N. Michigan Ave.

N. Garfield St.

MILLENNIUM PARK

W. Court Pl.

W. Washington St.

W. Calhoun Pl.

0 — 1/8 mile

0 — 100 meters

Ⓝ

W. Madison St. — E. Madison St.

The Versailles-inspired Ⓐ **Cadillac Palace Theatre** is a former movie palace that now hosts touring musicals, dance performances, and concerts. Another former movie palace, the spectacular Ⓑ **Ford Center for the Performing Arts Oriental Theatre,** opened in 1926 and was restored in the 1980s to its original over-the-top Indian-inspired decor; it's worth seeing, no matter what's playing on the stage. Marked by a nostalgic orange-lettered marquee, the landmark Ⓒ **Chicago Theatre** was once the crown jewel of the movie theater

The landmark Chicago Theatre is the oldest Beaux Arts building in the city.

empire of Balaban & Katz. It's the oldest Beaux Arts building in the city. The 3,800-seat hall opened in 1928 and was restored in 1986 as a showplace for Broadway musicals, concerts, and dramas. All three theaters use a number run by Broadway in Chicago (☎ 312/977 1700). Home of the city's oldest resident theater company, the Ⓓ **Goodman Theatre** opened in 2000, incorporating the landmark neo-Georgian and Palladian facades of the old Harris and Selwyn theaters. The facility includes 850- and 400-seat theaters (☎ 312/443 -3800; www.goodman-theatre.org). The large bar at Ⓔ **Petterino's** (150 N. Dearborn St.; ☎ 312/422-0150; $$), once frequented by Sinatra and Bogart, is ideal for a quick bite. Try the "shrimp de jonghe" appetizer, a Chicago original featuring six shrimp coated in garlicky bread crumbs. 🕐 *15 min. El: Red Line to Randolph.*

Mag Mile: An Architectural Tour

1 The Drake Hotel
2 Palmolive Building
3 Fourth Presbyterian Church
4 L'Appetito
5 John Hancock Center
6 Chicago Water Tower and Pumping Station
7 Women's Athletic Club
8 Medinah Temple
9 Tree Studios
10 William Wrigley Jr. Building
11 Billy Goat Tavern

M any of the signature buildings Chicago is famous for are found along the stretch of Michigan Avenue known as the Magnificent Mile, and hold a special place in the hearts of locals. From private clubs to posh condominiums and historic churches, this entire area rose from the ashes after the Great Fire of 1871. It is today one of the most architecturally significant avenues in the country. START: **Chicago/State El Station or Bus 151 (Michigan Ave.) to Walton Street.**

The Drake's Palm Court is one of the city's best spots for afternoon tea.

1 ★★ The Drake Hotel. Located at the transition point between the Gold Coast and Downtown Chicago, this landmark 13-story building was constructed in 1920 of Bedford limestone in a design inspired by the Italian palazzos of the late Renaissance. You can stroll through the ornate lobby or stop in for a cuppa at the serene Palm Court, one of the city's top spots for afternoon tea ($25 per person). ⏱ *20 min. 140 E. Walton St. www.the drakehotel.com. El: Red Line to Chicago/State. See p 137.*

2 ★ Palmolive Building. This "monument to cleanliness" was built in 1929 for Colgate–Palmolive, the world's leading soap manufacturer, but was known as the Playboy Building from 1965 to 1989, when it housed the famous skin mag (whose headquarters is now located at 680 N. Lake Shore Dr.). The picturesque Art Deco landmark was Chicago's first commercial skyscraper built outside the Loop. It has since been redeveloped and now houses luxury condos. ⏱ *5 min. 919 N. Michigan Ave. www.palmolivebuilding.com. El: Red Line to Chicago/State.*

3 ★★★ Fourth Presbyterian Church. This church, built in 1914, was the creation of Ralph Adams Cram—America's leading Gothic Revival architect, best known for New York's Cathedral of St. John the Divine—and parishioner Howard Van Doren Shaw (a prominent architect in his own right). The church is an amalgam of English and French Gothic styles, while the parish buildings are Tudor in form. The ornate sanctuary is generally open during the day and sometimes hosts concerts (signs outside will alert you to the latest offering, or you can check the website). The courtyard, known as the "garth" to

A stained glass window at the ornate Fourth Presbyterian Church.

Presbyterians, is a charming photo spot. ⏱ *15 min. 866 N. Michigan Ave. (at Delaware St.). www.fourth church.org. El: Red Line to Chicago/State.*

I recommend drinks and snacks at ⓸ ★ **L'Appetito**, on the lower level of the John Hancock Center. This family-owned Italian deli is known for its vast array of freshly baked Italian cookies. *875 N. Michigan Ave., plaza level. ☎ 312/337-0691. $.*

⓹ ★★★ John Hancock Center.
The first giant on the Chicago skyline was erected in 1969 and featured several structural innovations, including crisscross steel framing a tapering form that creates an illusion of super proportions, making the building look larger than it really is. The Hancock Observatory on the 94th floor offers spectacular views and is open to the public, as is a decent bar and restaurant duplex between the 95th and 96th floors. ⏱ *1 hr., if you visit the observatory. 875 N. Michigan Ave. ☎ 312/751-3681. Admission (to observatory) $15 adults, $13 seniors, $9 kids. Daily 9am–11pm. El: Red Line to Chicago/State.*

The John Hancock Center is notable for its crisscross steel framing.

The castellated Chicago Water Tower was the inspiration for White Castle's famous logo.

⓺ ★ Chicago Water Tower and Pumping Station.
Built in a castellated Gothic style that was wildly popular in the 1860s, these two National Historic Landmarks, which sit across from each other on Michigan Avenue (the Pumping Station on the east side, the Water Tower on the west), were the only ones in the area to survive the Great Fire of 1871. Why the duo escaped unscathed when virtually every other building in the vicinity was wiped out remains a mystery. Made of a distinct yellow-tinted Illinois limestone, the buildings now house a city art gallery (in the Water Tower), the Lookingglass Theatre Company (p 129), and a visitor center (in the old Pumping Station). ⏱ *30 min. Michigan Ave. at Chicago Ave. Visitor center open daily 7:30am–7pm, except Thanksgiving, Christmas, and New Year's Day. El: Red Line to Chicago/State.*

⓻ ★ Women's Athletic Club.
Modeled on elegant Parisian

buildings, this 1928 creation of Philip B. Maher (1894–1981) is marked by French Second Empire influences. The nine-story structure houses a private club and the oldest women's athletic facility in the United States. ⏱ 5 min. 626 N. Michigan Ave. El: Red Line to Grand.

8 ★★ Medinah Temple. Built in 1912, this Moorish-style palace was the regional headquarters of the Shriners and site of their annual circus until 1998. The building, one of the finest examples of the Islamic Revival style in the country, nearly fell into ruin before it was declared a historic landmark and restored as a Bloomingdale's furniture store. ⏱ 5 min. 600 N. Wabash Ave. El: Red Line to Grand.

9 Tree Studios. To encourage visiting artists working on the 1893 Columbian Exposition to stay in Chicago, this row of cottagelike buildings—the oldest artist studios in the country—was built in 1894.

This sculpture, by Pablo Picasso, dominates the Daley Plaza.

The Queen Anne–style buildings feature retail stores on the street level and artists' studios upstairs (the latter aren't open to the public). ⏱ 5 min. 601–623 N. State St. El: Red Line to Grand.

10 ★★★ William Wrigley Jr. Building. The Wrigley family, of chewing-gum fame, owns and operates this building (actually, two towers set side by side and connected via skywalks), which was erected between 1919 and 1924. Its white, terra cotta cladding (more than 250,000 tiles worth) glitters in the sunlight and reflects the water of the nearby river. Six shades of white, darkest at the base and lightening up to the roofline, distinguish the exterior tiles. The shading is especially beautiful when the building is illuminated after dark. Another highlight is the south tower's immense, four-faced clock, which was inspired by the Giralda Tower in Seville, Spain. ⏱ 15 min. 400 and 410 N. Michigan Ave. www.wrigley.com/about_us/the_wrigley_building.do. El: Red Line to Grand.

Look for a staircase from the Michigan Avenue sidewalk that descends to the street below. Here you'll find a tap room, the **11 ★ Billy Goat Tavern,** immortalized by John Belushi, who portrayed a cranky Greek short-order cook on *Saturday Night Live* ("cheezborger, cheezborger, no Coke, Pepsi"). Yes, you can still get a darned good cheeseburger here, though the quirky atmosphere is the best part of the experience. This local institution is especially popular with journalists (check out the wall honoring such famous columnists as Roger Ebert and the late, great Mike Royko). *430 N. Michigan Ave.* ☎ 312/222-1525. $. El: Red Line to Grand.

Navy Pier

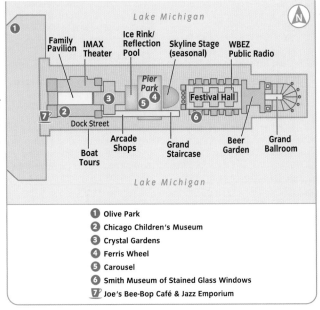

Lake Michigan

Family Pavilion
IMAX Theater
Ice Rink/ Reflection Pool
Skyline Stage (seasonal)
WBEZ Public Radio

Pier Park

Festival Hall

Dock Street

Boat Tours
Arcade Shops
Grand Staircase
Beer Garden
Grand Ballroom

Lake Michigan

1 Olive Park
2 Chicago Children's Museum
3 Crystal Gardens
4 Ferris Wheel
5 Carousel
6 Smith Museum of Stained Glass Windows
7 Joe's Bee-Bop Café & Jazz Emporium

Chicago's number-one tourist attraction, this 3,000-foot-long (900m) pier was built during World War I and has served as a ballroom, a training center for navy pilots during World War II, and a satellite campus of the University of Illinois. It's hugely popular with families, as it combines a carnival, food court, and boat dock. The pier is a fun place to stroll (if you don't mind crowds), though the commercialism of the place might be too much for some. START: **Red Line to Grand/State El Station, then Navy Pier's free trolley bus; or take Bus 29, 56, 65, or 66.**

Navy Pier Tip

Unless otherwise noted, all the attractions in this section are open Sunday through Thursday from 10am to 10pm, and Friday through Saturday from 10am to midnight. For more information on the Pier's many dining, shopping, and sightseeing opportunities, head online to **www.navypier.com**.

1 ★★★ kids **Olive Park.** Roam the most scenic sliver of parkland in the city. Fronted by a small beach, Olive Park is beloved by adults for its lovely city and lake vistas, and by kids, who like to point out the various boats that ply the waters of our Great Lake. ⏱ *30 min. Just north and west of Navy Pier, 600 N. Michigan Ave.* ☎ *312/742-PLAY (Chicago Park District).*

2 ★★ kids **Chicago Children's Museum.** This three-story museum is one of Chicago's most popular cultural attractions. It has areas designed especially for preschoolers as well as for children up to age 10. Several permanent exhibits allow kids a maximum of hands-on fun, and creative temporary exhibitions are always on tap as well. Don't miss **Dinosaur Expedition,** which re-creates an expedition to the Sahara, allowing kids to conduct scientific research and dig for the bones of a Saharan dinosaur. **WaterWays** allows visitors to learn about the uses and benefits of water resources by constructing fountains and teaming up with others to blast a stream of water 50 feet (15m) in the air. Finally, a tri-level **Schooner** lets kids climb from the crow's nest to the gangplank. 🕐 *2 hr. On Navy Pier, 700 E. Grand Ave.* ☎ *312/527-1000. www.chi childrensmuseum.org. Admission $9 adults and kids, $8 seniors; free admission Thurs 5–8pm. Tues–Sun 10am–5pm (Thurs until 8pm.)*

3 Crystal Gardens. Rest your feet and soak up the tropical atmosphere in this relatively quiet six-story glass atrium, home to 70 full-size palm trees, dancing fountains, and other flora. 🕐 *10 min. Free admission.*

4 ★★ kids **Ferris Wheel.** The pier's 15-story model is a replica of

The 15-story Ferris wheel at Navy Pier.

the world's first, which debuted at Chicago's 1893 World's Fair. Hop aboard this kid-magnet for fabulous views of the city and lakefront. 🕐 *10 min. $5 per ride.*

5 ★ kids **Carousel.** This colorful work of art features 36 hand-painted animals, fashioned in a variety of historical styles. The running boards depict scenes from Navy Pier's history. Young kids will be charmed; so will you. 🕐 *10 min., though lines can build up on busy days. $3 per ride.*

6 ★ **Smith Museum of Stained Glass Windows.** This remarkable installation of 150 colorful stained-glass windows (the only museum of its kind in the U.S.), set in illuminated display cases, will wow even a jaded visitor. The artists represented include Frank Lloyd Wright, Louis Sullivan, and Louis Comfort Tiffany. 🕐 *30 min.* ☎ *312/ 595-5024. Free admission.*

One of the colorful displays at the Smith Museum of Stained Glass Windows.

Grab lunch or a snack at **7** kids **Joe's Be-Bop Café & Jazz Emporium,** a casual Southern-style barbecue restaurant with a full kids' menu and a lively New Orleans–style atmosphere with a spicy jambalaya to match. ☎ *312/595-5299. www.joesbebop.com. $$.*

The Art Institute of Chicago

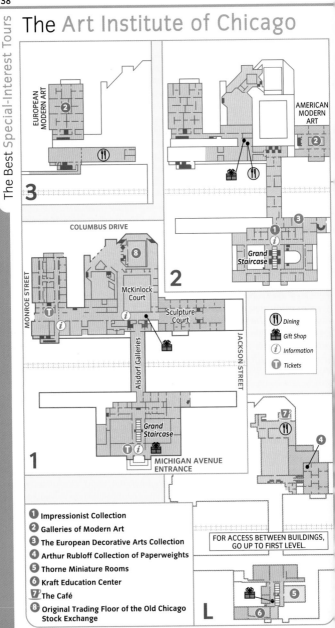

EUROPEAN MODERN ART ②

3

AMERICAN MODERN ART ②

COLUMBUS DRIVE

MONROE STREET

JACKSON STREET

8

2

McKinlock Court

Sculpture Court

① ③

Grand Staircase

Alsdorf Galleries

🍴 Dining

🎁 Gift Shop

ⓘ Information

🎟 Tickets

Grand Staircase

1

7

4

MICHIGAN AVENUE ENTRANCE

① Impressionist Collection
② Galleries of Modern Art
③ The European Decorative Arts Collection
④ Arthur Rubloff Collection of Paperweights
⑤ Thorne Miniature Rooms
⑥ Kraft Education Center
⑦ The Café
⑧ Original Trading Floor of the Old Chicago Stock Exchange

FOR ACCESS BETWEEN BUILDINGS, GO UP TO FIRST LEVEL.

L

⑤

⑥

Chicago's pride and joy is a warm, welcoming museum that's surprisingly unstuffy (during the holidays, the famous lion sculptures that guard its entrance sport wreaths around their necks). Founded in 1879 as the Chicago Academy of Fine Arts, the institute contains one of the world's great collections (more than 5,000 years' worth) of antiquities, paintings, and sculpture. Its current Beaux Arts home was constructed for the 1893 World's Columbian Exposition. In May 2009, the Art Institute will open its Modern Wing, a 264,000-square-foot (23,760-sq.-m) addition, the largest in the museum's history. A pedestrian bridge that leads from Millennium Park to the addition will also open in May 2009. START: **Monroe/State or Jackson/State El stations.**

Vincent van Gogh's Bedroom at Arles.

1 ★★★ **Impressionist Collection.** This is one of the more renowned, and therefore, highly trafficked, areas of the museum. It includes one of the world's largest collections of Monet paintings (the museum's *Arrival of the Normandy Train, Gare Saint-Lazare* is a rare urban scene by the painter). Other artists represented include Renoir, van Gogh, Manet, and Degas. Among the many treasures here is Seurat's pointillist masterpiece *Sunday Afternoon on the Island of La Grande Jatte.* 🕐 *45 min. Second floor.*

2 ★★★ **Galleries of Modern Art.** One of the world's greatest collections of modern art (more than 1,000 works). Items include paintings, sculpture, and mixed-media works from Pablo Picasso, Henri Matisse, and Salvador Dalí

through Willem de Kooning, Jackson Pollock, and Andy Warhol. Grant Wood's iconic *American Gothic* and Edward Hopper's *Nighthawks* are two very famous pieces that elicit double-takes from many visitors. René Magritte's thought-provoking *Time Transfixed* is another highlight. 🕐 *45 min. Second floor.*

3 ★★ **The European Decorative Arts Collection.** This extensive collection includes 25,000 objects (dating from A.D. 1100 to the

Grant Wood's famous American Gothic.

German sitting room (1815–1850) from the Thorne Miniature Rooms. Courtesy the Art Institute of Chicago ©.

present day), with special strengths in ceramics, glass, silver, and furniture. Highlights include a 1903 Viennese **Art Nouveau case clock** (note the metal bas-relief work); the 18th-century **Rococo Tredegar Cup** by Paul Lamerie, the most famous English silversmith of his day; an Oriental-themed 17th-century **Meissen porcelain centerpiece;** and the **Londonderry Vase,** a Sèvres porcelain masterpiece (and one of the finest examples of Empire style in the world) that was presented in 1814 to the Marquess of Londonderry by Louis XVIII. ⏱ *20 min. Lower level.*

❹ ★ **Arthur Rubloff Collection of Paperweights.** Don't miss this quirky collection, donated to the museum by Chicago real estate magnate Arthur Rubloff (1902–1983) in 1978. You'll find more than 1,500 of these charming and useful objects (most made of multi-colored glass), which became popular in the mid–19th century, when the establishment of a mail service made letter-writing, and letter-writing accessories, highly fashionable. ⏱ *15 min. Lower level.*

❺ ★★★ kids **Thorne Miniature Rooms.** Particularly entrancing to children and dollhouse fanatics, this must-see gallery

features 68 miniature rooms (the scale ranges from about 1 in./2.5cm to 1 ft./30cm) designed from 1937 to 1940 by Narcissa Ward Thorne, a miniaturist and the daughter-in-law of the founder of Montgomery Ward and Company. Each room is filled with tiny reproductions of furnished interiors from periods in European and American history. Styles run the gamut from the medieval 1300s to the modern 1930s. Especially noteworthy are the Louis XVI salon (inspired by Versailles's Petit Trianon) and the Georgian English Drawing Room (the keys on that tiny harpsichord actually move). The level of detail and masterful craftsmanship is extraordinary. ⏱ *20 min. Lower level.*

Art Institute Tips

Some tips for avoiding the rush hour: Many people don't realize the museum is open on Monday; keep this secret to yourself, and visit when the galleries are relatively subdued. Also, many visitors aren't aware that the museum stays open late on Thursdays, so consider stopping by after an early dinner.

❻ kids **Kraft Education Center.** Adjacent to the Thorne Miniature Rooms and under the Institute's Grand Staircase, this center offers special exhibits and games for kids. It also features numerous scheduled activities, which might include storytelling, puppet making, and poster drawing. All family programs are included in your admission fee. ⏱ *30 min. Lower level.*

A paperweight from the Rubloff Collection. Courtesy the Art Institute of Chicago ©.

Set inside an airy dining room, **7** **The Café** offers self-service dining that's a step above a typical museum's cafeteria in both quality and atmosphere. The menu features fresh fish, sandwiches, pizzas, Caesar salad, and a dessert station. In warm weather, take your meal outside to the seating area in McKinlock Court, a picturesque courtyard. *Lower level. $.*

8 ★ **Original Trading Floor of the Old Chicago Stock Exchange.** This room, originally built between 1893 and 1894, was salvaged and then reconstructed here when the Stock Exchange building was demolished in 1972. The room's elaborate stenciled decorations, molded plaster capitals, and art glass illustrate the work of Dankmar Adler and Louis Sullivan, two of Chicago's most important early architects. ⏱ *15 min. First level.*

9 **The Great Hall of European Arms and Armor.** At press time, it was uncertain where this exhibit would be located in the newly

One of the famous lion statues guarding the entrance to the Art Institute.

expanded museum, but it will be displayed in some form. The museum possesses 1,500 pieces of armor, one of the largest assemblages of its kind in North America. Most items are European and date from the 15th to the 19th centuries. Displays feature horse equipment, full and partial suits of armor, swords, daggers, and maces. There are also examples of armor from the Middle East and the Americas. ⏱ *30 min.*

Practical Matters

The Art Institute of Chicago (☎ 312/443-3600; www.artic.edu) is located at 111 S. Michigan Ave. (at Adams St.). Take Bus 3, 4, 60, 145, 147, or 151 to Michigan Avenue and Jackson Street or the Red Line El to the Jackson/State or Monroe/State stations.

Suggested admission is $12 for adults and $7 for seniors, children, and students with ID. Children 11 and under are free. There's an additional cost for special exhibitions. Admission is free on Thursday and Friday from 5 to 9pm. The museum is open Monday and Wednesday 10:30am to 5pm, Tuesday and Thursday 10:30am to 8pm (with free admission from 5 to 8pm on Thursday), and Friday, Saturday, and Sunday from 10am to 5pm. It's closed on Thanksgiving, December 25, and January 1.

Museum of Science & Industry

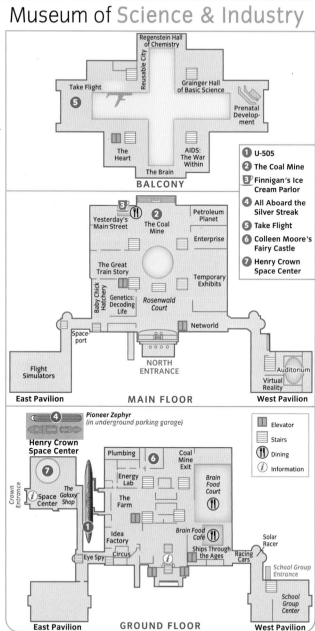

BALCONY

- Regenstein Hall of Chemistry
- Reusable City
- Take Flight **5**
- Grainger Hall of Basic Science
- Prenatal Development
- The Heart
- AIDS: The War Within
- The Brain

1. U-505
2. The Coal Mine
3. Finnigan's Ice Cream Parlor
4. All Aboard the Silver Streak
5. Take Flight
6. Colleen Moore's Fairy Castle
7. Henry Crown Space Center

MAIN FLOOR

- Yesterday's Main Street
- Finnigan's Ice Cream Parlor **3**
- The Coal Mine **2**
- Petroleum Planet
- Enterprise
- The Great Train Story
- Baby Chick Hatchery
- Genetics: Decoding Life
- Rosenwald Court
- Temporary Exhibits
- Networld
- Spaceport
- Flight Simulators
- NORTH ENTRANCE
- Auditorium
- Virtual Reality
- East Pavilion
- West Pavilion

GROUND FLOOR

- All Aboard the Silver Streak **4**
- Pioneer Zephyr (in underground parking garage)
- Henry Crown Space Center
- Plumbing
- Colleen Moore's Fairy Castle **6**
- Coal Mine Exit
- Brain Food Court
- Energy Lab
- Space Center **7**
- The Galaxy Shop
- The Farm
- Crown Entrance
- U-505 **1**
- Idea Factory
- Brain Food Café
- Eye Spy
- Circus
- Ships Through the Ages
- Racing Cars
- Solar Racer
- School Group Entrance
- School Group Center
- East Pavilion
- West Pavilion

Legend:
- Elevator
- Stairs
- Dining
- (i) Information

uilt as the only permanent structure for the 1893 World Columbian Exposition, the classical-style Palace of Fine Arts building is now home to 14 acres (5.6 hectares) of scientific wonders. Generations of children recount fond memories of this world-famous museum—the granddaddy of interactive museums, with some 2,000 exhibits. The good news: It still thrills kids (and adults, too). **START: Bus 6 or Metra Electric train to 57th Street and Lake Park Avenue.**

1 ★★★ U-505. The highlight of this 35,000-square-foot (3,252-sq.-m) exhibit is a German submarine (known as a U-boat) that sank a number of Allied ships during World War II before it was captured by the U.S. Navy in 1944. It was installed here in 1954 and remains the only German submarine on display in North America. The exhibit offers a fascinating look at the claustrophobic reality of underwater naval life. You have to pay $5 extra for a guided tour of the sub's interior, but this is still worth your time even if you don't go inside the actual submarine; there are interesting photos and exhibits that surround the sub. ⏱ *30 min. To avoid serious crowds, come at museum opening. Ground floor. Optional 15-min. guided tours cost $5.*

2 ★★ The Coal Mine. This exhibit, which dates back to 1934, now incorporates modern mining techniques—but the best part is a simulated trip down into a dark, mysterious re-created mine that's very lifelike (and not for the claustrophobic). Interactive stations focus on energy and conservation. A stop here is worth the inevitable theme park–like lines you'll face. ⏱ *30 min. First floor.*

3 Finnigan's Ice Cream Parlor is modeled on a real Hyde Park ice-cream shop that opened in 1917. Soak up the turn-of-the-20th-century atmosphere and indulge in awesome sundaes and shakes. For heartier appetites, there are sandwiches and chips, and great coffee. *Main floor, near the Coal Mine. $.*

Various transportation displays at the Museum of Science and Industry.

4 ★ kids All Aboard the Silver Streak. The Burlington Pioneer Zephyr—the world's first streamlined, diesel-electric train—was built in the 1930s and revolutionized train design. The 197-foot (60m) train, nicknamed the Silver Streak, is installed (along with a simulated train station) in the museum's three-story underground parking garage. This is a must for train buffs. ⏱ *15 min. Great Hall.*

5 kids Take Flight. This aviation-themed exhibit features a full-size Boeing 727 airplane that revs up its engines and replays voice recordings from a San Francisco–Chicago flight periodically throughout the day. Visitors can explore the interior and try some of the controls. ⏱ *15 min. Balcony.*

6 ★★ kids Colleen Moore's Fairy Castle. Colleen Moore, a popular silent film actress and miniatures fan, set out in 1928 to create her version of a dream dollhouse. It took more than 7 years and 700 craftsmen to create this lavishly decorated miniature palace, filled with priceless treasures. The rooms, filled with more than 2,000 miniatures, sport fairy-tale motifs and are incredibly detailed: King Arthur's Round Table in the dining room is set with a real gold service, and the princess's bathroom has running water. ⏱ *20 min. Ground floor.*

The dining room in Colleen Moore's Fairy Castle is set with gold tableware.

⑦ ★★★ Henry Crown Space Center. The story of space exploration is documented in copious detail inside this 35,000-square-foot

Classical statues on the exterior of the Museum of Science and Industry.

(3,150-sq.-m) addition to the museum—a must for space buffs. A highlight here is the **Apollo 8 Command Module,** the first manned craft to orbit the moon (check the exterior, and you'll spot the bumps and bruises it accumulated during the course of its journey to and from space). Other items of interest include astronaut training gear and a moon rock. Best of all is a 20-minute simulated space-shuttle experience at the center's five-story **Omnimax Theater.** Other science-related IMAX films are also screened at the theater; call the museum or check the website for show times. ⏱ *40 min. (more, if you see a film). Off ground level.* ●

Practical Information

The Museum of Science and Industry (☎ 800/468-6674 or 773/684-1414; www.msichicago.org) is located at 57th Street and Lake Shore Drive. Take Bus 6 or the Metra Rail to 57th Street and Lake Park Avenue.

Admission to the museum only is $13 adults, $12 seniors, $9 kids 3 to 11, and free for children under 3. Admission is free during various times of the year, especially in September and January. Check the website under "admission prices" for a full listing. Combination tickets to the museum and Omnimax Theater cost $20 adults, $19 seniors, $14 kids 3 to 11, and free for kids under 3 on an adult's lap.

The museum is open Monday through Saturday 9:30am to 5:30pm, and Sunday from 11am to 5:30pm. It is closed December 25.

The Gold Coast

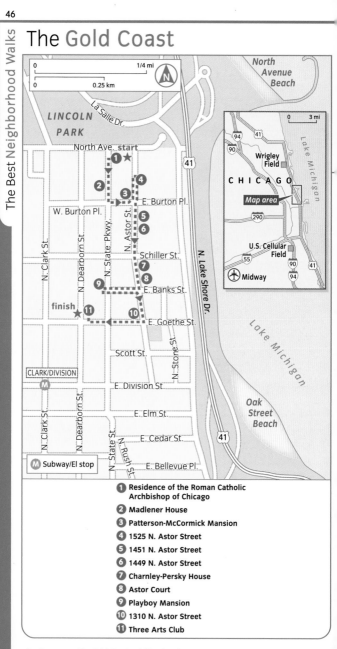

1 Residence of the Roman Catholic Archbishop of Chicago

2 Madlener House

3 Patterson-McCormick Mansion

4 1525 N. Astor Street

5 1451 N. Astor Street

6 1449 N. Astor Street

7 Charnley-Persky House

8 Astor Court

9 Playboy Mansion

10 1310 N. Astor Street

11 Three Arts Club

Previous page: The Gold Coast neighborhood.

This scenic and exclusive neighborhood of leafy streets and historic mansions fronts Lake Michigan and is home to some of Chicago's most famous and moneyed families. It dates back to the 1880s, when retailing wizard Potter Palmer built a lakeshore castle in the midst of what was then wild marshland (his spectacular home, at what is now 1450 N. Lake Shore Dr., was eventually torn down and a high-rise complex built in its place). After buying up the neighboring land, Palmer watched the city's most prominent social families follow his lead, turning his marshland into real estate gold. START: **Oak Street Beach, Lake Shore Drive just south of Oak Street. Bus: 151.**

❶ Residence of the Roman Catholic Archbishop of Chicago.

This 2½-story Queen Anne–style mansion dates back to 1880 and stands on the grounds of a former cemetery. One of the oldest and most notable residences on the Gold Coast, it's also one of the best preserved. Note the elaborate chimneys—there are 19 of them. The redbrick structure is the current home of Cardinal Francis George. *1555 N. State Pkwy. (at North Ave.).*

❷ Madlener House.

Designed as a private residence by Richard E. Schmidt in 1902, this National Historic Landmark foreshadowed the Art Deco style that would not emerge in Chicago for another 20

Madlener House is noted for both its Prairie and Chicago school influences.

The stately Residence of the Roman Catholic Archbishop in Chicago is one of the best-preserved mansions in Chicago.

years. The brick-and-limestone structure's clean lines and its doorways ornamented with delicate bronze grillwork offer hints of both the Prairie and Chicago schools of design. It's currently home to the Graham Foundation for Advanced Studies in the Fine Arts, which has installed a collection of fragments from famous Chicago buildings in the courtyard. It's a must for architecture buffs and historic home fans. ⏱ *90 min. for guided tour. 4 W. Burton Place.* ☎ *312/787-4071. www.graham foundation.org. Tours run by Society of Architectural Historians; for tour information, www.sah.org,* ☎ *312/ 573-1365. Tours of interior are offered Sat in conjunction with guided tour of local historic homes. $10 adults, $5 seniors and kids.*

③ Patterson–McCormick Mansion. Designed by New York architect Stanford White, this palazzo-style mansion was commissioned in 1893 by Joseph Medill, owner of the *Chicago Tribune,* as a wedding present for his daughter. The Georgian structure is faced with Roman bricks of burnt yellow and terra cotta trim, and marked the beginning of an architectural movement towards classical exteriors. The home was purchased in 1914 by Cyrus McCormick, Jr., son of the inventor of the reaper and the first president of International Harvester. McCormick had it enlarged to its current size in 1927. The building now houses condominiums. *20 E. Burton Place.*

④ ★★ 1525 N. Astor Street. This attractive town house (on a block full of multimillon-dollar homes) is the former home of Robert Todd Lincoln (1843–1926), the son of Abraham and Mary Todd Lincoln. Lincoln operated a private law practice in Chicago before moving on to serve as secretary of war to presidents Garfield and Arthur. Upon the death of George Pullman,

The 1893 palazzo-style Patterson–McCormick mansion marked the start of a Chicago trend focusing on Classic exteriors.

Frank Lloyd Wright called the Charnley-Persky House "the first modern house in America."

one of his clients, Lincoln became president of the Palace Car Company in 1897.

⑤ ★★ 1451 N. Astor Street. Designed by Howard Van Doren Shaw, who built several of the mansions on ritzy Astor Street, this mansion showcases the unique "Jacobethan" style (a mixture of 16th- and 17th-c. features of Elizabethan and Jacobean architecture). It was originally built for brewer Peter Fortune in 1912.

⑥ ★★ 1449 N. Astor Street. The origins of this grandiose château remain a mystery, though it was definitely built around 1890. The exterior features, including an intimidating stone porch, decorative friezes, and a large front bay make for worthwhile viewing.

⑦ ★★ Charnley-Persky House. This 1892 National Historic Landmark was built by the firm of Adler and Sullivan, back when a 19-year-old draftsman named Frank Lloyd Wright was laboring there in obscurity. Wright's role in designing the building (he called it "the first modern house in America") is evident in its progressive shape, especially when compared to its fanciful neighbors, homes that drew on styles based in antiquity. Even today, this home is an excellent illustration of the timelessness of Wright's ideas. Charles Persky donated the building to the Society of Architectural Historians in 1995, and the society runs public tours on Wednesdays (45 min.) and Saturdays (90 min.). Call for information. 🕐 *1 hr. 1365 N. Astor St.* ☎ *312/915-0105. www.sah.org. Tours are free Wed. at noon; Sat tours at 10am include other historic neighborhood residences and cost $10 adults, $5 seniors and kids.*

8 Astor Court. If this building evokes images of England when you look at it, that's because of its Georgian formality, typical of the architecture you'd find in London. It was designed over 1914 by Howard Van Doren Shaw, the architect also responsible for the Goodman Theatre (p 128). Look up at the ornament over the central drive, which leads to a formal inner court surrounded by residential units: The ornament is the source of the structure's nickname, "The Court of the Golden Hands." *1355 N. Astor St.*

The almost sedate-looking Playboy Mansion was home to Hugh Hefner and his bunnies during Playboy's heyday.

9 Playboy Mansion. Built in 1899, this very traditional-looking mansion was home to *Playboy*'s Hugh Hefner during his Chicago heyday in the 1960s. The building has been converted into private condos, so you'll need your imagination to envision Hugh romping here with his bunnies. (Playboy Enterprises, now run by Hugh's daughter, Christie Hefner, is still headquartered in Chicago.) *1340 N. State Pkwy.*

10 1310 N. Astor Street. John Wellborn Root (1850–91), one of the founders of the Chicago School of Architecture and a former director of the American Institute of Architects, is best known for his work on skyscrapers with Daniel Burnham (their collaborations include the Monadnock and Rookery buildings). But this lovely brick town house, built by Root in 1887, must have struck a chord with the architect—he moved in and lived here with his family (including his son, John Root, Jr., a renowned architect in his own right) until he died of pneumonia at the young age of 41.

11 Three Arts Club. Currently under renovation to become a luxury hotel and club, this four-story Chicago landmark was built in 1914 by architect John Holabird to house a club dedicated to providing women with a suitable environment for the study of painting, music, and drama. Many of the club's founders were prominent women of the time, including social reformer Jane Addams and socialite Edith Rockefeller McCormick. The club's residential units were arranged around a central courtyard, much in the style of a Tuscan villa (a lot of the exterior ornamentation is also Byzantine in nature). The ornamental mosaics over the terra cotta entrance salute the three branches of the arts that the club is named for. *1300 N. Dearborn St.*

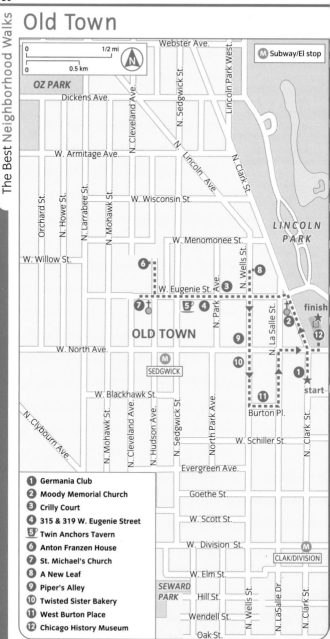

Old Town

The Best Neighborhood Walks

M Subway/El stop

1. Germania Club
2. Moody Memorial Church
3. Crilly Court
4. 315 & 319 W. Eugenie Street
5. Twin Anchors Tavern
6. Anton Franzen House
7. St. Michael's Church
8. A New Leaf
9. Piper's Alley
10. Twisted Sister Bakery
11. West Burton Place
12. Chicago History Museum

Old Town is an eclectic residential neighborhood that mixes frame cottages, brick town houses, historic taverns, and churches. Home to the city's German immigrant population at the turn of the 20th century, Old Town became famous in the '60s as a Hippie Haven (a time that saw the birth of the area's most famous landmark, The Second City comedy theater). After falling down on its luck in the '70s, the area has been gentrified and is now a top destination for boutique shopping, dining, and theater. START: **Intersection of Clark Street and North Avenue. Bus: 22 (Clark).**

① **Germania Club.** This lovely red-brick building, built in 1889, was the original home of a German-American *Sangverein* (singing society), a social outlet for immigrants in Chicago. Today, it's home to a bank and several stores. Note the elaborate terra cotta ornamentation on the exterior and the oversize, arched windows on the second floor. *1536 N. Clark St.*

Moody Memorial Church incorporates both Romanesque and Byzantine elements in its design.

② **Moody Memorial Church.** Dwight L. Moody came to Chicago from Massachusetts in 1856 to work as a shoe salesman, but eventually became one of the city's most colorful evangelists. He worked as a missionary mostly in the city's poorer sections, notably the area that later became known as Cabrini Green, one of the nation's most notorious housing projects (located at Clybourn St., Cabrini Green is nearly disassembled, and its residents have moved to low-rise, mixed-income housing). The church he founded was originally at Chicago Avenue and LaSalle Drive, where the Moody Bible Institute is now located. This building, dating from 1925, incorporates Byzantine (the decorative exterior) and Romanesque (the arched stained-glass windows) designs. Visitors are welcome to attend services. A free tour of the building is offered after the Sunday morning service. *1630 N. Clark St.* ☎ *312/943-0466. www.moodychurch.org.*

③ **Crilly Court.** Resembling homes in an old quarter of New Orleans (complete with wrought-iron balconies in the back), these well-maintained row houses sit on one of Chicago's oldest streets. The houses (and the apartment buildings opposite them) were built by contractor Daniel F. Crilly around 1885, when he cut a lane, named it for himself, and offered cottages to working families on the lower end of the economic scale. The owl-eyed among you might spot the names of the Crilly's children carved into the entrances to the Queen Anne–style buildings. *Block of Eugenie St., just west of Wells St.*

④ **315 & 319 W. Eugenie Street.** These privately owned homes are excellent examples of the wooden dwellings built outside the city limits in the years immediately following the Great Fire (wooden buildings were outlawed in the city proper following the conflagration).

A little taste of the Big Easy can be found amidst the wrought-iron balconies of Crilly Court.

They are noteworthy for their fanciful exterior trim work, not a rare sight in this immigrant neighborhood, where so many skilled artisans once made their homes.

Stop in for a burger at **5** ★★★ **Twin Anchors Tavern,** a neighborhood watering hole. This down-home spot, decorated with memorabilia dating back to the days when Frank Sinatra was a frequent visitor, is a favorite of locals. I suspect you'll feel at home here, too. *1655 N. Sedgwick St.* ☎ *312/266-1616. www.twin anchorsribs.com. $.*

6 Anton Franzen House. This classic Chicago cottage measures a story and a half and features a broad gabled facade. Built in 1880 of brick (as opposed to the prevailing wood), it is not so different in appearance from Frank Lloyd Wright's original Oak Park cottage (p 147). If you want to see a prime example of the typical late–19th-century Chicago house, this is it. *1726 N. Hudson Ave.*

7 ★★ St. Michael's Church. It's said that if you can hear the bells of St. Michael's, you know that you're

in Old Town. Indeed, the clock tower of this monumental church presides over the neighborhood, casting a long shadow over the courtyard that leads to the entrance. Historically a German parish (as opposed to the Irish parishes found elsewhere in the city during the early 1900s), St. Michael's (named for the Archangel who drove Adam and Eve from paradise) is a massive Romanesque church that reveals a strong southern European influence. The latter is especially evident in the stained-glass windows, embellished with Catholic iconography, that were imported from Munich at the turn of the 20th century. *1633 N. Cleveland Ave. (between North Ave. and Eugenie St.).* ☎ *312/642-2498. www. st-mikes.org.*

8 ★★ A New Leaf. North Wells Street offers great window shopping, and this store is a standout. The loft-style space is filled with cut flowers, vintage plant varieties, tropical foliage, succulents, and everything else you need to make a house a home, including candles in a rainbow of colors, ribbons to match, votive holders, and other tabletop necessities. *1818 N. Wells St.* ☎ *312/642-8553.*

9 Piper's Alley. This entertainment space was the site of a bakery owned by Henry Piper in 1880. During the 1960s, it was Old Town's

Frank Sinatra was a regular at the historic Twin Anchors Tavern, which still remains a local favorite.

Monumental St. Michael's Church presides over Old Town.

most popular tourist zone, filled with boutiques and bead shops. Today it's home to an art film cinema, several theaters and shops, and, since the 1950s, The Second City comedy club (p 126). *1616 N. Wells St.*

🔟 **Twisted Sister Bakery.** Located just south of North Avenue on Wells Street, this bakery's appearance—marble tabletops, exposed brick walls, hardwood floors—suggests "cozy neighborhood bakery," but the treats are a cut above. Pull a chair up to the fireplace and enjoy your choice of cupcakes, cookies, eclairs, cakes, and tarts, with a cup of Chicago's best local brew, Intelligensia Coffee. *1543 N. Wells St.* ☎ *312/932-1128. www.twistedsisterbakery.com.*

⓫ **West Burton Place.** What was once a short block of cookie-cutter Victorian homes was remodeled in 1927 into inspired apartment buildings by Sol Kogen and Edgar Miller, two Old Town artists who had studied together at the Art Institute in 1917. The heavily embellished

structures were rehabbed with an assortment of salvaged materials (glass, marble, terra cotta, and so on) from various demolished buildings in the area. Miller's masterpiece is 155 W. Burton Place (observe the bounty of transparent stained glass—Miller's favorite medium). Leases on the apartments within are zealously guarded.

⓬ ★ **Chicago History Museum.** Founded in 1856, the History Museum (formerly the Chicago Historical Society) is one of Chicago's oldest cultural institutions. Its handsome Georgian red-brick headquarters on the southwestern tip of Lincoln Park (just on the edge of Old Town) recently underwent a massive renovation. New galleries feature interactive exhibits, including a re-creation of an 1890s El station; an exhibit on "Chicago in Crisis" (covering everything from the Great Chicago Fire of 1871 to the Democratic Convention riots in 1968); and a section on Illinois's most famous native son, Abraham Lincoln. There's a special gallery just for kids, where you can dress up like a giant Chicago hot dog with all the fixings and admire yourself, hot peppers and all, in the mirror. *1601 N. Clark St. (at North Ave.).* ☎ *312/642-4600. www.chicagohistory.org.*

Kids love the interactive hot dog exhibit at the Chicago History Museum.

Bucktown & Wicker Park

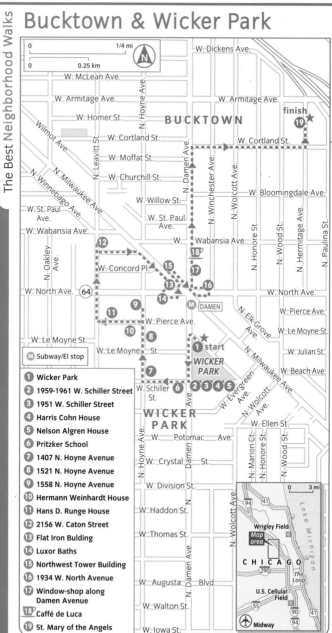

1 Wicker Park
2 1959-1961 W. Schiller Street
3 1951 W. Schiller Street
4 Harris Cohn House
5 Nelson Algren House
6 Pritzker School
7 1407 N. Hoyne Avenue
8 1521 N. Hoyne Avenue
9 1558 N. Hoyne Avenue
10 Hermann Weinhardt House
11 Hans D. Runge House
12 2156 W. Caton Street
13 Flat Iron Bulding
14 Luxor Baths
15 Northwest Tower Building
16 1934 W. North Avenue
17 Window-shop along
    Damen Avenue
18 Caffé de Luca
19 St. Mary of the Angels

M Subway/El stop

Wicker Park is an artists' community filled with trendy shops, funky restaurants, and side streets lined with pricey mansions and other examples of Victorian architecture. Bucktown, traditionally working-class, is alive with new development. Both are favorite nighttime destinations of Chicagoans in search of the latest and greatest clubs and bars, but many don't get to see the neighborhoods' historic architecture, which is best viewed during the day. START: **Take El's Blue line to Damen station, then go 1 block south to Wicker Park.**

① Wicker Park. The smallest park in the city (a mere 4 acres/1.6 hectares) gave its name to one of Chicago's most famous neighborhoods. The park was donated to the city around 1870 by siblings Charles (an alderman who made his money building railroads) and Joel Wicker. The brothers had extensive real estate holdings in the area and figured the park could only enhance the value of their property. *At the intersection of N. Damen Ave. and Schiller St.*

② 1959–1961 W. Schiller Street. This double home was built in 1886 in the fashionable Second Empire–style (note the large mansard roof and decorative sawtooth pattern in the brickwork). Its owner was a ship's captain and medical doctor. In the 1920s it

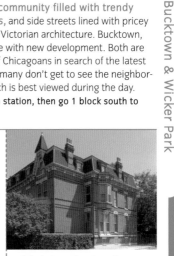

Built in the Second Empire–style, 1959–1961 W. Schiller has been restored to its original splendor.

became a rooming house. It has thankfully been restored with lively Victorian colors.

③ 1951 W. Schiller Street. Built as the residence of Dr. Nels T. Quales, a Norwegian immigrant and humanitarian who founded Chicago's Lutheran Deaconess Hospital, this house dates from 1873

Picturesque Wicker Park is the namesake for one of the city's most famous neighborhoods.

and features Italianate styling and a Romanesque exterior noted for its use of arches and truncated columns. The addition of Moorish windows on the first and second stories altered the facade around 1890, and the house is currently being restored to its original condition.

4 Harris Cohn House. This mansion (built in 1890–91) was the home of a partner in the Cohn Brothers Clothing Company. The Italian Romanesque facade features square columns of granite (polished to resemble marble) and a turret resting on a shell-shaped base. Stonework on the second-floor balcony follows a checkerboard pattern, and handrails are scrolled with a motif of oak leaves. The residence was reconverted from a boarding house into a single-family home after a fire damaged it around 1980, and underwent extensive interior restoration and beautification in the 1990s. *1941 W. Schiller St.*

5 Nelson Algren House. The exterior stonework on this three-story home is worth a look, but more interesting than the facade is

The Harris Cohn House features top-notch stone- and woodwork.

The cannon in the yard of 1558 N. Hoyne Ave. is a remnant of the home's time as an American Legion headquarters.

the fact that novelist Nelson Algren (1909–1981) lived in one of the building's third-floor apartments from 1959 to 1975. The National Book Award–winner (for his landmark *The Man with the Golden Arm*) and journalist drew inspiration for his writing from the surrounding neighborhood. A sidewalk marker provides info about Algren's life and writings. *1958 W. Evergreen St.*

6 Pritzker School. This Chicago public school is named for its most famous alumnus. A. N. Pritzker, the son of a Russian immigrant, grew up in the neighborhood and graduated from this school when it was known as Wicker Park School (Pritzker's family went on to found the Hyatt hotel chain). *2009 W. Schiller St.*

7 1407 N. Hoyne Avenue. In the late 19th century, so many vintners and brewers built mansions along the stretch of Hoyne running from Evergreen Avenue to North Avenue, that it became known as **Beer Baron Row.** This mansion, built in 1880 by German wine merchant John Rapp, was the largest single-family estate in Wicker Park at the time (the estate's Coach House is now a separate residence at 2044 W. Schiller St.). The mansard roof and wrought-iron fence are characteristic of the Second Empire–style of the estate. For all of its grandeur, however, this was not a happy home: Rapp was murdered here by his bookkeeper, his wife went insane, and their son was convicted of embezzlement. Note that locals refer to this place as either the Goldblatt or Wieboldt Mansion, though no member of these two prominent Chicago mercantile families (both Wicker Park fixtures) ever resided here.

8 1521 N. Hoyne Avenue.

German manufacturing executive Adolph Borgmeier was definitely behind the design of this fetching mansion, built in 1890 (though some claim it was actually built by a war profiteer who scammed the federal government for millions during the Civil War). The design is a brilliant mix of Romanesque and Queen Anne elements; look closely at the metal trim, and you'll spot a host of decorative symbols (flowers, scrolls, and so on). The likeness of a woman carved into the exterior is a typical embellishment on German-built houses.

9 1558 N. Hoyne Avenue.

Ever fearful of another conflagration after the events of the Great Fire of 1871, the designers of this 1877 mansion stuck to ornamental pressed metal when creating its decorative trim. The Queen Anne–style home was originally built for Hermann Plautz, the president of the Northwestern Brewing Company. From 1927 to 1972, it served as the headquarters for the local American Legion (which is why that seemingly out-of-place cannon is still in the front yard).

10 Hermann Weinhardt House.

When furniture company exec Hermann Weinhardt commissioned a home that would remind him of his German roots, this must-see mix of fairy-tale Victorian and Bavarian gingerbread was the result. The 1888 mansion features three stories of extraordinary detailing, including an elaborately carved balcony and an unusual juxtaposition of green stone and redbrick limestone. *2135 W. Pierce Ave. (between N. Hoyne Ave. and N. Leavitt St.).*

11 Hans D. Runge House.

This 1884 home, built by the treasurer of the Wolf Brothers Milling Company, is considered a prime example of the intricate Eastlake style (named for 19th-c. English designer Charles Eastlake) of ornamentation and features lots of elaborate woodwork. Architecture aside, the house is best known for a 1930 concert given by the great Polish pianist and statesman Ignacy Paderewski from the upper level of the building's two-story porch, when the home functioned as the Polish consulate. *2138 W. Pierce Ave. (between N. Hoyne Ave. and N. Leavitt St.).*

Paderewski gave a piano concert on the Hans D. Runge House's balcony in 1930.

The Northwest Tower Building is one of the finest examples of Art Deco architecture in Chicago.

12 2156 W. Caton Street. Import-export entrepreneur Ole Thorpe built this German-influenced Romanesque mansion in 1892. The most obvious feature is the round, domed turret rising from the flared and rough-surfaced foundations. Other highlights include a host of stained-glass windows and a notable sunburst design over the door on the second-story porch.

13 Flat Iron Building. Wicker Park is known for its artistic bent, and this office building, designed in 1929 by the firm of Holabird & Root, is best known as the home of many artists' lofts and galleries (most are open to the public, so feel free to wander around inside). *1569 N. Milwaukee Ave. (at W. North Ave.).*

14 Luxor Baths. Also known as the North Avenue Baths, this building dates back to the 1920s, when public baths were all the rage. The baths were a popular meeting spot for wheelers and dealers back in the day, and, according to legend, were also a mob hangout. The gleaming terra cotta exterior is all that remains of the past; the interior has been transformed into a bunch of private yuppie apartments. *2041 W. North Ave.*

15 Northwest Tower Building. One of the finest examples of Art Deco architecture in Chicago, this handsome 12-story office building was built in 1929 and was the tallest structure outside of the downtown area at the time. It's often called the Coyote Building because it's the site of the annual "Around the Coyote" arts festival. During the Prohibition era, the building was the terminus for a secret underground tunnel (now closed) that allowed patrons to escape a speak-easy across the street during raids. *1600 N. Milwaukee Ave.*

16 kids 1934 W. North Avenue. The coolness quotient of the Wicker Park/Bucktown area may have soared in 2001, when MTV selected it as the site of that season's hit reality soap opera, *The Real World*, but quite a number of

The Flat Iron Building is home to many artists' lofts and galleries.

Picturesque St. Mary of the Angels dominates the Bucktown skyline.

The warmly lit 18 ★ **Caffé de Luca** features deep wooden booths and aims to replicate the small town of Cindente, Italy. Almond sodas, pastries, coffee, gelato, plus a selection of beers and wines are on the menu, and you can sit outside in good weather. *1721 N. Damen Ave.* ☎ *773/342-6000. $.*

19 St. Mary of the Angels.
The dome on this Renaissance-style Roman Catholic church dominates the neighborhood's skyline, and was modeled on the Vatican's St. Peter's Basilica. The immense building—it takes up an entire block—opened in 1920 to serve Bucktown's Polish parish, but by the 1980s had deteriorated to the point that it had been slated for demolition. A massive outcry from the local community led instead to a huge restoration campaign (the repairs cost more than the price of the original construction). Today, the church, from the carved angels on its rooftop to its stained-glass windows, is in picture-perfect shape. *1850 N. Hermitage Ave. (at W. Cordlandt St.).* ☎ *773/278-2644. www.smachicago.org.*

Window-shop your way down Bucktown's major commercial street, Damen Avenue.

locals were anything but thrilled by the accompanying publicity. This Wicker Park loft apartment will be familiar to viewers as the spot where the young and the restless lived during filming (several of the seven cast members worked a few doors down, at the hip pizzeria, Piece).

17 Window-shop along
Damen Avenue. The best way to travel from Wicker Park into Bucktown is to window-shop along Damen Avenue, the street that marks the heart of the neighborhood. Start at its intersection with North Avenue and work your way up. The busy thoroughfare is loaded with vintage and designer clothing stores, cozy coffee shops, and trendy bars. Good shopping bets include **Belly Dance Maternity** (p 77), **Riley** (p 79), and **Psychobaby** (p 78). It's also fabulous for people-watching.

Andersonville

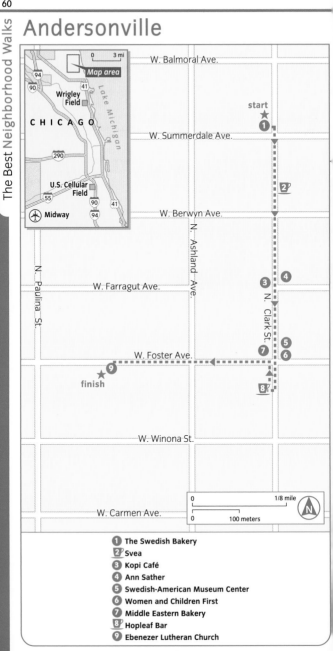

1 The Swedish Bakery
2 Svea
3 Kopi Café
4 Ann Sather
5 Swedish-American Museum Center
6 Women and Children First
7 Middle Eastern Bakery
8 Hopleaf Bar
9 Ebenezer Lutheran Church

Chicago's Swedish immigrants left their mark on this now-gentrified neighborhood, which has the feel of a small Mid-western village—albeit with an eclectic mix of Middle Eastern restaurants and a burgeoning gay and lesbian community. The architecture isn't particularly special, though on the side streets east of Clark Street, you'll find typical Chicago-style redbrick three-flats (three-floor buildings, one apartment to a floor) and bungalows. Come here to stroll, shop, eat, people-watch, and soak up a unique neighborhood's flavor. START: **Clark and Foster streets. El: Red Line to Berwyn.**

1 ★★★ **The Swedish Bakery.** Many locals consider this 80-year-old bakery the best in Chicago. Handmade Swedish butter cookies are available year-round, and at the holidays, you'll find festive heart-shaped spicy ginger cookies (*pepparkakor*), spice cookies (*pfeffernuesse*), and *marzariner* almond tarts. Don't let the crowds of loyal customers dissuade you; take a number and get in line—it moves quickly. *5348 N. Clark St.* ☎ *773/561-8919. www.swedish bakery.com.*

The storefront **2** **Svea** serves only breakfast and lunch, featuring honest, simple home cooking: cre-pelike Swedish pancakes with lin-gonberry sauce; grilled *falukorv*, a mild pork sausage; and, of course, Swedish meatballs. *5236 N. Clark St.* ☎ *773/275-7738. $.*

The Swedish Bakery's cakes and cookies make it a favorite with locals.

3 **Kopi Café.** Plan your next travel adventure at this travel bookstore, global boutique, and cof-feehouse. It has a worldly charm (and a sort of Moroccan atmos-phere), with pillows and floor-level tables for lounging, and boutique items (many are travel-themed) for browsing. Clocks on the walls keep the time for several countries around the world. They make a mean mango smoothie. *5317 N. Clark St.* ☎ *773/989-5674.*

4 ★★ **Ann Sather.** Say the words "Ann Sather" to a Chicagoan, and the reply will be "cinnamon buns." The gigantic, gooey buns (two for $3) are synonymous with one of the city's most popular brunch spots (there are additional locations on Belmont, Broadway, and Southport). For my money, though, the pecan rolls are even better, and best of all are the heav-enly Swedish pancakes with lin-gonberries. Swedish folk art murals provide the ideal backdrop for your meal. There will be a wait, but don't worry: lines move quickly. *5207 N. Clark St.* ☎ *773/271-6677. www.annsather.com.*

5 kids **Women and Children First.** This feminist and children's bookstore holds a huge selection of titles (more than 30,000) for, by, and about women. Better yet, it's a warm, inviting place that welcomes browsers. The store often sponsors

Keeping Warm with Swedish Glögg

Swedes and Chicagoans have one major thing in common: cold weather—and plenty of it. When icy winds blow off Lake Michigan, head to Andersonville for a piping-hot mug of *glögg* at Simon's Tavern, 5210 N. Clark St. (☎ 773/878-0894). The Swedish-inspired bar (originally owned by a Swedish immigrant, then run by his son until 1994, when it was sold to some very friendly folks) mixes up quite a concoction of port wine, brandy, oranges, raisins, and spices, served in a glass coffee mug with almonds and wine-soaked raisins. While you're sipping, make sure to check out the bulletproof glass booth, where the original owner, acting as a bootlegger, cashed people's paychecks during Prohibition. When you're touring and the temp starts dropping, Simon's is the perfect spot for staying warm.

writing workshops and events featuring notable feminist authors (past guests have included Margaret Atwood and Maxine Hong Kingston). *5233 N. Clark St. (between Foster and*

The striking Gothic Ebenezer Lutheran Church, known as the "Swedish Cathedral."

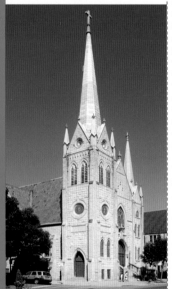

Bryn Mawr aves.). ☎ *773/769-9299. www.womenandchildrenfirst.com.*

6 ★★ kids **Swedish-American Museum Center.** This storefront museum chronicles the Swedish immigrant contribution to American life. The museum is a hub of activity, offering cultural lectures, concerts, classes, and folk dancing geared to Swedish Americans, some of whom still live in the surrounding Andersonville neighborhood. On the third floor, you'll find a highly worthwhile **Children's Museum of Immigration,** where Swedish craft demonstrations and classes, as well as language classes, are offered. Geared toward kindergarteners through sixth graders, the museum lets kids experience the journey to North America from the Old World. They can step inside an authentic Swedish farmhouse, board a steamship for America, and begin a new life in a log cabin. There's also a nice gift shop that offers Orrefors glassware; books on Swedish folk art, decorating, and cooking; children's toys; and holiday knick-knacks. ⏱ *30 min. 5211 N. Clark St. (near Foster Ave.).* ☎ *773/728-8111.*

No visit to Anne Sather is complete without its famous cinnamon buns.

www.samac.org. Admission $4 adults, $3 seniors and kids over age 3, free for kids under 3. Tues–Fri 10am–4pm; Sat–Sun 11am–4pm. Subway/El: Red Line to Bryn Mawr.

7 Middle Eastern Bakery. This grocery is known for its deli counter, which features spinach pies, fresh falafel, trays of baklava, pickled vegetables, olives, and soups. If you're looking to stock up on snacks to carry on your travels or something to munch on as you stroll the neighborhood, you'll find plenty of bulk goods in wooden barrels: dried fruits, nuts, and candies. *1512 W. Foster Ave. ☎ 773/561-2224.*

The **8 Hopleaf Bar,** a European-style pub, is the perfect spot to end your shopping tour of Clark Street. Choose a Belgian brew (there's a selection of 200 varieties) and a plate of some of the best fries in the city—perfectly crispy and served with sides of aioli (garlicky mayonnaise) and ketchup. *5148 N. Clark St. ☎ 773/334-9851. $$.*

9 Ebenezer Lutheran Church. This striking, Gothic-style limestone church (nicknamed the "Swedish Cathedral") was built in 1908 by the neighborhood's Swedish Lutherans (the congregation, however, was founded in 1892). During the height of the Scandinavian immigration wave in the late 1890s and early 1900s, it served as a center for religion, culture, and family activities. Today, the church serves quite a diverse congregation (from Swedes to Nigerians) and is known for welcoming gays and lesbians. You will, however, still find evidence of the congregation's Swedish heritage: On December 13, there's a St. Lucia Day celebration, and on Christmas morning, there's a traditional service conducted in Swedish. *1650 W. Foster Ave. ☎ 773/561-8496. www. ebenezerchurch.org.*

Andersonville's Hopleaf Bar serves some of the best fries in the city.

Hyde Park

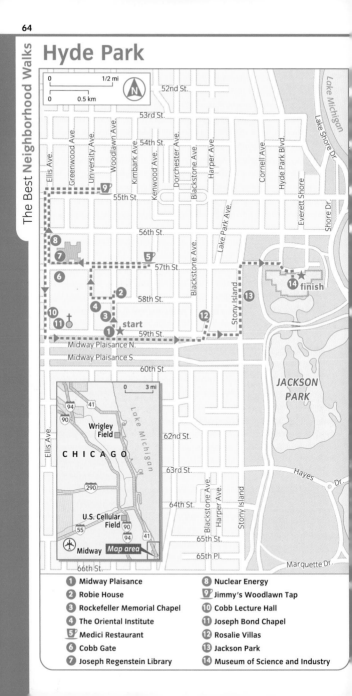

1 Midway Plaisance
2 Robie House
3 Rockefeller Memorial Chapel
4 The Oriental Institute
5 Medici Restaurant
6 Cobb Gate
7 Joseph Regenstein Library
8 Nuclear Energy
9 Jimmy's Woodlawn Tap
10 Cobb Lecture Hall
11 Joseph Bond Chapel
12 Rosalie Villas
13 Jackson Park
14 Museum of Science and Industry

Hyde Park combines a top attraction for kids—The Museum of Science and Industry—with the University of Chicago's 175 acres of gorgeous Gothic buildings and some of the city's most distinctive residential architecture. It's a truly racially integrated neighborhood and well worth visiting, but be aware that just beyond its borders lie some of the blighted areas of the city. START: **Take the Metra to 56th Street and walk 4 blocks south to 60th Street.**

1 Midway Plaisance. The heart of the University of Chicago campus is a broad (1-block wide), grassy thoroughfare designed by Frederick Law Olmsted, the famous landscape architect behind New York City's Central Park. The mile-long (1.6km) stretch was the site of the 1893 World Columbian Exposition's Bazaar of Nations, which featured the world's first Ferris wheel and carnival sideshow attractions. The term "midway" has been used ever since to refer to the heart of a carnival. *At 60th St. and Stony Island Ave., west to Cottage Grove Ave.*

2 ★★★ Robie House. Considered a masterpiece of 20th-century American architecture, this National Historic Landmark features the open layout, linear geometry of form, and craftsmanship that are typical of Frank Lloyd Wright's Prairie School design. Completed in 1909 for inventor Frederick Robie, a bicycle and motorcycle manufacturer, the home is also notable for its exquisite leaded- and stained-glass doors and windows. It's also among the last of Wright's Prairie School–style homes: During its construction, Wright abandoned both his family and his Oak Park practice to follow other pursuits, most prominently the realization of his Taliesin home and studio in Spring Green, Wisconsin. Docents from Oak Park's Frank Lloyd Wright Home & Studio Foundation (p 147, **2**) lead tours here, even though the house is currently undergoing a massive, 10-year restoration. A Wright specialty bookshop is located in the building's former three-car garage—a structure that was highly unusual for the time in which it was built. ⏱ *2 hr. 5757 S. Woodlawn Ave. (at 58th St.).* ☎ *773/ 834-1847. www.wrightplus.org. Admission $12 adults, $10 seniors and $5 kids 4–10. Mon–Fri tours at 11am, 1pm, and 3pm; Sat–Sun every half-hour 11am–3:30pm. Bookshop open daily 10am–5pm. Bus: 6.*

3 ★★★ Rockefeller Memorial Chapel. John D. Rockefeller founded the University of Chicago in cooperation with the American Baptist Society, and his bequest to the university included funds for this magnificent Gothic minicathedral (a mere chapel, it isn't). The building was designed by Bertram Goodhue (who was also the architect behind Cal Tech's campus) and dedicated in 1928; it was renamed for its benefactor upon his death in 1937. Outstanding features include the

Robie House, among the last of Frank Lloyd Wright's Prairie School–style homes.

The Assyrian winged bull from the palace of Sargon II, at the Oriental Institute.

circular stained-glass window high above the main altar, a series of statues depicting important figures in religion, and the world's second-largest carillon (72 bells). *5850 S. Woodlawn Ave.* ☎ *773/702-2100. http://rockefeller.uchicago.edu. Free admission. Daily 8am–4pm. Bus: 6.*

④ ★★ **The Oriental Institute.** The Oriental Institute houses one of the world's major collections of Near Eastern art (some of the exhibits here date back to 9000 B.C.). Many of the galleries have been renovated since the Institute's opening in 1931, but this is still a traditional museum: lots of glass cases, very few interactive exhibits. The must-see Egyptian Gallery includes a monumental 17-foot (5.2m) solid-quartzite statue of King Tutankhamen (the boy king who ruled Egypt from about 1335–24 B.C.), the largest Egyptian sculpture in the Western Hemisphere (tipping the scales at 6 tons/5,443k). The highlight of the Mesopotamian Gallery is a massive, 16-foot-tall (4.9m) sculpture of a winged bull with a human head, which once stood in the palace of Assyrian King Sargon II. Many of the gallery's other works have become one-of-a-kind since the looting of the National Museum in Baghdad in 2003. ⏱ *1 hr. 1155 E. 58th St. (at University Ave.).* ☎ *773/702-9514.*

http://oi.uchicago.edu. Free admission; suggested donation $5 adults, $2 children under 12. Tues and Thurs–Sat 10am–6pm; Wed 10am–8:30pm; Sun noon–6pm. Bus: 6.

The casual ⑤ **Medici Restaurant,** near the university campus, has fed generations of students, who've carved their names into the tables while chowing down on the house specialty—pizza. Great salads and baked goods, too. *1327 E. 57th St.* ☎ *773/667-7394. $.*

⑥ **Cobb Gate.** Enter the campus of the world-renowned University of Chicago (more than 75 Nobel Laureates have graced its halls) through Cobb Gate (movie buffs might recognize it as the place where Harry met Sally in *When Harry Met Sally*), which features lots of Gothic detailing. The mythic figures climbing to the tip of the gate's pointed gable are said to represent the admissions counselor and college examiner, defying students an easy passage into the university. You, however, can pass through without problem, and can stroll around the campus's dramatic stone buildings (most of them designed by renowned Gothic architect Henry Ives Cobb),

The University of Chicago's Rockefeller Memorial Chapel, a Gothic masterpiece.

patterned after England's Oxford University. *57th St. between Ellis and University aves.*

7 Joseph Regenstein Library. This building is a behemoth that was ostensibly designed to blend in with its neighbors, but does nothing of the sort. The building's textured limestone (it looks like slab concrete) and vertical glass windows are not beloved by critics, but the users of this seven-floor research library (the largest on campus) give it high marks. It is home to one of the most extensive map collections in the world. The library is generally closed to the public, but out-of-state visitors with a valid photo ID can get a day pass at the library's Privileges Office (worth it if you're a bookworm or a map fan). *1100 E. 57th St. (between S. University and S. Ellis aves.).* ☎ *773/702-8782. www.lib.uchicago.edu.*

8 Nuclear Energy. This abstract sculpture (representing a skull and a mushroom cloud) by Henry Moore was installed in 1967 to commemorate the site of the world's first controlled nuclear chain reaction. In 1942, Nobel Laureate Enrico Fermi supervised that historic event in a makeshift underground laboratory beneath what was then the grandstand of the university's Stagg Field sports stadium. *Ellis Ave. between 56th and 57th sts.*

The Cobb Gate entrance to the University of Chicago campus.

Nuclear Energy marks the site of the world's first controlled nuclear chain reaction.

9 Jimmy's Woodlawn Tap is the University of Chicago's most famous watering hole. This 50-year-old bar and grill doesn't offer much in the way of atmosphere (it's famously rough around the edges), but it's a great place to grab a drink, burger, or barbecue beef or reuben sandwich. *1172 E. 55th St.* ☎ *773/643-5516. $.*

10 Cobb Lecture Hall. This distinctive Gothic building, the first of 19 that Henry I. Cobb (1859–1931) designed for the campus, was all there was to the University of Chicago when it opened for business in 1892. Classes are still held here today (the interior was revamped in 1963), and the building is also home to the Renaissance Society, Chicago's oldest contemporary art museum (founded in 1915). The Society holds frequent exhibitions that are open to the public in the Bregman Gallery on the fourth floor. *5811 S. Ellis Ave.* ☎ *773/702-8670. www.renaissance society.org. Free admission. Gallery open Tues–Fri 10am–5pm; Sat–Sun noon–5pm.*

11 ★★ Joseph Bond Chapel. Even nonbelievers applaud the exquisite interiors of this showcase for ecclesiastical architecture. The 300-seat chapel was donated to the university in 1926 in honor of the memory of Joseph Bond, a former trustee of the Baptist Theological Union, a precursor to the university's Divinity School (which uses the building for services on Wed mornings). The structure is richly decorated with detailed carvings, etchings, sculptures, stained glass, and detailed woodwork—all of it themed to messages from the New Testament and the Gospels. The picturesque chapel is a very popular venue for weddings. *1050 E. 59th St.* ☎ *773/702-8200. http://divinity.uchicago.edu/student/bond.shtml.*

⓬ **Rosalie Villas.** In 1883, a developer named Rosalie Buckingham purchased this land and planned to build a subdivision of 42 houses on spacious lots to re-create a semi-rural environment. She hired George Pullman's architect, Solon S. Berman, who had recently completed building the Pullman planned community, just to the south. Today, many of the cottages they constructed remain, in various states of repair, and line both sides of the block. Their eclectic color schemes and overgrown gardens give the street a distinctive countercultural flavor. ***Harper Ave. between 59th and 57th sts.***

One of the eclectically designed and visually striking Rosalie Villas.

⓭ **Jackson Park.** Originally known as South Park (in 1880 it was renamed in honor of President Andrew Jackson), this 1,055-acre (4.3-sq.-km) park was laid out in 1871 by Olmsted and Vaux, the team that designed Central Park in New York City. The full plan for the park, however, wasn't carried out until 1890, when Olmsted returned to Chicago to work with Daniel Burnham on the World's Columbian Exposition. Together, the two architects mapped out broad boulevards and built fountains and temporary, ornate, white buildings (the park was nicknamed The White City during the fair). Today, few of the Beaux Arts structures and gardens erected for the Exposition remain (an exception is the Fine Arts Palace, which now houses the Museum of Science and Industry; see p 42), though the park has aged quite gracefully and is a popular spot for strolling, fishing, golf, tennis, and boating. ***6401 S. Stony Island Ave. Bus: 1 or 6.***

⓮ ★★★ kids **Museum of Science and Industry.** Cap your walking tour with a stop at this museum's stellar Henry Crown Space Center. If time allows, rest your legs while taking in a movie at the center's Omnimax Theater. See p 44, ❼. ●

Shopping Best Bets

Best Place for Take-Home Gifts
★★★ Chicago ArchiCenter, 224 S. Michigan Ave. (p 81)

Best Bargain Shoes
★★ Lori's Discount Designer Shoes, 824 W. Armitage Ave. (p 78)

Best Art Supplies
★★ Pearl Paint Art Supplies, 255 W. Chicago Ave. (p 75)

Best Home Furnishings
★★★ Primitive Art Works, 130 N. Jefferson St. (p 82)

Best Wood Furniture
★★★ Sawbridge Studios, 153 W. Ohio St. (p 82)

Biggest Collection of Blues and Jazz
★★★ Jazz Record Mart, 27 E. Illinois St. (p 83)

Best Art Gallery
★★★ Rhona Hoffman Gallery, 118 N. Peoria St. (p 82)

Best Variety of Clothing
★★★ Mark Shale, 900 N. Michigan Ave. (p 78)

Best Department Store Values
Nordstrom, 55 E. Grand Ave. (on Michigan Ave., p 80)

Best Glassware
★★ P.O.S.H., 613 N. State St. (p 82)

Best Children's Books
Unabridged Bookstore, 3251 N. Broadway (p 77)

Best Place for Men's High Fashion
Ultimo, 116 E. Oak St. (p 79)

Best Place for Women's High Fashion
Ikram, 873 N. Rush St. (p 77)

Best Hip and Wearable Women's Fashion
★★ Sugar Magnolia, 34 E. Oak St. (p 79)

Best Wine Store
★★ House of Glunz, 1206 N. Wells St. (p 81)

Best Museum Shop
★★ Art Institute of Chicago, 111 S. Michigan Ave. (p 81)

Best Vintage Clothing
★★★ Wacky Cats, 3012 N. Lincoln Ave. (p 79)

Best Designer Vintage
★★★ McShane's Exchange, 815 W. Armitage Ave. (p 78)

Best Place for Antiques
★★★ Griffins & Gargoyles Ltd., 2140 N. Lawrence Ave. (p 75)

Best Gourmet Food Store
★★★ Fox & Obel Food Market, 401 E. Illinois St. (p 80)

Best Chocolates
★★★ Vosges Haut-Chocolat, 520 N. Michigan Ave. (p 81)

Fox & Obel Food Market, the city's top spot for gourmet foods.

Magnificent Mile Shopping

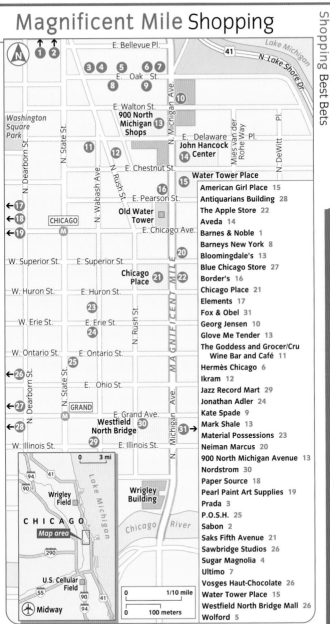

American Girl Place 15
Antiquarians Building 28
The Apple Store 22
Aveda 14
Barnes & Noble 1
Barneys New York 8
Bloomingdale's 13
Blue Chicago Store 27
Border's 16
Chicago Place 21
Elements 17
Fox & Obel 31
Georg Jensen 10
Glove Me Tender 13
The Goddess and Grocer/Cru
  Wine Bar and Café 11
Hermès Chicago 6
Ikram 12
Jazz Record Mart 29
Jonathan Adler 24
Kate Spade 9
Mark Shale 13
Material Possessions 23
Neiman Marcus 20
900 North Michigan Avenue 13
Nordstrom 30
Paper Source 18
Pearl Paint Art Supplies 19
Prada 3
P.O.S.H. 25
Sabon 2
Saks Fifth Avenue 21
Sawbridge Studios 26
Sugar Magnolia 4
Ultimo 7
Vosges Haut-Chocolate 26
Water Tower Place 15
Westfield North Bridge Mall 26
Wolford 5

p 69: The Paper Source in River North.

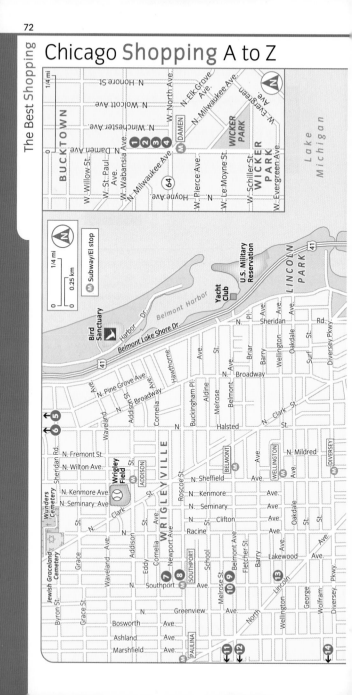

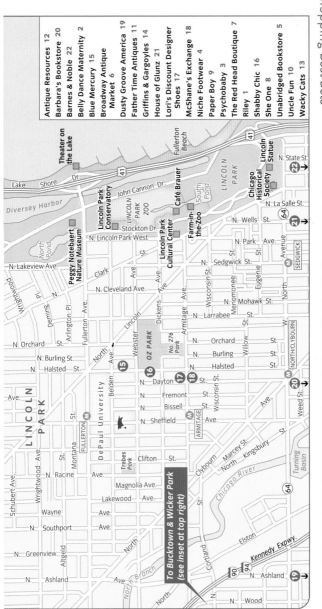

Antique Resources 12
Barbara's Bookstore 20
Barnes & Noble 22
Belly Dance Maternity 2
Blue Mercury 15
Broadway Antique
  Market 6
Dusty Groove America 19
Father Time Antiques 11
Griffins & Gargoyles 14
House of Glunz 21
Lori's Discount Designer
  Shoes 17
McShane's Exchange 18
Niche Footwear 4
Paper Boy 9
Psychobaby 3
The Red Head Boutique 7
Riley 1
Shabby Chic 16
She One 8
Unabridged Bookstore 5
Uncle Fun 10
Wacky Cats 13

To Bucktown & Wicker Park
(see inset at top right)

Loop & River North Shopping

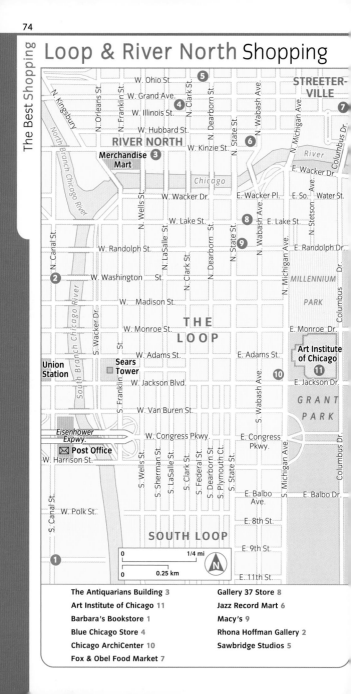

The Antiquarians Building 3	Gallery 37 Store 8
Art Institute of Chicago 11	Jazz Record Mart 6
Barbara's Bookstore 1	Macy's 9
Blue Chicago Store 4	Rhona Hoffman Gallery 2
Chicago ArchiCenter 10	Sawbridge Studios 5
Fox & Obel Food Market 7	

Shopping A to Z

Antiques

The Antiquarians Building

RIVER NORTH   Some 30 dealers on four floors proffer fine antiques for big bucks. Offerings include silver, jewelry, and Asian, Art Deco, Old English, and mid–20th-century furnishings. *159 W. Kinzie St.* ☎ *312/527-0533. AE, DISC, MC, V. El: Brown Line to Merchandise Mart. Map p 71.*

Antique Resources WEST LAKEVIEW

This spot specializes in antique lighting fixtures, especially French chandeliers, and also features a good array of Georgian furniture. *1741 W. Belmont Ave.* ☎ *773/871-4242. www.antiqueresources inc.com. MC, V. El: Red or Brown line to Belmont. Map p 72.*

Broadway Antique Market

WEST LAKEVIEW   Two floors of funky, fun, and somewhat pricey antiques and collectibles. *6130 N. Broadway.* ☎ *773/743-5444. www. bamchicago.com. AE, DISC, MC, V. El: Red Line to Granville. Map p 72.*

Father Time Antiques WEST

LAKEVIEW   This family-owned shop, in business since 1979, sells the Midwest's largest variety of antique timepieces. *2108 W. Belmont Ave.* ☎ *773/880-5599. www. fathertimeantiques.com. MC, V. El: Red or Brown line to Belmont. Map p 72.*

★★★ Griffins & Gargoyles Ltd.

RAVENSWOOD   Family-owned since 1975, this shop specializes in Western European furniture dating from 1880 to 1930. Come for dining tables, bureaus and dressers, benches, and cabinets. Customizing is one of their specialties: a friend recently had a wonderful kitchen table fashioned from a zinc top and a whitewashed picnic table-style base. *2140 W. Lawrence Ave. (at Diversey Pkwy.).* ☎ *773/769-1255. www.griffins-gargoyles.com. MC, V. El: Brown Line to Diversey. Map p 72.*

Art Supplies

★★ Paper Source RIVER NORTH

Now a national chain, Chicago is home to the original Paper Source store. Learn how to make your own scrapbooks, buy cards and small gifts, choose among reams of exotic papers, or add to your collection of rubber stamps. *232 W. Chicago Ave.* ☎ *312/337-0798. www.paper-source. com. AE, DISC, MC, V. El: Brown Line to Chicago. Map p 71.*

★★ Pearl Paint Art Supplies

RIVER NORTH   The Midwestern outpost of New York's famous Canal Street store carries everything from canvases and egg-tempera paints for serious artists to glue guns and glitter for rainy-day arts and crafts. *255 W. Chicago Ave. (at Franklin St.).* ☎ *312/915-0200. www.pearlpaint. com. AE, DISC, MC, V. El: Brown Line to Chicago. Map p 71.*

Father Time Antiques offers a quality selection of antique clocks and watches.

Shopping in Chicago: Just the Facts

Chicago stores usually open for business at 9 or 10am. Smaller stores usually close by 5 or 6pm. Traditionally, larger stores stay open latest—until 8pm or so—on Thursday night. On all other nights, except Sundays, when they open around 11am and close around 6pm, department stores stay open until about 7pm.

The biggest sales of the year take place in January, when retailers slash prices on winter clothing to make room for spring offerings. This is the best time to shop (if you didn't blow all your bucks over the holidays), especially because Chicago has the highest total sales tax of any major city in the country at 10.25%. Car rentals are taxed at 20%, hotel rooms at 15.4%, and soft drinks 13.25%. Ouch. Grocery items and medications are much less, at 2%.

Beauty Products & Cosmetics

Aveda MAGNIFICENT MILE   This branch of the eco-friendly Minnesota-based cosmetics company sells all-natural scents, lotions, hair care products, and makeup. Come here and breathe in the aromatherapy. *875 N. Michigan Ave., in the plaza of the John Hancock Center Observatory.* ☎ *312/664-0417. www.aveda.com. AE, DISC, MC, V. El: Red Line to Chicago/State. Map p 71.*

★★★ Blue Mercury LINCOLN PARK   Both a luxury apothecary and spa chain, this shop carries a huge range of cosmetics, from Diptyque, Fresh, Creed, Laura Mercier, and more, including hard-to-find brands. *2208 N. Halsted St.* ☎ *773/327-6900. www.bluemercury.com. AE, DISC, MC, V. El: Brown Line to Armitage. Map p 72.*

Sabon GOLD COAST   Known for its body scrubs and minimalist packaging, this is the place to pop into for a free Dead Sea hand scrub. You'll also find home scents, facial bars, and—perfect for those long Chicago winters—a deep moisturizing body butter. *1152–1154 N. State St.* ☎ *312/981-1234.*

www.sabonchicago.com. MC, V. El: Red Line to Chicago/State. Map p 71.

Books & Stationery

Barbara's Bookstore WEST LOOP   This flagship store of a popular local chain is known for hosting numerous author readings for kids and adults. *1218 S. Halsted (at Roosevelt Rd.).* ☎ *312/413-2665. www.barbarasbookstore.com. AE, DISC, MC, V. Subway/El: Blue Line to UIC/Halsted. Map p 72.*

Barnes & Noble GOLD COAST   Buy a book and sip coffee at the ground-level cafe in this well-situated store, just steps away from the hustle and bustle of Michigan Avenue. *1130 N. State St.* ☎ *312/280-8155. AE, DISC, MC, V. El: Red Line to Clark/Division. Map p 71.*

Borders MAGNIFICENT MILE   This enormously popular and well-trafficked bookstore has a cafe that overlooks Michigan Avenue and a lower level offering a colorful selection of writing accessories. *830 N. Michigan Ave.* ☎ *312/573-0564. AE, DISC, MC, V. El: Red Line to Chicago/State. Map p 71.*

★★ Paper Boy WRIGLEYVILLE A card and gift store with some of the most offbeat and artsy greeting cards in the city, plus exquisite gift wrap and stationery. *1351 W. Belmont Ave.* ☎ *773/388-8811. AE, MC, V. El: Brown Line to Southport. Map p 72.*

kids Unabridged Bookstore LAKEVIEW This independent bookseller is known for its gay and lesbian specialty section, and also its award-winning range of children's books. Their full-time, knowledgeable staff handwrites recommendations. Chicago's largest children's bookstore is a must-see, and features special events such as sidewalk chalk drawing and visits from book characters and authors. *3251 N. Broadway.* ☎ *773/883-9119. www. unabridgedbookstore.com. AE, MC, V. El: Red Line to Addison. Map p 72.*

Clothing & Shoes

★★★ Barneys New York MAGNIFICENT MILE A miniversion of New York's Barneys, this is the place in town to buy top-of-the-line men's suits. Not for those who faint at high prices, but excellent for spotting trends and people-watching. (For items skewing younger and lower-priced, check out the Barney's Co-op at 2209-11 N. Halsted St.) *25 E. Oak St.* ☎ *312/587-1700. www. barneys.com. MC, V. El: Red Line to Chicago/State. Map p 71.*

★★ Belly Dance Maternity BUCKTOWN/WICKER PARK Hip maternity clothes for stylish moms-to-be, from Japanese Weekend, Michael Stars, Earl Jeans, and Citizens of Humanity. The Storksak diaper bags and blankets from Little Giraffe make great baby shower gifts. *1647 N. Damen Ave.* ☎ *773/ 862-1133. AE, DISC, MC, V. El: Blue Line to Damen. Map p 72.*

Head for Glove Me Tender to stock up on accessories that will help you combat the city's windy winters.

★★ Elements MAGNIFICENT MILE High-end, high-design gifts, jewelry, handbags, kitchen and bath accessories, and tabletop items are what you'll find at this cutting-edge retailer. *741 N. Wells St.* ☎ *312/642-6574. AE, MC, V. El: Red Line to Chicago/State. Map p 71.*

Glove Me Tender MAGNIFICENT MILE If you lost your mittens somewhere in your travels up and down Michigan Avenue, this boutique has a huge selection to help you replace them—along with hats, scarves, and other accessories. *900 N. Michigan Ave., 5th Floor.* ☎ *312/ 664-4022. www.glovemetender.com. AE, DISC, MC, V. El: Red Line to Chicago/State. Map p 71.*

★★★ Hermès Chicago MAGNIFICENT MILE Hermès makes the world's most sought-after scarves and ties. Don't be intimidated, even if you're not buying: It's fun to walk through and gaze at the colorful designs that make these silk scarves and ties perennial favorites. *110 E. Oak St.* ☎ *312/787-8175. www. hermes.com. AE, DC, MC, V. El: Red Line to Chicago/State. Map p 71.*

Ikram MAGNIFICENT MILE This boutique stocks all the big names, from Valentino to Yves St. Laurent. Among the high-priced offerings are jewelry, stationery, and decorative accessories that give the place a personal touch. *873 N. Rush St.* ☎ *312/587-1000. www.ikramonline. com. AE, DC, DISC, MC, V. El: Red Line to Chicago/State. Map p 71.*

★★ **Kate Spade** MAGNIFICENT MILE Head here for designer handbags, ranging in style from plaid and gingham to snakeskin and basic black. Her shoes and stationery goods are adorable, too. *101 E. Oak St.* ☎ *312/654-8853. www.kate spade.com. AE, DISC, MC, V. El: Red Line to Chicago/State. Map p 71.*

★★ **Lori's Discount Designer Shoes** LINCOLN PARK This mecca for shoe lovers features discounted footwear from major designers. On weekends, the store swarms with shoppers. Happy hunting! *824 W. Armitage Ave.* ☎ *773/281-5655. AE, DISC, MC, V. El: Brown Line to Armitage. Map p 72.*

★★★ **Mark Shale** MAGNIFICENT MILE Chicago's own upscale clothing chain, with a fine selection of men's and women's casual and dressy clothing and labels you won't find in most department stores. The menswear is especially good, and the service is excellent. *900 N. Michigan Ave., 3rd and 4th floors.* ☎ *312/440-0720. www.markshale.com. AE, DC, DISC, MC, V. El: Red Line to Chicago/State. Map p 71.*

★★★ **McShane's Exchange** LINCOLN PARK This consignment shop sells designer clothes at real-person prices. Sorry guys: They only carry women's clothing. *815 W. Armitage Ave.* ☎ *773/525-0282. AE, DISC, MC, V. El: Brown Line to Armitage. Map p 72.*

★★ **Niche Footwear** BUCKTOWN/ WICKER PARK Fashionable European footwear, including Moma boots from Italy, Chie Mahara from Spain, Paul Smith from the U.K., and France's Costume National. You might even find a pair of boots that are warm enough to stand up to Chicago winters while being cute enough to stand out in a crowd. *1566 N. Damen Ave.* ☎ *773/489-2001. AE, DISC, MC, V. El: Blue Line to Damen. Map p 72.*

Prada MAGNIFICENT MILE A boutique so chic it's almost painful. Chicago's top spot for buying the famous Italian designer's signature bags. *30 E. Oak St.* ☎ *312/951-1113. AE, DC, MC, V. El: Red Line to Chicago/State. Map p 71.*

Psychobaby BUCKTOWN/WICKER PARK Cool, crazy clothing for babies and kids up to size 6X. Everything your creative kid needs to express his or her individuality, from shoes to toys to T-shirts that read "Half-Pint Hipster." *1630 N. Damen Ave.* ☎ *773/772-2815. AE, DC, DISC, MC, V. El: Blue Line to Damen. Map p 72.*

The Red Head Boutique WRIGLEYVILLE Women's specialty boutique featuring trendy clothes, purses, and jewelry. *3450 N. Southport Ave.* ☎ *773/325-9898. www. redheadboutique.com. AE, MC, V. El: Brown Line to Southport. Map p 72.*

Psychobaby sells hip clothes for the young set.

★★ **Riley** BUCKTOWN/WICKER PARK   Modern, casual clothing for men and women in a clean-cut store, with ochre wood and black leather furniture. Popular picks for men include Jet Lag cargos and separates by Phil Moor and Kenneth Cole. For women, you'll find a huge selection of Michael Stars T-shirts. *1659 N. Damen Ave.* ☎ *773/489-0101. MC, V. El: Blue Line to Damen. Map p 72.*

★ **She One** WRIGLEYVILLE   Shop at this boutique for chic yet inexpensive women's clothing. *3402 N. Southport Ave.* ☎ *773/549-9698. AE, DISC, MC, V. El: Brown Line to Southport. Map p 72.*

★★ **Sugar Magnolia** MAGNIFICENT MILE   This women's clothing boutique sells casual attire for relaxing, and sexy clothes for going out. It also offers small gifts, jewelry, and handbags. *34 E. Oak St.* ☎ *312/944-0885. AE, DISC, MC, V. El: Red Line to Chicago/State. Map p 71.*

Ultimo MAGNIFICENT MILE   Chicago's best-known upscale clothier offers women's clothing by big-time labels such as John Galliano, Dolce & Gabbana, and Agnona. *114 E. Oak St.* ☎ *312/787-1171. AE, DC, DISC, MC, V. El: Red Line to Chicago/State. Map p 71.*

★★★ **Wacky Cats** LAKEVIEW   Mannequins in various eccentric outfits greet you at this shop, featuring such 1950s-era vintage items as taffeta cocktail dresses and bowling shirts. *3012 N. Lincoln Ave. (at Wellington Ave.).* ☎ *773/929-6701. www.wackycats.com. AE, MC, V. El: Brown Line to Wellington. Map p 72.*

Wolford MAGNIFICENT MILE   Slip into this lingerie boutique for sleek bodysuits and durable hosiery from Europe. *54 E. Oak St.* ☎ *312/642-8787. MC, V. El: Red Line to Chicago/State. Map p 71.*

Stylish moms-to-be flock to Belly Dance Maternity for hip attire.

Consumer Electronics

The Apple Store MAGNIFICENT MILE   The four-story mecca for all technological gadgets beginning with "i": iPod, iMac, and more. The prices are retail, but the store offers in-house computer (Macs only, of course) workshops and an extremely knowledgeable sales staff. *679 N. Michigan Ave.* ☎ *312/981-4104. www.apple.com. AE, DC, DISC, MC, V. El: Red Line to Grand/State. Map p 71.*

Department Stores

Bloomingdale's MAGNIFICENT MILE   The first Midwestern branch of the famed upscale New York department store features six manageably sized floors of shopping. The store carries its own in-house brands as well as the full range of designers that you'd expect, with especially good shoe and jewelry selections. *900 N. Michigan Ave. (at Walton St.).* ☎ *312/440-4460. www.blooming dales.com. AE, DISC, MC, V. El: Red Line to Chicago/State. Map p 71.*

Macy's THE LOOP   Federated Department Stores changed the legendary Marshall Field's flagship store into a Macy's in 2006 (many locals still refuse to use any name but the original). The name may be different, but this landmark (opened in 1852) still offers 73 acres (30 hectares) of shopping. Chicago traditions include meeting under the store's clock and viewing the famous animated holiday window displays. Take afternoon tea in the gracious Walnut Room. *111 N. State St.* ☎ *312/781-1000. www.macys.com. AE, DISC, MC, V. El: Red Line to Randolph. Map p 74.*

Neiman Marcus MAGNIFICENT MILE Yes, you'll pay top dollar for designer names here, but Neiman's has a broader price range than many of its critics care to admit. It also has some great sales. Once you've shopped 'til you've dropped, get your blood sugar back up by eating a popover in the Zodiac Room. *737 N. Michigan Ave. (at Superior St.).* ☎ *312/642-5900. www.neimanmarcus.com. AE. El: Red Line to Chicago. Map p 71.*

Nordstrom MAGNIFICENT MILE A spacious, airy design and trendy touches complement this store's famed focus on service. Cafe Nordstrom offers a shopping break, with salads and sandwiches. *Westfield North Bridge Mall, 55 E. Grand Ave. (at Rush St.).* ☎ *312/464-1515. www.nordstrom.com. AE, DISC, MC, V. El: Red Line to Grand. Map p 71.*

Saks Fifth Avenue MAGNIFICENT MILE This upscale department store is best known for its varied fragrance selection and designer collections. The men's department gets high marks for personalized service and is located in a separate building on the east side of Michigan Avenue. *Chicago Place, 700 N. Michigan Ave. (at Superior St.).* ☎ *312/944-6500. www.saksfifthavenue.com. AE, DC, DISC, MC, V. El: Red Line to Chicago/ State. Map p 71.*

Food, Chocolates & Wine

★★★ Fox & Obel Food Market STREETERVILLE This local gourmet store features a butcher, fresh fish counter, deli, bakery, produce market, and a prepared foods area. There's even a cafe, which serves a knockout New York strip-loin sandwich. The hours (6am–midnight daily) will accommodate your urge for a late-night gourmet snack. *401 E. Illinois St.* ☎ *312/410-7301. www. fox-obel.com. AE, DC, DISC, MC, V. Bus: 151 to Illinois. Map p 71.*

The Goddess and Grocer/Cru Wine Bar and Cafe MAGNIFICENT MILE At once a wine bar, restaurant, and upscale grocer, here you can pick up wine, liquor, beer, cheeses, pâtés, crackers, and anything else you might need to make a romantic picnic or a take-home

The venerable Marshall Field's department store is now a Macy's, but it still sells everything from crystal to Cubs shirts.

Farmers' Markets

From mid-May to late October, Chicago's downtown plazas and neighborhoods overflow with fruits, vegetables, flowers, and food from farms outside the city—even from outside the state. Markets in residential neighborhoods, such as the gourmet market at Lincoln Park High School, 2001 N. Orchard, usually take place on Saturdays. The farmers' markets that are held downtown—including those listed here—take place during the week. Schedules may vary, so contact the Mayor's Office of Special Events (☎ 312/744-3315) for more information. Downtown markets include:

- Daley Plaza, 55 W. Randolph St., on Thursdays
- Federal Plaza, Adams Street and Jackson Street, on Tuesdays
- Park at Jackson Street and Wacker Drive, across from the Sears Tower, on Thursdays
- Prudential Plaza, 130 E. Randolph St., every other Tuesday

snack to eat in your hotel room. On the other side of the store, you'll find Cru, a wine bar where you can nosh on cheese plates and the Cru Club sandwich, with lobster, avocado, and beef tenderloin. *888 N. Wabash St.* ☎ *312/337-4001. AE, DC, DISC, MC, V. El: Red Line to Chicago/State. Map p 71.*

★★ House of Glunz OLD TOWN Chicago's oldest wine shop carries an inventory of some 1,500 wines, some of which date back to 1811. Ask the knowledgeable owners to steer you to the right bottle for your budget. *1206 N. Wells St.* ☎ *312/642-3000. www.houseofglunz.com. AE, DISC, MC, V. El: Red Line to Clark/Division. Map p 72.*

★★★ Vosges Haut-Chocolat MAGNIFICENT MILE Exotic-flavored truffles (including paprika, candied violets, and Cointreau) in pretty packaging, and the best toffee I've ever had. *520 N. Michigan Ave. (Westfield North Bridge Mall).* ☎ *312/644-9450. www.vosgeschocolate.com. AE, DISC, MC, V. El: Red Line to Grand/State. Map p 71.*

Gift Shops

★★ Art Institute of Chicago THE LOOP This museum's bustling gift shop is a great place to shop for jewelry, glassware, books, and quality reproductions. *111 S. Michigan Ave.* ☎ *312/443-3600. www.artic. edu. AE, DISC, MC, V. El: Green, Brown, Purple, or Orange line to Adams, or Red Line to Monroe or Jackson. Map p 74.*

★★★ Chicago ArchiCenter THE LOOP The best gift shop in the city offers architecture-focused books, decorative accessories, and gifts. You'll also find "Architecture Ambassadors" providing information on the wide range of tours on offer. *224 S. Michigan Ave.* ☎ *312/922-3432. www.architecture.org. AE, DISC, MC, V. El: Red Line to Monroe or Jackson. Map p 74.*

Gallery 37 Store THE LOOP The paintings, jewelry, ceramics, decorated furniture, textiles, and sculptures sold here are made by Chicago residents, ages 14 to 21, participating in a nonprofit arts training program. Proceeds benefit the program. *66 E. Randolph St.* ☎ *312/744-7274. www.gallery37. org. AE, DISC, MC, V. El: Red Line to Randolph. Map p 74.*

Housewares, Furnishings & Art

★★★ **Georg Jensen** MAGNIFICENT MILE This branch of the famous Danish company sells Scandinavian designs in silver, silverware, other household items, and jewelry. *In The Drake Hotel, 959 N. Michigan Ave.* ☎ *312/642-9160. www.georg jensen.com. AE, MC, V. El: Red Line to Chicago/State. Map p 71.*

★★ **Jonathan Adler** RIVER NORTH Known for his needlepoint throw pillows, you can find all of those "home-made" touches you need to make a house a very hip home. *676 N. Wabash St.* ☎ *312/274-9920. www .jonathanadler.com. AE, DISC, MC, V. El: Red Line to Grand. Map p 71.*

★★ **Material Possessions** RIVER NORTH Shop here for unusual table settings, including pottery and glass, custom dinnerware, and a selection of artistic jewelry. *704 N. Wabash St.* ☎ *312/280-4885. www. materialpossessions.com. AE, MC, V. El: Red Line to Grand. Map p 71.*

★★ **P.O.S.H.** RIVER NORTH Never-used vintage silver and commercial-grade china from European and American hotels will inspire you to set a fun, quirky table. *613 N. State St.* ☎ *312/280-1602. www.posh chicago.com. MC, V. El: Red Line to Chicago. Map p 71.*

★★★ **Primitive Art Works** WEST LOOP Winding your way through this 31,000-square-foot (2,880-sq.-m) store, you'll feel as if you've taken an exotic worldwide journey. Packed with furniture, rugs, jewelry, and beads from various cultures, this store might yield a giant Buddha head acquired from a Korean temple that was being destroyed on one

day; on another, you might discover an exquisite embroidered rug from Turkmenistan. *130 N. Jefferson St.* ☎ *312/575-9600. www.beprimitive. com. AE, DC, DISC, MC, V. El: Brown Line to Chicago.*

★★★ **Rhona Hoffman Gallery** BUCKTOWN/WICKER PARK This gallery has a high profile on the international scene and is a purveyor of works by blue-chip players such as Cindy Sherman, Sol LeWitt, and Jenny Holzer. Hoffman has also added pieces by up-and-comers such as Dawoud Bey. *118 N. Peoria St.* ☎ *312/455-1990. No credit cards. Bus: 20 (Madison). Map p 74.*

★★★ **Sawbridge Studios** RIVER NORTH Stunningly crafted furniture with stunning prices to boot. Some of the most beautiful woodworking I've ever seen. *153 W. Ohio St.* ☎ *312/828-0055. www.sawbridge. com. AE, DISC, MC, V. El: Brown Line to Merchandise Mart. Map p 74.*

Shabby Chic LINCOLN PARK Everything you need to achieve the famous, feminine decorating look

Quirky china and vintage silver are the major buys at P.O.S.H.

Sawbridge Studios sells magnificent woodwork and beautifully crafted furniture.

created by English designer Rachel Ashwell is for sale in this furniture and furnishings store. *2146 N. Halsted St. ☎ 773/327-9372. www.shabbychic.com. AE, DC, DISC, MC, V. El: Brown Line to Armitage. Map p 72.*

Michigan Avenue's Vertical Shopping Malls

Chicago Place MAGNIFICENT MILE Inaugurated in 1991, Chicago Place has been looking for an identity ever since. The mall is mainly notable as the home of Saks Fifth Avenue. *700 N. Michigan Ave. ☎ 312/266-7710. www.chicago-place.com. El: Red Line to State/Grand. Map p 71.*

900 North Michigan Avenue MAGNIFICENT MILE The most upscale of the Magnificent Mile malls is often called the "Bloomingdale's building" for its most prominent tenant. There are about 70 stores, a few good restaurants, and a chic salon named for well-known local hairdresser Mario Tricoci; book well in advance, as it's always bustling. *900 N. Michigan Ave. ☎ 312/915-3916. www.shop900.com. El: Red Line to Chicago/State. Map p 71.*

Water Tower Place MAGNIFICENT MILE Chicago's first—and busiest—vertical mall, this seven-floor building has about 100 mostly upscale stores that reportedly account for roughly half of all the retail trade transacted along the Magnificent Mile. *835 N. Michigan Ave. ☎ 312/440-3165. www.shopWaterTower.com. El: Red Line to Chicago/State. Map p 71.*

kids Westfield North Bridge Mall MAGNIFICENT MILE The best concentration of kids' stores on the Mag Mile—The Lego Store (☎ 312/494-0760) being my top pick—is located on the third floor of this mall, anchored by Nordstrom. *520 N. Michigan Ave. ☎ 312/327-2300. www.westfield.com/northbridge. El: Red Line to State/Grand. Map p 71.*

Music

kids Blue Chicago Store RIVER NORTH Here's a store that's dedicated to teaching kids about the blues. Pick up some books and CDs, and consider attending the Saturday night dance-a-thons that are open to all ages. *534 N. Clark (at W. Grand Ave.). ☎ 312/661-1003. www.bluechicago.com. AE, DISC, MC, V. El: Red Line to State/Grand. Map p 71.*

Dusty Groove America LAKEVIEW Soul, funk, jazz, Brazilian, lounge, Latin, and hip-hop music on new and used vinyl. All the new CDs are rare or imported—or both. *1120 N. Ashland Ave. ☎ 773/342-5800. www.dustygroove.com. AE, DISC, MC, V. El: Blue Line to Division. Map p 72.*

★★★ Jazz Record Mart RIVER NORTH Arguably the best jazz record store in the country, and confirmably the largest. The first of four rooms in this extensive store houses the "Killers Rack," albums that the store's owners consider essential to any jazz collection. *27 E. Illinois. ☎ 312/222-1467. AE, DISC, MC, V. El: Red Line to Grand. Map p 71.*

preteen set, this store recently moved to the former Lord & Taylor space in the Water Tower Place mall and lures in thousands of shoppers each year with selections of clothing, dolls, books, and accessories. Call ahead to book a lunch or afternoon tea in the cafe. *835 N. Michigan Ave. (Water Tower Place).* ☎ *312/255-9876. www.americangirlplace.com. AE, DC, DISC, MC, V. El: Red Line to Chicago/State. Map p 71.*

★★ **Uncle Fun** LAKEVIEW Uncle Fun and his staff travel the world to bring home bobbing head figurines, accordions, and stink bombs from all corners of the Earth—for the sole purpose of tickling your fancy. If you can't make it in person, check out the "Famous 12-Step Plan for Fun" on the website. *1338 W. Belmont Ave. (near Southport Ave.).* ☎ *773/477-8223. www.unclefunchicago. com. AE, MC, V. El: Red or Brown line to Belmont. Map p 72.* ●

There's no better place in town for novelty goods than Uncle Fun.

Toys

American Girl Place MAGNIFI-CENT MILE The "in" place for the

Art Fairs

Browse alongside locals at these quality juried art fairs, for which artists from all over the country apply to be accepted:

Around the Coyote, at the intersection of Damen, North, and Milwaukee avenues (☎ 773/342-6777; www.aroundthecoyote.org), takes place the second weekend in September. Your entrance fee entitles you to enter local art galleries, as well as many artists' homes and studios in Wicker Park and Bucktown.

Bucktown Arts Fest, near Fullerton and Western avenues (☎ 312/409-8305; www.bucktownartsfest.com), is held the last weekend in August in a comfortable park setting.

The **57th Street Art Fair,** 57th Street in downtown Hyde Park (☎ 773/493-3247; www.57thstreetartfair.org), is a long-standing fair that's a natural outgrowth of the intellectual and artsy enclave of Hyde Park. The action takes place on the third weekend in June.

Old Town Art Fair, Lincoln Avenue and Wisconsin Street (☎ 312/337-1938; www.oldtownartfair.org), is held the second weekend in June. The most high-end of Chicago's art-fair offerings, it boasts art prices to match.

Indiana Dunes

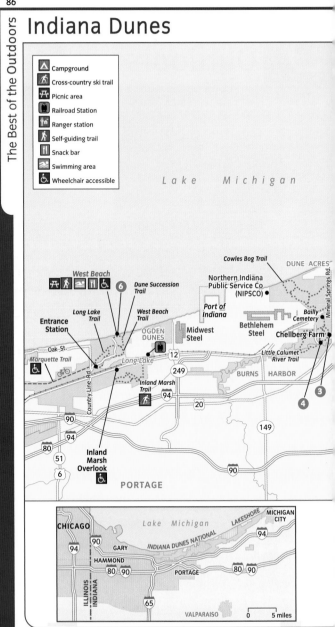

Campground

Cross-country ski trail

Picnic area

Railroad Station

Ranger station

Self-guiding trail

Snack bar

Swimming area

Wheelchair accessible

Lake Michigan

Cowles Bog Trail

DUNE ACRES

West Beach

Dune Succession Trail

Northern Indiana Public Service Co (NIPSCO)

Mineral Springs Rd

Bailly Cemetery

Long Lake Trail

West Beach Trail

Port of Indiana

Bethlehem Steel

Chellberg Farm

Entrance Station

OGDEN DUNES

Midwest Steel

Oak St.

12

Little Calumet River Trail

Marquette Trail

Long Lake

249

BURNS HARBOR

Inland Marsh Trail

94

20

90

94

80

149

51

6

Inland Marsh Overlook

90

PORTAGE

CHICAGO

Lake Michigan

LAKESHORE

MICHIGAN CITY

94

90

GARY

INDIANA DUNES NATIONAL

HAMMOND

80 90

PORTAGE

80 90

ILLINOIS INDIANA

65

VALPARAISO

0   5 miles

Previous page: North Avenue Beach offers a great view from its lakefront path.

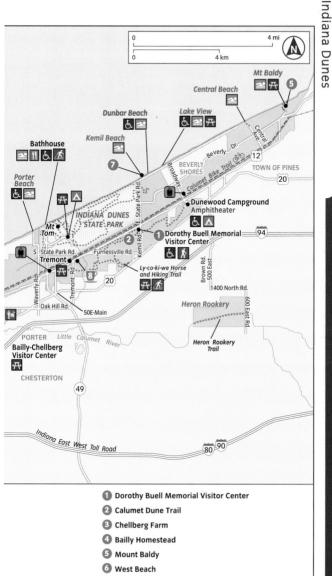

1 Dorothy Buell Memorial Visitor Center
2 Calumet Dune Trail
3 Chellberg Farm
4 Bailly Homestead
5 Mount Baldy
6 West Beach
7 Kemil Beach
8 Campground Grocery

My favorite outdoor escape is Indiana Dunes National Lakeshore, 53 miles (85km) southeast of Chicago. You may not associate the Midwest with sand dunes, but a trip here will change your mind. The landscape includes 15 miles (24km) of dunes and grasses fronting Lake Michigan, reminiscent of Cape Cod, as well as maple and oak forests, marshes, and bogs. START: You'll need to drive, so this is the day to rent a car if you didn't bring yours along. Take I-94 East to Ind. 49 North (east of Porter). Follow Ind. 49 North to Rte. 12. Travel east on Rte. 12 for 3 miles to the Dorothy Buell Memorial Visitor Center.

❶ Dorothy Buell Memorial Visitor Center.

Stop by the information desk for a free map covering the National Lakeshore. Both kids and adults will enjoy the 10-minute orientation slide show; there are also interactive video terminals for youngsters. You'll also find restrooms and a gift shop. ⏲ *20 min.* ☎ *219/926-7561, ext. 225. www.nps.gov/indu. Park admission $8 per vehicle. Open Memorial Day to Labor Day daily 8am–6pm; rest of the year daily 8am–5pm.*

You can step back into the 19th century when you visit the fully restored brick farmhouse on Chellberg Farm.

❷ Calumet Dune Trail.

Perfect for novices and the mobility-impaired, this .8-mile (1.2km) paved trail starts behind the Dorothy Buell Memorial Visitor Center and winds through a forest of yellow sassafras and oaks. Signs describe the flora and fauna along the way. If you only have time for one short hike, this is the trail to walk to get a good, representative sample of the natural wonders of the lakeshore, from the gently rolling dunes to a swamp, and, finally, the majestic red and white oak trees that create a dense canopy in summer months. ⏲ *20–30 min.*

❸ kids Chellberg Farm.

Those with a historical bent will enjoy touring this restored 1885 brick farmhouse, which belonged to a Swedish immigrant family that lived and worked on this farm for three generations. The Chellberg family sold their farm to the National Park Service in 1927, and their home has been restored to its original late–19th-century appearance (forget electricity and indoor plumbing). There's also a barn filled with farm animals; you can help farmers feed them on Saturdays and Sundays. ⏲ *1 hr. www.nps.gov/indu. For information on Chellberg Farm, see www.nps.gov/archive/indu/history/chellberg.htm. Free admission. Open 8am to sunset year-round.*

❹ Bailly Homestead.

This National Historic Landmark, the former residence of a French Canadian fur trader, dates back to 1822, when it served as a meeting and trading center for Native Americans and Euro-Americans. On Sundays from 1 to 4pm, volunteers dress in period clothing and offer up lots of historical tidbits and insights into life on the homestead. For history buffs, this is a rare opportunity to catch a glimpse into the lives of early settlers. While you're here, don't miss the unusual family cemetery. ⏲ *1 hr. www.nps.gov/indu. Open Memorial*

Day to Labor Day daily 11am–4:30pm; Mar 1 to Memorial Day and Labor Day to Oct Sat–Sun 11am–4:30pm.

5 Mount Baldy. At 125 feet (38m), this is the largest "living" sand dune in the park, meaning that the dune is kept in constant motion by wind and water. Mt. Baldy actually creeps several inches (7.5cm) farther from Lake Michigan each year. It got its name thanks to its lack of vegetation, which is the reason why it's mobile—there are no plants anchoring it. The dune is one of the best attractions in the park, popular with everyone from kids to experienced hikers. Climb to the top for a real aerobic workout; you'll be rewarded with a sweeping view of the lake, and on a clear day, you can see all the way to Chicago. Kids love to race to the top; on the southern slope, you'll see half-buried trees (as they move, the dunes bury forests, and erosion exposes them again). Once you climb down the "mountain," head for the lake; if it's July or August, the water will be warm enough for a refreshing dip. 🕐 *30 min. Open May–Sept daily 6am–9pm; Oct–Apr daily 8am–sunset.*

6 West Beach. This top attraction is not only one of the lakeshore's most popular beaches, but also the starting point for a scenic 3-mile (4.8km) boardwalk trail that leads you through dunes, an oak savanna, and jack pine forests on your way to Lake Michigan. It's the perfect trail for sampling the many landscapes found in the National Lakeshore. The beach is my favorite at the lakeshore; it's very popular with swimmers, though you should use caution, as the lake bottom can be uneven and there can be dangerous rip currents (a concern at all of the lakeshore's beaches). This is the only beach where lifeguards are on duty (summer months only), and there's a bathhouse, picnic facilities, vending

Take time to explore the many beaches along the Indiana Dunes National Lakeshore.

machines, and restrooms, too. 🕐 *2 hr.* ☎ *219/926-7561, ext. 668 for swimming info. May–Sept $6 parking fee until 8pm; Oct–Apr free parking. Open May–Sept daily 9am–9pm; Oct–Apr daily 8am–sunset.*

7 Kemil Beach. If it's beach-going that you're focused on, check out Kemil Beach, a long stretch of beautiful white sand. While West Beach is my favorite for swimming and sunbathing, this is the best spot in the national lakeshore to watch the sunset. If you get here early enough for one last hike before the sun goes down, don't miss the Dune Ridge Trail, which starts right off the parking lot. This moderate, 1-mile loop requires some climbing, but is nothing a reasonably fit person can't handle, and will take you through a lovely forested area. Restrooms are available. 🕐 *1 hr. Open May–Sept daily 6am–9pm; Oct–Apr daily 8am–sunset.*

It's nothing fancy, but there is a **8 concession and campground grocery** that's open during the summer months (you can buy wood, ice, groceries, and picnic supplies), and a small fast-food outlet. The crowd tends to include a nice mix of older people, singles, teenagers, and families. *1600 N. Hwy. 25E, Chesterton, IN.* ☎ *219/926-1952. $.*

Chicago Lakeshore

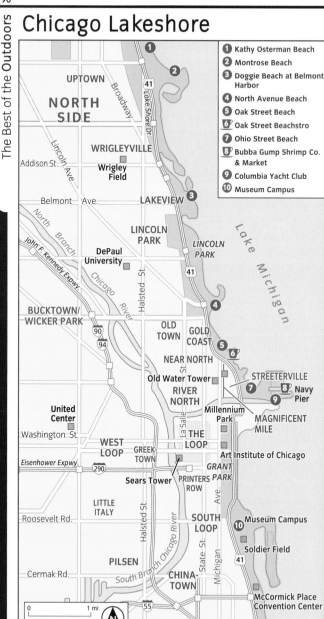

1. Kathy Osterman Beach
2. Montrose Beach
3. Doggie Beach at Belmont Harbor
4. North Avenue Beach
5. Oak Street Beach
6. Oak Street Beachstro
7. Ohio Street Beach
8. Bubba Gump Shrimp Co. & Market
9. Columbia Yacht Club
10. Museum Campus

One of the things Chicagoans love most about their city is the scenic lakefront path that extends 18 miles (29km) along Lake Michigan's shore, from Hollywood Beach in the north (the neighborhood of Edgewater) to the Museum of Science and Industry (Hyde Park) in the south. It's perfect for biking, strolling, spreading a beach towel on the sand or grass, or simply sitting on a park bench and watching the world go by. If the weather is fine and you want to stop for a dip along the way, all beaches officially open about June 20 (although the water temperature is at its best in August, when it hovers just above 70°F/21°C). START: **Hollywood-Ardmore Beach, Berwyn El Station.**

Tip

For picnic supplies, do as the locals do and head to **Bockwinkel's**, 222 N. Columbus Drive (☎ 312/482-9900). Known for its lunch specials (sandwiches, a superior salad bar, and really great fruit), you'll find it on the ground floor of the Park Millennium building, located one block north of Millennium Park, and one block east of Michigan Avenue.

① Kathy Osterman Beach.

Known to locals as Hollywood-Ardmore Beach, this lovely crescent of sand is less congested than many of the city's other beaches. If you're looking for relative quiet and seclusion (relative because this is a big city, after all), you'll find a like-minded, tanned-and-toned crowd here, sunning themselves. The beach's south end has steadily become popular with gays, who've moved up the lakefront from their longtime hangout at Belmont Rocks. Facilities include bathrooms and drinking fountains. This is one of the city's nine wheelchair-accessible beaches. ⏲ *30 min. 5700 N. Lake Shore Dr. (at Hollywood St.).* ☎ *312/742-PLAY. www.chicago parkdistrict.com.*

② Montrose Beach. This

unsung treasure is midway between Hollywood-Ardmore and North Avenue beaches. Long popular with the city's Hispanic community, it offers an expanse of sand mostly uninterrupted by jetties or piers (unlike North Ave. Beach), a huge adjacent park with soccer fields, and one big hill that's great for kite flying. If you're interested in having some green space for tossing a baseball, or want to watch a soccer game, this beach is your best choice—no other beach in the area boasts such proximity to a park. As at North Avenue Beach, you'll find bathrooms, drinking fountains, bike racks, and concession stands. It's also a popular spot for fishing. ⏲ *30 min. Lake Shore Dr. at Montrose Ave.* ☎ *312/742-PLAY. www.chicagoparkdistrict.com.*

③ Doggie Beach at Belmont Harbor. Chicago is a town of dog

The Chicago Lakeshore is a scenic spot for a stroll, bike ride, or picnic.

Many a Chicagoan has taken a four-legged friend to Doggie Beach for a game of fetch.

lovers, many of whom bring their pooches here for a dip. Nestled in a small corner of a harbor near Hawthorne and Lake Shore Drive, this is not so much a beach as an enclosed strip of sand where locals take their dogs to fetch sticks and play in the water. Facilities are minimal. ⏱ *10 min. 3200 N. Lake Shore Dr. (just south of Addison St.).* ☎ *312/742-PLAY. www.chicagopark district.com.*

4 North Avenue Beach. I'm one of many Chicagoans who can't get enough of the view from the lakefront bike path here, looking south to the John Hancock Center— a view so famous it's often featured on the cover of guide books. To get a snapshot of the picture-perfect scene, walk north on Lake Shore Drive to North Avenue, and take the tunnel to North Avenue Beach. Once on the lakefront path, turn south toward the city, and you will have your Kodak moment. (Just watch out for all the cyclists, skaters, runners, and dog walkers if it's a nice summer day.) Accessible to both the mobility-impaired and to families toting strollers, the beach also offers an array of facilities, including restrooms, concession stands, drinking fountains, bike racks, volleyball courts, and a chess pavilion. ⏱ *30 min. Lake Shore Dr.*

and North Ave. ☎ *312/742-PLAY. www.chicagoparkdistrict.com.*

5 Oak Street Beach. The city's best-known beach, and my personal favorite, is a perfect place to get back in touch with the world. Its location, at the northern tip of the Magnificent Mile, creates some interesting people-watching moments: In season, check out the local sun worshippers wearing flip-flops and carrying coolers as they make their way up tony Michigan Avenue toward this curving slice of sand. The beach is accessible to families with strollers and the mobility-impaired, but this trendy spot can get crowded on summer afternoons. Facilities include volleyball courts and bathrooms. ⏱ *30 min. Lake Shore Dr. and Oak St.* ☎ *312/742-PLAY. www.chicagoparkdistrict.com.*

The warm-weather-only beachfront cafe, **6 Oak Street Beachstro,** is set right on the sands of Oak Street Beach. It serves inventive cafe fare, including fresh seafood, sandwiches, and pastas. Beer and wine are available. *1000 N. Lake Shore Dr. at Oak Street Beach.* ☎ *312/915-4100. $$.*

Unsung Montrose Beach is much loved by soccer players, who love to play in its adjacent park.

The protected harbor of Ohio Street beach attracts many a sailor.

7 Ohio Street Beach. If it's seclusion you're seeking, you'll enjoy Ohio Street Beach, an intimate sliver of sand just west of Navy Pier. Thanks to buoys marking a 1-mile (1.6km) swimming course and a location in a protected harbor (making for calmer waters than you'll find elsewhere on the lake), Ohio Street Beach is also the place for serious open-water swimming. On most summer mornings, you'll see athletes (often in wet suits) training in the water, many of them preparing for the annual Chicago Triathlon in August. ⏱ *20 min. 400 N. Lake Shore Dr.* ☎ *312/742-PLAY. www. chicagoparkdistrict.com.*

A theme restaurant inspired by the film *Forrest Gump*, **8 kids Bubba Gump Shrimp Co. & Market** is a casual family seafood joint that looks just like a southern shrimp shack, complete with metal pails on the tables (for paper towels). Tasty smoothies for the kids (or try the speckled lemonade, freshly squeezed and made with strawberries), peel-and-eat shrimp, and hush puppies make this a great lunch stop at Navy Pier. *600 E. Grand Ave. (at Lake Michigan).* ☎ *312/252-4867. www.bubbagump.com. $$.*

9 Columbia Yacht Club. Housed in a 372-foot (113m) Canadian icebreaker and ferry named *Abegweit* (often called *Abby* by locals), this private club dates back to 1891, and is now the premier spot for sailing lessons on Lake Michigan. Even if you're not a yachting fan, the harbor area offers lovely views. ⏱ *5 min., unless you're taking a lesson. In Monroe Harbor, at the foot of Randolph Dr. and Lake*

Park Planning

Chicago's lakefront is forever free and clear of development thanks in no small part to Daniel H. Burnham (1846–1912), a renowned architect and city planner. Burnham, architect of the Rookery (p 29, **7**), the Monadnock Building (p 30, **9**), the "White City" of the 1893 World's Columbian Exposition, New York's Flatiron Building, and Washington, D.C.'s Union Station, presented his most ambitious work, the *Plan of Chicago*, in 1909 with architect Edward H. Bennett. (There's a big centennial celebration planned for 2009, with two architects selected to build special pavilions in Millennium Park). The plan set the standard for urban design in the United States and anticipated the city's need to control random urban growth and create a system of city parks and lakefront recreation areas.

The Museum Campus is home to several major attractions, including the Adler Planetarium.

Shore Dr. ☎ *312/938-3625. www. columbiayachtclub.com. Sailing school rates vary; contact the club or check the website.*

⑩ Museum Campus. Created by the relocation of Lake Shore Drive, this beautiful park was opened in 1998 with the goal of being recognized as one of the most innovative cultural playgrounds in the country. The Campus connects three Chicago cultural institutions: The Adler Planetarium, Field Museum of Natural History (p 22, ⑨), and John G. Shedd Aquarium (p 21, ⑧). Today, broad walkways make it easier for pedestrians to visit the museums, and the reclaimed parkland and terraced gardens offer new space for picnicking, theater, and museum education activities. *Word to the wise:* Traffic tends to get hectic and the Museum Campus congested on Chicago Bears game days (Soldier Field is just south of the Field Museum). Plan your visit accordingly. 🕓 *30 min., more if you visit some of the museums. 18th St. and Lake Shore Dr.* ☎ *312/742-PLAY. www.museum campus.org. Bus: 12, 127, or 146.* ●

Bikes & Safety

Biking the Chicago lakefront is a wonderful way to while away a sunny afternoon. Except for an occasional construction barrier and the occasional crowd, the lakefront offers smooth and flat terrain that makes for an easy ride.

The biggest challenge to riders is the wind, which can get downright nasty. Try to ride against the wind at the beginning of your ride when your legs are still fresh (this may mean shifting your route to ride north first—the wind is often out of the northwest). You might also encounter an east wind off the lake, which means you'll be leaning to one side for the entire ride. Keep in mind that on very windy days, inexperienced cyclists have been known to take a spill.

To rent bikes or in-line skates, head over to **Bike Chicago** (☎ 312/595-9600; www.bikechicago.com), which has locations at Millennium Park, Navy Pier, Riverwalk, North Avenue Beach, and Foster Beach. Bike rentals start at $8 an hour. The company also offers easy 2- to 3-hour bike tours of the lakefront; tours cost $30 adults, $25 seniors, $15 kids under 12. The latest and greatest addition is Segway tours, $49 for a 2½ hour tour on the lakefront.

Dining Best Bets

Best Brazilian Steakhouse
★ Texas de Brazil $$$ *51 E. Ohio St. (p 106)*

Best Burger
★★ Mike Ditka's Restaurant $$$ *100 E. Chestnut St. (p 103)*

Best Fondue
★ Geja's Cafe $$ *340 W. Armitage Ave. (p 101)*

Best Sushi
★★ Mirai Sushi $$$ *2020 W. Division St. (p 104)*

Best Chicago-Style Pizza
★ Lou Malnati's $ *439 N. Wells St. (p 103)*

Best Celebrity-Chef Meal
★★★ Frontera Grill & Topolobampo $$–$$$ *445 N. Clark St. (p 101)*

Best Special-Occasion Restaurant
★★★ L20 $$$$ *2300 N. Lincoln Park West (p 102)*

Chicago is renowned for its pizza, and there's no better place to sample it than Lou Malnati's.

Best French Bistro
★★ Bistro Campagne $ *4518 N. Lincoln Ave. (p 100)*

Best Baby Back Ribs
★★ Twin Anchors Tavern $ *1655 N. Sedgwick St. (p 106)*

Most Romantic
★★★ North Pond Café $$$ *2610 N. Cannon Dr. (p 104)*

Best Outdoor Dining
★ Piccolo Sogno $$ *464 N. Halsted St. (p 104)*

Best Italian
★★ Merlo $$ *2638 N. Lincoln Ave. (p 103)*

Best Steakhouse
★★★ RL $$$ *115 E. Chicago Ave. (p 105)*

Best Asian
★★★ Shanghai Terrace (in the Peninsula Hotel) $$$ *108 E. Superior St. (p 105)*

Best Brunch
★ Milk & Honey Cafe $ *1920 W. Division St. (p 104)*

Best Vegetarian
★★★ Green Zebra $ *1460 W. Chicago Ave. (p 102)*

Best Ice Cream
★ Margie's Candies $ *1960 N. Western Ave. (p 103)*

Best View
★★★ Everest $$$$ *440 S. LaSalle St. (p 101)*

Best Pre-Theater Meal
★★ Trattoria No. 10 $$ *10 N. Dearborn St. (p 106)*

Previous page: Lou Mitchell's, known for its generous and tasty breakfasts.

Bucktown & Wicker Park Dining

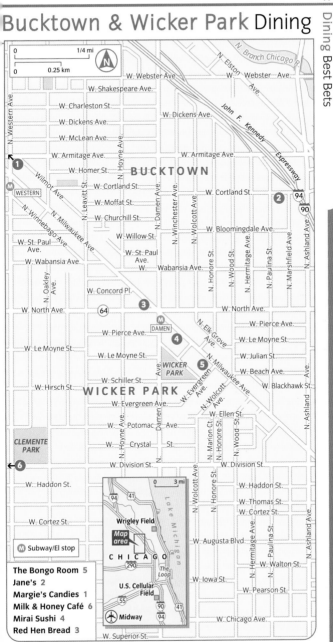

The Bongo Room 5
Jane's 2
Margie's Candies 1
Milk & Honey Café 6
Mirai Sushi 4
Red Hen Bread 3

Chicago Dining

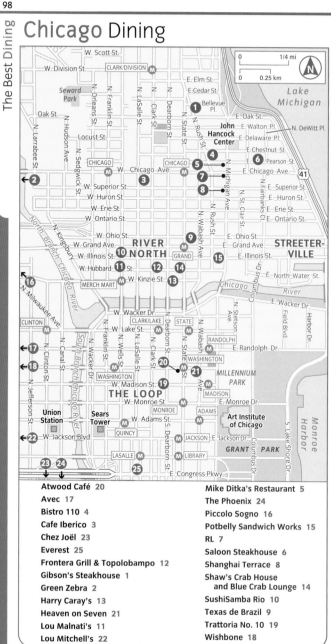

Lincoln Park Dining

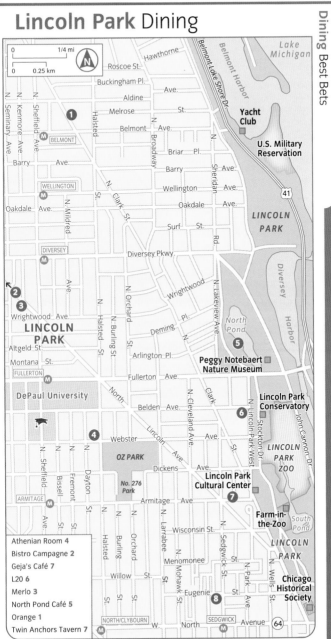

Athenian Room 4
Bistro Campagne 2
Geja's Café 7
L20 6
Merlo 3
North Pond Café 5
Orange 1
Twin Anchors Tavern 7

Restaurants A to Z

★ **kids** **Athenian Room** LINCOLN PARK *GREEK* Swing by this family-owned Greek taverna for chicken kalamata with a side of tasty fries smothered in olive oil, lemon, and red-wine vinegar, and topped with oregano, salt, and pepper. *807 W. Webster Ave. (at Halsted St.).* ☎ *773/348-5155. Entrees $4.50–$11. MC, V. Lunch & dinner daily. El: Brown Line to Armitage. Map p 99.*

★★ **Atwood Café** THE LOOP *AMERICAN* Colorful and offbeat, this stylish hotel restaurant serves fresh takes on American comfort food; try my personal favorite, the mussels in garlicky tomato sauce. *In the Hotel Burnham, 1 W. Washington St. (at State St.).* ☎ *312-368-1900. www.atwoodcafe.com. Entrees $18–$26. AE, DISC, MC, V. Breakfast & lunch Mon–Sat; brunch Sun; dinner daily. El: Red Line to Washington/State. Map p 98.*

★★★ **Avec** RANDOLPH STREET MARKET DISTRICT *FRENCH* Dine in tight, modern quarters at this hot spot, which features small plates (the specialty of the house is homemade charcuterie) and matching wines, served carafe-style. *615 W. Randolph St.* ☎ *312/377-2002. Entrees $15–$25. AE, DC, MC, V. Dinner daily. El: Green Line to Clinton. Map p 98.*

★★★ **Bistro Campagne** LINCOLN SQUARE *FRENCH* The best bistro in town sports a rich-wood, Prairie-school interior with a lovely garden space for outdoor dining. Expect excellently prepared but simple fare at a reasonable price. *4518 N. Lincoln Ave.* ☎ *773/271-6100. Entrees $8–$15. MC, V. Dinner daily; brunch Sun. El: Brown Line to Western. Map p 99.*

The Hotel Burnham's Atwood Café serves fresh takes on American comfort food.

★ **kids** **Bistro 110** MAGNIFICENT MILE *FRENCH* A neighborhood crowd gathers here for tasty wood-grilled vegetable platters and bouillabaisse. The Sunday brunch offers a New Orleans flair and live jazz. *110 E. Pearson St. (just west of Michigan Ave.).* ☎ *312/266-3110. www.levy restaurants.com. Entrees $13–$28. AE, DC, DISC, MC, V. Lunch Mon–Sat; brunch Sun; dinner daily. El: Red Line to Chicago/State. Map p 98.*

★ **kids** **The Bongo Room** WICKER PARK *BREAKFAST* This brightly colored brunch mecca offers tasty and creative treats such as lemon ricotta pancakes and bittersweet cocoa-espresso pancakes with Butterfinger-cashew butter. The menu changes every 4 months, so you'll have to visit to discover their latest concoction. *1470 N. Milwaukee Ave.* ☎ *773/489-0690.*

www.bongoroom.com. Entrees $8–$15. MC, V. Breakfast/brunch daily until 2:30pm. El: Blue Line to Damen. Map p 97.

★ **Cafe Iberico** RIVER NORTH *SPANISH* This tapas joint is boisterous and crowded, but the food is authentic and inexpensive—perfect for a late-night dinner. *739 N. LaSalle St. (between Chicago Ave. and Superior St.).* ☎ *312/573-1510. www.cafe iberico.com. Entrees $8–$13; tapas $2–$7. DC, DISC, MC, V. Lunch & dinner daily. El: Red Line to Chicago/ State. Map p 98.*

★★ **Chez Joël** LITTLE ITALY *FRENCH* Cozy and romantic, this tiny piece of France serves up such classics as steak frites, braised lamb shank, and coq au vin. *1119 W. Taylor.* ☎ *312/ 226-6479. Entrees $12–$22. AE, DC, DISC, MC, V. Lunch Mon–Fri; dinner daily. El: Blue Line to Polk. Map p 98.*

★★★ **Everest** THE LOOP *FRENCH* Forty stories above Chicago, this stylish Relais & Châteaux member astounds with spectacular views and earthy Alsatian cuisine to match. *440 S. LaSalle St. (at Congress Pkwy.).* ☎ *312/663-8920. www.everest restaurant.com. Reservations required. Entrees $27–$46. AE, DC, DISC, MC, V. Dinner Tues–Sat. El: Brown Line to LaSalle/Van Buren or Red Line to Adams. Map p 98.*

★★★ **Frontera Grill & Topolobampo** RIVER NORTH *MEXICAN* Owners Rick and Deann Bayless run one of North America's best Mexican restaurants. The older Frontera Grill dining room offers a casual atmosphere and classic cuisine; the newer and dressier Topolobampo room features more upscale fare. *445 N. Clark St. (between Illinois and Hubbard sts.).* ☎ *312/661-1434. www.frontera kitchens.com. Reservations accepted at Topolobampo; call Frontera at 8:30am the day-of for a limited* number of reservations. Entrees: Frontera $15–$25; Topolobampo $24–$35. AE, DC, DISC, MC, V. Frontera Grill: Lunch Tues–Fri; brunch Sat–Sun; dinner Tues–Sat. Topolobampo: Lunch Tues–Fri; dinner Tues–Sat. El: Red Line to Grand/State. Map p 98.

★ **Geja's Cafe** LINCOLN PARK *FONDUE* A dark, romantic hideaway, Geja's (pronounced gay-haz) might strike some as too gloomy, and the cook-it-yourself technique won't appeal to everyone, but for fondue fans, it's heaven. Choose the Prince Geja's combination dinner, the best Geja's has to offer, including cheese fondue appetizer, followed by a platter of raw lobster, shrimp, chicken, beef, and scallops to cook at your table, plus veggies and dipping sauces. When the flaming chocolate fondue arrives for dessert, with fresh fruit and pound cake for dipping and marshmallows for roasting, you'll want to beg for mercy. *340 W. Armitage Ave. (between Lincoln Ave. and Clark St.).* ☎ *773/281-9101. www.gejascafe.com. 3-course dinners $25–$45 per person. AE, DC, DISC, MC, V. Mon–Thurs 5–10pm; Fri 5–11:30pm; Sat 5pm–midnight; Sun*

The stylish Topolobampo is one of the best Mexican restaurants in the country.

4:30–9:30pm. *Subway/El: Brown Line to Armitage. Map p 99.*

★ **Gibson's Steakhouse** GOLD COAST *STEAKHOUSE* Chicagoans come to this steakhouse to see and be seen (check out the celebrity photo wall). Giant-size, well-aged steaks are the stars of the show. *1028 N. Rush St. (at Bellevue Place).* ☎ *312/266-8999. www.gibsons steakhouse.com. Entrees $22–$35. AE, DC, DISC, MC, V. Lunch & dinner daily. El: Red Line to Clark/Division. Map p 98.*

★ **Green Zebra** WEST TOWN *VEGETARIAN* A "small plates" approach offers creative veggie delights; count on ordering two miniportions if you want to fill up. The menu has a few chicken dishes, so it's a good compromise for groups with both carnivores and vegetarians. *1460 W. Chicago Ave. (at Greenview St.).* ☎ *312/243-7100. www.greenzebrachicago.com. Entrees $7–$14. AE, DC, DISC, MC, V. Dinner daily. Bus: 66. Map p 98.*

★ kids **Harry Caray's** RIVER NORTH *ITALIAN/STEAKHOUSE* Named for the legendary Chicago Cubs announcer, this restaurant's showcases are filled with baseball memorabilia. The good steaks, chops, and Italian basics are served in enormous portions. *33 W. Kinzie St. (at Dearborn St.).* ☎ *312/828-0966. www.harrycarays.com. Entrees $11–$33. AE, DC, DISC, MC, V. Lunch & dinner daily. El: Brown Line to Merchandise Mart, or Red Line to Grand/State. Map p 98.*

★★ kids **Heaven on Seven** THE LOOP *CAJUN* The best Cajun and Creole cooking north of New Orleans. Opt for the po' boy sandwiches (oyster and soft-shell crab). *111 N. Wabash Ave. (at Washington St.), 7th floor.* ☎ *312/263-6443. www.heavenonseven.com. Entrees $8–$11. No credit cards. Breakfast*

Celebrate a Cubs win with Harry Caray's enormous portions of Italian food.

Mon–Fri; brunch Sat; dinner 3rd Fri of each month. El: Orange, Brown, or Green line to Madison/Wabash. Map p 98.

★★ **Jane's** BUCKTOWN/WICKER PARK *AMERICAN* Bucktown residents pack this place (set inside an old but charming two-story home) for its pan-roasted grouper and goat cheese, and the herb-stuffed chicken breast. *1655 W. Cortland St. (west of Ashland Ave.).* ☎ *773/862-5263. Entrees $9–$20. AE, MC, V. Brunch Sat–Sun; dinner daily. El: Blue Line to Damen. Map p 97.*

★★★ **L20** LINCOLN PARK Pronounced el-two-oh, this seafood-centric spot has replaced Ambria as the jewel in the crown of Lettuce Entertain You's restaurant chain. Your choices are $110 for a four-course prix-fixe menu or $165 for a 12-course menu, with raw, warm, and main courses, all set in splendorous surroundings. *2300 N. Lincoln Park West (in the Belden-Stratford Hotel).* ☎ *773/868-0002. www.l20restaurant.com. Prix fixe. Dinner daily. Closed Tues. Bus: 151 to Belden. Jackets recommended for men. Map p 99.*

★★★ **kids** **Lou Malnati's** RIVER NORTH *PIZZA* Choose between Chicago deep dish or thin crust pizza at this branch of the popular Illinois chain. If you find yourself hooked, you can have a frozen pie mailed to your home. *439 N. Wells St.* ☎ *312/828-9800. www.loumalnatis.com. Pizzas start at $11. AE, DC, DISC, MC, V. Lunch & dinner daily. El: Brown Line to Merchandise Mart. Map p 98.*

★ **kids** **Lou Mitchell's** THE LOOP *AMERICAN/DINER* A Chicago tradition since 1923, this quirky restaurant features attentive service and large portions. The airy omelets served in sizzling skillets (you'll double your pleasure—and cholesterol—with Mitchell's use of double-yolk eggs) are a standout. *565 W. Jackson Blvd. (at Jefferson St.).* ☎ *312/939-3111. Entrees $5–$12. No credit cards. Breakfast & lunch daily. El: Blue Line to Clinton St. Map p 98.*

★★★ **kids** **Margie's Candies** BUCKTOWN *ICE CREAM* A kitschy ice-cream parlor circa 1921 that serves sundaes in giant-size conch shell dishes and makes its own hot fudge, butterscotch, and caramel. It also serves a limited menu of

sandwiches and salads. *1960 N. Western Ave. (at Armitage Ave.).* ☎ *773/384-1035. Entrees $8–$15. V. Breakfast, lunch & dinner daily. El: Blue Line to Milwaukee/Western. Map p 97.*

★ **Merlo** LINCOLN PARK *SOUTHERN ITALIAN* Dine on authentic (the owners hail from Bologna) Bolognese cuisine in a re-created salon from an Emilia-Romagna villa. House specialties include tagliatelle with Bolognese ragu, and *torta della nonna* (a cake with cream filling and wild berry cream sauce). *2638 N. Lincoln Ave.* ☎ *773/529-0747. Entrees $15–$25. AE, DISC, MC, V. Dinner daily. El: Red Line to Fullerton or Brown Line to Diversey. Map p 99.*

★★ **Mike Ditka's Restaurant** MAGNIFICENT MILE *STEAKHOUSE* Named for "Da Coach" of the 1985 Super Bowl champ Bears, this football memorabilia-filled gathering place attracts local celebs and a sophisticated crowd. Go for the "fullback size" filet mignon with spinach and homemade onion rings. *100 E. Chestnut St.* ☎ *312/587-8989. www. mikeditkaschicago.com. Entrees $15–$30. AE, DC, DISC, MC, V. Lunch Mon–Fri; brunch Sat–Sun; dinner*

Giant, well-aged steaks steal the show at Gibson's Steakhouse.

daily. El: Red Line to Chicago/State. Map p 98.

★ **Milk & Honey Café** UKRAINIAN VILLAGE *BREAKFAST* Set on a hopping strip of restaurants and shops in this newly gentrified neighborhood, this cafe offers a refreshing twist on breakfast and lunch in a bright and airy setting. Don't miss the orange brioche French toast or crab cake with chipotle mayo on a baguette. *1920 W. Division St.* ☎ *773/395-9434. Entrees under $9. AE, MC, V. Breakfast & lunch daily from 8am; weekend brunch from 8am. Map p 97.*

★★★ **Mirai Sushi** BUCKTOWN/WICKER PARK *JAPANESE* Blending a serious devotion to sushi and sake with a youthful and funky ambience, here's the best place in town to slurp down sushi and "red ones," the house cocktail of vodka with passion fruit, lime, and cranberry juices. *2020 W. Division St.* ☎ *773/862-8500. Sushi $1.75–$4 per piece. AE, DC, DISC, MC, V. Dinner daily. El: Blue Line to Division. Map p 97.*

★★★ **North Pond Café** LINCOLN PARK *AMERICAN* This secluded, Arts and Crafts–style retreat offers dramatic vistas from its location inside Lincoln Park. Meals are crafted from organic, locally grown ingredients. The All-American wine list focuses on boutique vintages. *2610 N. Cannon Dr. (south of Diversey Pkwy.).* ☎ *773/477-5845. www.northpondrestaurant.com. Entrees $24–$30. AE, DC, MC, V. Dinner Tues–Sun; brunch Sun. Bus: 151. Map p 99.*

★★ **kids** **Orange** LAKEVIEW *AMERICAN* Breakfast, lunch, and multiple combinations of the two is all that this casual (and orange) restaurant serves. Creative variations on traditional favorites include pan-seared cut oatmeal with dried fruit compote and apple cider–brown

sugar syrup. *3231 N. Clark (north of Belmont).* ☎ *773/549-4400. Entrees $5–$12. DISC, MC, V. Breakfast & lunch Tues–Sun. El: Red Line to Belmont. Map p 99.*

★★ **kids** **The Phoenix** CHINATOWN *CHINESE/DIM SUM* Expect speedy and friendly service, immense dining rooms, and tables filled with families enjoying Cantonese cuisine ranging from shrimp dumplings to sticky rice wrapped in leaves. Arrive early if you want to sample the dim sum. *2131 S. Archer Ave.* ☎ *312/328-0848. Entrees $8–$15. AE, DC, DISC, MC, V. Breakfast, lunch & dinner daily. Dim sum service: Mon–Fri 9am–3pm, Sat–Sun 8am–3pm. El: Red Line to Cermak/Chinatown. Map p 98.*

★★ **Piccolo Sogno** WEST TOWN *ECLECTIC* The most beautiful alfresco dining spot in the city is the 150-seat garden full of plants and light-illuminated trees at this Italian restaurant. Try the wood-fired white pizza or slow-roasted pork. *464 N. Halsted St. (at Grand Ave.).* ☎ *312/2421-0077. Entrees $15–$25. AE, DC, MC, V. Dinner daily. El: Blue Line to Grand Ave. Map p 98.*

Posh RL is a prime dining spot for steaks and other classic American dishes.

★ **kids** **Potbelly Sandwich Works** MAGNIFICENT MILE *SAND-WICHES* This popular branch of a local chain serves up a mean grilled sub sandwich, prepared on home-made rolls with turkey, Italian meats, veggies, and more. *520 N. Michigan Ave. (in the Westfield North Bridge shopping center).* ☎ *312/664-1008. www.potbelly.com. Sandwiches under $5. No credit cards. Lunch & dinner daily. El: Red Line to Grand/State. Map p 98.*

★★★ **kids** **Red Hen Bread** WICKER PARK *BAKERY* Choose from more than 24 varieties of freshly baked breads, including multigrain, Italian roasted garlic ring, and chocolate. You can also order tasty sandwiches or pastries and eat them at this tiny storefront shop. They've also opened a Lake-view location, at 500 W. Diversey St. (☎ 773/248-6025). *1623 N. Milwau-kee Ave.* ☎ *773/342-6823. Loaves under $5. AE, MC, V. Open 7am–7pm Mon–Sat; 8am–5pm Sun. El: Blue Line to Damen. Map p 97.*

★★★ **RL** MAGNIFICENT MILE *STEAK-HOUSE* Ralph Lauren's first venture into the restaurant business is this posh and clubby spot adjacent to his Michigan Avenue emporium. It serves excellent steaks and classic American retro dishes (flaming steak Diane, Waldorf salad, Dover sole). *115 E. Chicago Ave.* ☎ *312/475-1100. www.rlrestaurant.com. Entrees $15–$31. AE, DC, DISC, MC, V. Lunch & din-ner daily. El: Red Line to Chicago/State. Map p 98.*

★★ **Saloon Steakhouse** STREETERVILLE *STEAKHOUSE* Warm and cheery, this place is usu-ally filled with happy, animated car-nivores eating the specialty 16-ounce bone-in filet mignon and bacon-scallion mashed potatoes. *200 E. Chestnut St. (at Mies van der Rohe Way).* ☎ *312/280-5454.*

Fresh crabs are just one of the many tasty seafood offerings on the menu at Shaw's Crab House.

www.saloonsteakhouse.com. Entrees $13–$35. AE, DC, DISC, MC, V. Lunch Mon–Fri; dinner daily. El: Red Line to Chicago/State. Map p 98.

★★★ **Shanghai Terrace** MAGNIF-ICENT MILE *ASIAN* The Cantonese cuisine and Shanghai supper club decor reflect the Peninsula Hotel Group's renowned Asian properties. The outdoor terrace overlooking Michigan Avenue is ideal for a warm-weather cocktail. *In the Penin-sula Hotel, 108 E. Superior St. (at Michigan Ave.).* ☎ *312/337-2888. Reservations recommended. Entrees $15–$25. AE, DC, DISC, MC, V. Dinner Tues–Sat. El: Red Line to Chicago/ State. Map p 98.*

★ **Shaw's Crab House and Blue Crab Lounge** RIVER NORTH *SEAFOOD* A 1940s-style local insti-tution, Shaw's has a lively atmos-phere and an extensive seafood menu featuring fried smelt, sautéed sea scallops, and grilled fish, among other fare. The adjacent Blue Crab Lounge offers an extensive raw bar that will please even the most sophisticated seafood lover, and live jazz or blues. *21 E. Hubbard St. (at State St.).* ☎ *312/527-2722. www. shawscrabhouse.com/chicago.html. Reservations accepted. Entrees $14–$31. AE, DC, DISC, MC, V. Lunch Mon–Fri; dinner daily. El: Red Line to State/Grand. Map p 98.*

★ **SushiSamba Rio** RIVER NORTH *ASIAN/SOUTH AMERICAN* A mix of Japanese-Brazilian-Peruvian cuisine, a dramatic dining room, a sushi bar, and a *caipirinha* (traditional Brazilian cocktail) bar makes this one of the trendiest restaurants in town. *504 N. Wells St.* ☎ *312/595-2300. www. sushisamba.com. Reservations required for main dining room. Entrees $15–$25. AE, MC, V. Lunch & dinner daily. El: Brown Line to Chicago. Map p 98.*

★★ **Texas de Brazil** RIVER NORTH *STEAKHOUSE* This crazy-huge restaurant seats 500 guests and features aerial wine artists, who bring your bottle while affixed to a trapeze-like system. That, plus an unending supply of grilled meats and 75-item salad bar, makes this $48 prix-fixed eal entertaining as well as filling. *51 E. Ohio St.* ☎ *312/670-1006. Prix fixe. $28 salad bar only. AE, DISC, MC, V. Dinner nightly. El: Red Line to Chicago/State. Map p 98.*

★★ **Trattoria No. 10** THE LOOP *ITALIAN* This ideal pre-theater dinner spot has a Tuscan feel, with a warm, orangey glow. The real bargain is the wonderful (and cheap) after-work (5–8pm) all-you-can-eat buffet. *10 N. Dearborn St. (at Madison St.).* ☎ *312/984-1718. Entrees $14–$27; buffet $12, with a $6 drink minimum. AE, DC, DISC, MC, V. Lunch Mon–Fri; dinner Mon–Sat. El: Red or Blue line to Dearborn. Map p 98.*

★★★ kids **Twin Anchors Tavern** OLD TOWN *BARBECUE* This

Italian favorites complement the al fresco dining space at Piccolo Sogno.

unpretentious pub dates back to Prohibition and preserves the style of old Chicago in dark mahogany and serviceable Formica. The restaurant's slow-cooked baby back ribs (go for the zesty sauce) keep people coming back. *1655 N. Sedgwick St. (1 block north of North Ave.).* ☎ *312/266-1616. www. twinanchorsribs.com. Entrees $10–$20. AE, DC, DISC, MC, V. Lunch Sat–Sun; dinner daily. El: Brown Line to Sedgwick. Map p 99.*

★★★ kids **Wishbone** RANDOLPH STREET MARKET DISTRICT *CAJUN/ SOUTHERN* Primitive art decorates this bright, open restaurant, which is always bustling with loyal locals. The down-home Southern fare is reasonably priced and hearty, and the excellent Sunday brunch is justifiably popular (but can get very crowded). *1001 W. Washington St. (at Morgan St.).* ☎ *312/850-2663. www.wishbonechicago.com. Entrees $5.25–$14. AE, DC, DISC, MC, V. Breakfast & lunch daily; dinner Tues–Sat. Bus: 20. Map p 98.* ●

Nightlife Best Bets

Best Viennese Coffee
★★ Julius Meinl Café, *3601 N. Southport Ave. and 4363 N. Lincoln Ave.* (p 117)

Best Bar Food
★★ The Hopleaf Bar, *5148 N. Clark St.* (p 63)

Most Kitsch
★ Marie's Rip Tide Lounge, *1745 W. Armitage Ave.* (p 114)

Best Happy Hour
★★ J Bar, *in The James Hotel, 610 N. Rush St.* (p 114)

Best Late-Night Noshing
★★★ BIN 36, *339 N. Dearborn St.* (p 113)

Best View
★★ Signature Lounge, *875 N. Michigan Ave.* (p 115)

Best Irish Pub
★★ Kitty O'Shea's, *720 S. Michigan Ave.* (p 114)

Best Place to Watch Soccer
★★ Sheffield's, *3258 N. Sheffield Ave.* (p 115)

Best Rock Club
★★ Elbo Room, *2871 N. Lincoln Ave.* (p 118)

Best Restored Tavern
★★★ The California Clipper, *1002 N. California Ave.* (p 118)

Best Blues Club
★★★ Buddy Guy's Legends, *754 S. Wabash Ave.* (p 116)

Best Sports Bar
★ Cubby Bear, *1059 W. Addison St.* (p 113)

Best Neighborhood Hangout
★ Old Town Ale House, *219 W. North Ave.* (p 115)

The Green Mill is the place in Chicago for jazz music.

Best Scottish Pub
★ The Duke of Perth, *2913 N. Clark St.* (p 113)

Best Champagne Bar
★★ Pops for Champagne, *601 N. State St.* (p 115)

Best Martini
★★ The Matchbox, *770 N. Milwaukee Ave.* (p 115)

Best Bowling and Lounge Combo
★★ 10pin *330 N. State St.* (p 116)

Best Wine Bar
★★★ Bin 36, *339 N. Dearborn St.* (p 113), and Bin Wine Café, *1559 N. Milwaukee Ave.* (p 113)

Best Mecca for Beer Lovers
★★★ The Map Room, *1949 N. Hoyne Ave.* (p 114)

Best Find
★★★ The Hideout, *1354 W. Wabansia Ave.* (p 118)

Best Hotel Bar
★★★ J Bar, *in The James Hotel, 610 N. Rush St.* (p 114)

Best Jazz Club
★★★ The Green Mill, *4802 N. Broadway* (p 118)

Previous page: The blues can be heard at venues around the city.

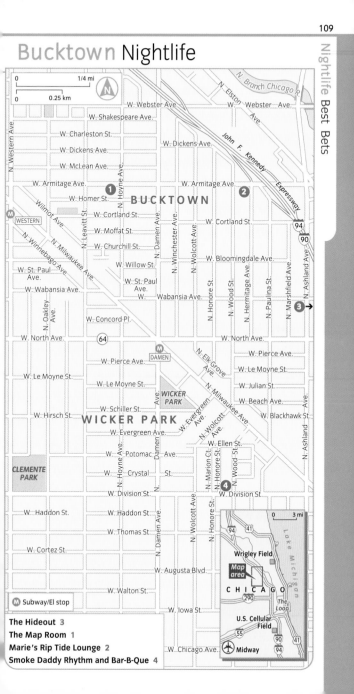

Bucktown Nightlife

The Hideout 3
The Map Room 1
Marie's Rip Tide Lounge 2
Smoke Daddy Rhythm and Bar-B-Que 4

Chicago Nightlife

B.L.U.E.S. 14
The California Clipper 16
Cubby Bear 7
Cullen's Bar and Grill 5
The Duke of Perth 12
Elbo Room 13
Goose Island 9
The Green Mill 2
Hopleaf Bar 1
Julius Meinl Café 6
Kingston Mines 15
Matchbox 17
Old Town Ale House 18
Roscoe's Tavern 10
Sheffield's 11
Smart Bar 3
Uncommon Ground 4
The Wild Hare 8
Zebra Lounge 19

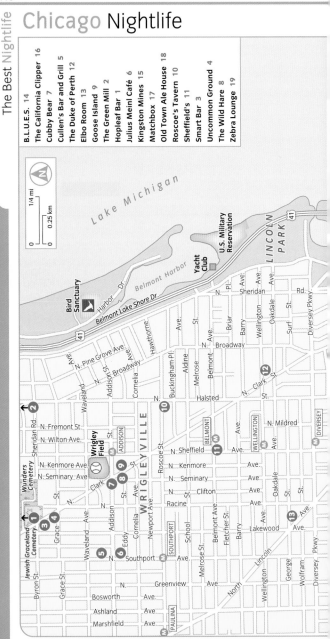

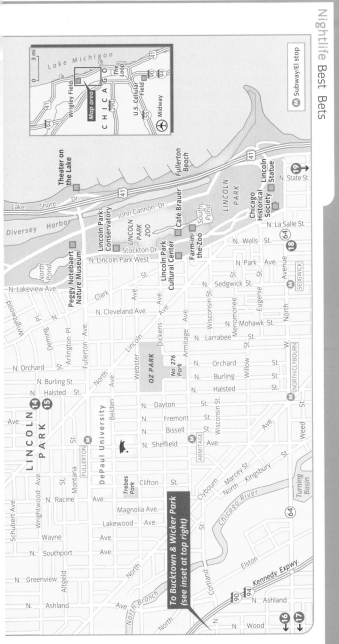

River North Nightlife

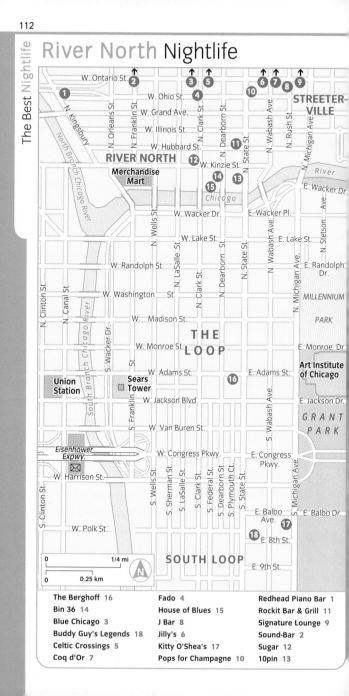

The Berghoff 16
Bin 36 14
Blue Chicago 3
Buddy Guy's Legends 18
Celtic Crossings 5
Coq d'Or 7
Fado 4
House of Blues 15
J Bar 8
Jilly's 6
Kitty O'Shea's 17
Pops for Champagne 10
Redhead Piano Bar 1
Rockit Bar & Grill 11
Signature Lounge 9
Sound-Bar 2
Sugar 12
10pin 13

Nightlife A to Z

Bars

★★ The Berghoff THE LOOP This local institution attracts an older, pin-stripe-wearing crowd, and holds Chicago liquor license no. 1, issued at the end of Prohibition. It features a good selection of German beers, 20-foot (6m) ceilings, a checked linoleum floor, and sepia photos of old Chicago. German and Austrian food, plus some standard American items, are on the menu. Don't hesitate—go for the schnitzel. *17 W. Adams St. (at State St.).* ☎ *312/427-3170. www.berghoff.com. El: Red or Blue line to Jackson/State or Monroe/State. Map p 112.*

★★★ Bin 36 RIVER NORTH It's all about wine at this bistro, located in a lofty, airy space in the Marina Towers complex that attracts young professionals and others on their way to concerts at the adjacent House of Blues. Several wine flights (four half-glasses of various vintages) are available, or try one of the suggested wine-and-cheese pairings (they serve a huge selection of American artisan cheeses until 1:30am and make for ideal late-night noshing). A second location, the Bin Wine Café, has opened in Wicker Park at 1559 N. Milwaukee Ave. (☎ 773/486-2233). *339 N. Dearborn St.* ☎ *312/755-9463. www.bin36.com. El: Red Line to Grand/State. Map p 112.*

★★ Celtic Crossings RIVER NORTH A diverse crowd of the young and the old, the corporate and the artistically minded, gathers around this Irish pub's fireplaces for quiet conversation over pints of Guinness and Harp. *751 N. Clark St. (near Chicago Ave.).* ☎ *312/337-1005. El: Red Line to Chicago/State. Map p 112.*

★ Cubby Bear WRIGLEYVILLE Cubs fans and the surrounding

neighborhood's young professionals head to this tri-level landmark to vent before and/or after games. Pool tables, darts, and TV screens offer diversions. At night, the club is one of Chicago's premier rock venues. *1059 W. Addison St. (across from Wrigley Field).* ☎ *773/327-1662. www.cubbybear.com. Concert tickets under $10. El: Red Line to Addison. Map p 110.*

★★★ Cullen's Bar and Grill LAKEVIEW This Irish watering hole attracts a diverse crowd, from singles to families, and features a large selection of beer and great food, including tasty grilled shrimp and huge Caesar salads. After you've downed a pint or two, stick around for the live Celtic music or take in a movie at the old-time Music Box Theatre next door (p 127). *3741 N. Southport Ave.* ☎ *773/975-0600. El: Brown Line to Southport. Map p 110.*

★ Duke of Perth LINCOLN PARK This congenial Scottish pub attracts a young crowd with its reasonably priced all-you-can-eat fish-and-chips special on Wednesdays and Fridays, its selection of single-malt scotch,

The Berghoff, a local institution, got the first liquor license in Chicago after Prohibition ended.

and an outdoor beer garden that's inviting on summer nights. *2913 N. Clark St. (at Wellington Ave.).* ☎ *773/477-1741. El: Brown Line to Diversey. Map p 110.*

Fado RIVER NORTH This multilevel reproduction of an Irish pub features various themed rooms (country cottage, Victorian Dublin, and so on) bursting with people drinking Guinness and eating standard pub grub. Live, traditional Irish music is featured on many nights. *100 W. Grand Ave. (at Clark St.).* ☎ *312/836-0066. www.fadoirishpub.com. El: Red Line to State/Grand. Map p 112.*

★★★ kids Goose Island Brewing Company WRIGLEYVILLE The best-known brewpub in town has its own brews on tap (sample three for $5). The enclosed patio is especially family-friendly and provides a beautiful setting for casual dining. There's a kids' menu (the baked mac and cheese is popular) if you couldn't snag a babysitter for the night. Don't miss the freshly baked pretzels with a choice of Dusseldorf mustard, cheese spread, or marinara sauce. *3535 N. Clark St. (at Sheffield Ave.).* ☎ *773/832-9040. www.gooseisland.com. El: Red Line to Addison. Map p 110.*

Holiday Club UPTOWN Home to Chicago's most diverse jukebox, plus Golden Tee golf and video poker. This laid-back joint attracts a good-looking young crowd and shakes out gallons of martinis and Manhattans every night. *4000 N. Sheridan Rd.* ☎ *773/486-0686. www. swingersmecca.com. El: Red Line to Sheridan.*

★★ J Bar The gathering place for stylish locals in their 20s and 30s, this lounge is just off the lobby of The James Hotel. Low-slung leather couches and high-concept drinks (the house martini blends blue raspberry vodka and elderflower cordial)

Head over to Fado for live Irish music, pub grub, and a pint of Guinness.

give this the vibe of an upscale urban club. *610 N. Rush St. (at Wabash Ave.)* ☎ *312/660-7200. El: Red Line to Grand. Map p 112.*

★★ Kitty O'Shea's THE LOOP The brogues at this hotel bar are as authentic as the Guinness on tap. You'll find live Irish entertainment, a jukebox stacked with favorite Gaelic tunes, and an older crowd enjoying the excellent Irish pub food. *In the Chicago Hilton and Towers, 720 S. Michigan Ave. (between Balbo and 8th sts.).* ☎ *312/922-4400. El: Red Line to Harrison. Map p 112.*

★★★ The Map Room BUCKTOWN/WICKER PARK Nearly 200 beers are offered (20 or so are on tap) at this tavern, frequented by an artistic and eclectic crowd of 30-somethings from the neighborhood. In the morning, this is a coffee bar; in the late afternoon, the drinks start flowing. Sunday night at 8pm is movie night. *1949 N. Hoyne Ave. (at Armitage Ave.).* ☎ *773/252-7636. www.maproom.com. El: Blue Line to Damen. Map p 109.*

★ Marie's Rip Tide Lounge BUCKTOWN/WICKER PARK The retro cool of this late-night dive bar on the after-dark circuit makes

Marie's a hoot. It seems like everything here (from the decor to the jukebox music) hasn't been updated since the '60s, though charming owners Shirley and Marie do decorate for the holidays—don't miss their Christmas and Valentine's Day decor. *1745 W. Armitage Ave. (at Hermitage Ave.).* ☎ *773/278-7317. El: Blue Line to Damen. Map p 109.*

★★ The Matchbox RIVER WEST This tiny corner bar (3 ft./.9m wide at its narrowest; 10 ft./3m at its widest) claims to be "Chicago's most intimate bar." It's not for the claustrophobic, but it's the perfect spot for a late-night martini. *770 N. Milwaukee Ave. (at Ogden Ave.).* ☎ *312/666-9292. El: Blue Line to Chicago. Map p 110.*

★ Old Town Ale House OLD TOWN This legendary saloon has played host to many a Second City comedian, including John Belushi, who commanded the pinball machines here during his Second City (p 126) days. A bit dingy, but full of local flavor. *219 W. North Ave. (at Wells St.).* ☎ *312/944-7020. El: Brown Line to Sedgwick. Map p 110.*

★★ Pops for Champagne RIVER NORTH A hot date spot for everyone from 20-somethings on up, this romantic lounge offers more than 100 labels of bubbly, plus live jazz at 9pm nightly in the downstairs jazz lounge. Courtyard and sidewalk cafe, raw bar, jazz lounge—this place has it all. *601 N. State St. (at Ontario St.).* ☎ *312/266-7677. www.popsforchampagne. com. Jazz lounge cover varies. El: Red Line to Grand. Map p 112.*

★★ Rockit Bar & Grill RIVER NORTH This former lamp factory has exposed brick walls, beams, and a 75-foot (23m) skylight. Dine on upscale grill items (a Kobe beef burger topped with foie gras), then grab a cocktail and hit the pool tables and plasma TVs in the lounge upstairs. *22 W. Hubbard St.* ☎ *312/645-6000. El: Brown Line to Merchandise Mart. Map p 112.*

★★ Roscoe's Tavern LAKEVIEW One of Chicago's best-known gay nightspots (though everyone's welcome) has six bars, a huge dance floor, and an antique tavern decor. Check out the patio garden when the weather's cooperative. *3356 N. Halsted St. (at Roscoe St.).* ☎ *773/281-3355. www.roscoes. com. $4 cover after 10pm on Sat. El: Red, Brown, or Purple line to Belmont. Map p 110.*

★★ Sheffield's LINCOLN PARK Play pool, golf, or board games at this welcoming neighborhood bar. In the winter, cozy up to the fireplace; in the summer, the outdoor beer garden is one of the city's best. Choose from 100 beers, including the tongue-in-cheek "bad beer" (think cheap domestic) of the month. *3258 N. Sheffield Ave. (at Belmont Ave.).* ☎ *773/281-4989. www.sheffieldschicago.com. El: Red or Brown line to Belmont. Map p 110.*

★★ Signature Lounge MAGNIFICENT MILE On the 95th floor of the John Hancock Center, this bar is a good place to perch for a drink before or after dinner. Because the

A hot spot for romance, Pops for Champagne serves more than 100 varieties of bubbly.

restaurant is on the pricey side, it attracts an older crowd. The view, as you'd expect, is dazzling. *875 N. Michigan Ave. ☎ 312/787-7230. www.signatureroom.com. El: Red Line to Chicago/State. Map p 112.*

★★ **10pin** RIVER NORTH   A modern interpretation of the classic bowling alley, this lounge is tucked away under the Marina Towers complex on the Chicago River. Everything feels bright and new, and there's a full menu of designer beers and upscale snacks. A giant video screen overlooking the 24 bowling lanes give the place a nightclub vibe. *330 N. State St. (between Kinzie St. and the Chicago River). ☎ 312/664-0300. www.10pinchicago.com. El: Red Line to Grand or Brown Line to Merchandise Mart. Map p 112.*

Blues Clubs

Blue Chicago RIVER NORTH This popular tourist spot features exposed brick walls, a good sound system, and an intimate atmosphere. It showcases top female blues talent. *736 and 536 N. Clark St. ☎ 312/642-6261. www.bluechicago.com. $5–$8 cover. El: Red Line to State/Grand. Map p 112.*

B.L.U.E.S. LINCOLN PARK   Live music plays 365 days a year in a dark, narrow club that seats patrons up close to the performers. *2519 N. Halsted St. (at Wrightwood Ave.). ☎ 773/528-1012. $5–$8 cover. El: Brown Line to Diversey. Map p 110.*

★★★ **Buddy Guy's Legends** THE LOOP   If Chicago is the body and soul of blues music, then this club—owned and operated by rock-'n'-roll Hall-of-Famer Buddy Guy—is its heart. The club's renowned guitar collection features instruments played by the likes of Eric Clapton and John Lee Hooker. *754 S. Wabash Ave. (between Balbo and 8th sts.).*

Mojo Mama, *a mural by artist John Carroll Doyle at Blue Chicago, one of the city's top clubs for female blues artists.*

☎ 312/427-0333. www.buddyguys.com. Usually under $10 cover. El: Red Line to Harrison/State. Map p 112.

★★★ **House of Blues** RIVER NORTH   One of Chicago's premier concert venues, this multi-level music hall books a wide variety of acts. It stages a popular Sunday gospel brunch featuring good southern fare ($43, with seatings at 10am and 12:30pm; reservations highly recommended). *329 N. Dearborn St. (at Kinzie St.). ☎ 312/923-2000. Tickets $10–$50. El: Red Line to State/Grand. Map p 112.*

Kingston Mines LINCOLN PARK This veteran roadhouse attracts hard-core fans and celebs with two stages' worth of down-home blues. Performances last until 4am on Saturdays. *2548 N. Halsted St. (at Wrightwood Ave.). ☎ 773/477-4646. www.kingstonmines.com. $12 cover Sat–Wed. El: Brown Line to Diversey. Map p 110.*

★★ Smoke Daddy Rhythm and Bar-B-Que
BUCKTOWN/WICKER PARK A great bar with live music 7 nights a week (mostly gritty, Chicago-style blues and jazz, played by small combos, due to the bar's intimate size). Arrive early if you want to sample the excellent slow-cooked barbecue, which arrives in retro plastic baskets. *1804 W. Division St.* ☎ *773/772-6656. No cover with dinner; cover varies for entertainment only. El: Blue Line to Damen. Map p 109.*

Cabaret & Piano Bars

Coq d'Or MAGNIFICENT MILE This piano bar and lounge showcases pianists and vocalists 7 nights a week, from 9:30pm to 1:30am. It's a classy place, where you can join the older crowd and indulge in a martini, a specialty of the house, and enjoy the dark, speak-easy atmosphere. *In The Drake Hotel, 140 E. Walton St.* ☎ *312/787-2200. No cover. El: Red Line to Chicago/State. Map p 112.*

Jilly's GOLD COAST Jazz trios and piano stylists play this dark room, named after Frank Sinatra's manager. It attracts a middle-aged crowd, as well as the occasional celeb. Drink prices aren't cheap, but there's no cover charge. *1007 N. Rush St. (at Oak St.).* ☎ *312/664-1001. www.jillyschicago.com. No cover. El: Red Line to Clark/Divison. Map p 112.*

Redhead Piano Bar RIVER NORTH A favorite with locals, this upscale lounge features top-notch pianists and makes a great spot for after-dinner cocktails. Dress well. *16 W. Ontario.* ☎ *312/640-1000. www.redheadpianobar.com. El: Red Line to State/Grand. Map p 112.*

★ Zebra Lounge GOLD COAST Black-and-white striped walls are the key to the decor at this shoe box–size piano bar. The multi-generational, loyal crowd gets raucous late in the evening; arrive by 9:30pm if you want to get a seat. *1220 N. State Pkwy. (between Division and Goethe sts.).* ☎ *312/642-5140. Subway/El: Red Line to Clark/Division. Map p 110.*

Cafes

★★ Julius Meinl Café LAKEVIEW The venerable Austrian coffee empire chose Chicago for its first attempt at re-creating a Viennese coffeehouse in the U.S., and has since opened a second location. The excellent coffee is served on a silver tray with a glass of water, but the luscious desserts are why locals flock here. *3601 N. Southport Ave. (at Addison St.;* ☎ *773/868-1857), and 4363 N. Lincoln Ave. (*☎ *773/868-1876). www.meinl.com. El: Brown Line to Southport. Map p 110.*

★★★ Uncommon Ground WRIGLEYVILLE More than just a coffeehouse, this bohemian cafe's soul-warming bowls of coffee are accompanied by California-influenced cuisine that's heavy on vegetarian dishes, accompanied by live music nightly. Local artists display their work here on a rotating basis. A second location has opened in Edgewater. *3800 N. Clark St. (at Grace St.;* ☎ *773/929-3680), and 1401 W. Devon Ave. (*☎ *773/465-9801). www.uncommonground.com. El: Red Line to Addison. Map p 110.*

A local favorite, the Redhead Piano Bar features top-notch pianists.

Live Music

★★★ The California Clipper

HUMBOLDT PARK   This lovingly restored 1940s tavern, with a gorgeous Art Deco bar and red walls, is worth a trip out to Humboldt Park on the weekends for its live rockabilly and "country swing." *1002 N. California Ave. ☎ 773/384-2547. www.californiaclipper.com. El: Blue Line to California, then take a cab. Map p 110.*

★★ Elbo Room LINCOLN PARK

The eclectic acts at this small live music venue range from hip-hop to Goth to rockabilly. The crowds are equally diverse. *2871 N. Lincoln Ave. (at George St.). ☎ 773/549-5549. www.elboroomchicago.com. $3 and up cover; no cover in the upstairs lounge. El: Brown Line to Diversey. Map p 110.*

★★★ The Green Mill UPTOWN

Known for offering great jazz in a historical setting, this former speakeasy was established in 1907 and frequented by infamous mobster Al Capone. Today you can hear Latin jazz, big band jazz, jazz piano, and more. Sunday nights it hosts the famous Uptown Poetry Slam with

Though it's off the beaten path, The Hideout features a friendly crowd and the best folk bands in the city.

Marc Smith (p. 129). *4802 N. Broadway (at Lawrence Ave.). ☎ 773/878-5552. Free–$8 cover. El: Red Line to Lawrence. Map p 110.*

★★★ The Hideout NEAR NORTH

SIDE   Head to this friendly tavern for the best lineup of folk and "alt country" bands in the city. The location epitomizes the term "out of the way," but it's worth the trip (about a $10 cab ride from the Magnificent Mile). *1354 W. Wabansia Ave. (between Elston Ave. and Throop St.). ☎ 773/227-4433. www.hideoutchicago.com. Usually $5–$10 cover. El: Blue Line to Damen. Map p 109.*

Nightclubs

★★★ Smart Bar WRIGLEYVILLE

One of the coolest clubs in Chicago is tucked away in the dimly lit basement of Metro, one of Chicago's best live rock venues. DJs here do some serious spinning; every night features a different style of music. *3730 N. Clark St. ☎ 773/549-0203. www.smartbarchicago.com. Cover usually $5–$15. El: Red Line to Addison. Map p 110.*

★ Sound-Bar RIVER NORTH   DJs

are the draw at this multilevel, high-tech dance club, which prides itself on booking top nightlife names. The young, club-savvy crowd comes for electronic dance, trance, and house music. If you want a primer on Chicago house music, this is a good place to start. *226 W. Ontario St. (at Franklin St.). ☎ 312/787-4480. Cover $10–$20. El: Red Line to Grand. Map p 112.*

The Wild Hare WRIGLEYVILLE

Dreadlocks and Red Stripe beer abound at Chicago's premier reggae club, which has hosted such notables as the Wailers and Yellowman. *3530 N. Clark St. (at Addison St.). ☎ 773/327-4273. No cover until 9:30pm Mon–Tues; otherwise $8–$12. El: Red Line to Addison. Map p 110.* ●

Arts & Entertainment Best Bets

Best Theater Company
★★★ Steppenwolf Theatre Company, *1650 N. Halsted St. (p 129)*

Best Rising Star on the Theater Scene
★★★ Lookingglass Theatre Company, *821 N. Michigan Ave. (p 129)*

Best Opera Company
★★★ Lyric Opera of Chicago, *20 N. Wacker Dr. (p 127)*

Best Ballet
★★ Joffrey Ballet of Chicago, *10 E. Randolph St. (p 126)*

Best Modern Dance
★★ Hubbard Street Dance Chicago, *205 E. Randolph St. (p 126)*

Best Symphony
★★ Chicago Symphony Orchestra, *220 S. Michigan Ave. (p 125)*

Best Late-Night Comedy
Late-Nite Catechism, *1641 N. Halsted St. (p 129)*

Best Guaranteed Laugh
★★★ Blue Man Group, *3133 N. Halsted St. (p 127)*

Best Up-and-Coming Comedians
★★★ ImprovOlympic, *3541 N. Clark St. (p 125)*

If you need a good laugh, the Blue Man Group's the best place in town to get it.

Best Free Live Music Performances
★ Chicago Cultural Center, *78 E. Washington St. (p 125)*

Wackiest Place to Watch a Film
★★★ Music Box Theatre, *3733 W. Southport Ave. (p 127)*

Best Movie Theater for Cinema Buffs
★ Gene Siskel Film Center, *164 N. State St. (p 126)*

Best Venue for World-Premiere Theater
★★★ Victory Gardens Biograph Theater, *2243 N. Lincoln Ave. (p 130)*

Best Children's Film Festival
Facets Multi-Media, *1517 W. Fullerton Ave. (p 126)*

Best Dinner Theater Show
Tommy Gun's Garage, *2114 S. Wabash Ave. (p 129)*

Best Venue for Popular Music
★★ Park West, *322 W. Armitage Ave. (p 125)*

Best Sports Experience
★★★ Wrigley Field, *1060 W. Addison St. (p 130)*

Best Sunday Night Activity
★★ Uptown Poetry Slam with Marc Smith, *4802 N. Broadway (p 129)*

Best Cheap Ticket in Town
Too Much Light Makes the Baby Go Blind, *5153 N. Ashland Ave. (p 129)*

Best Children's Theater
★★ Emerald City Theater Company, *2540 N. Lincoln Ave. (p 128)*

Previous page: Hubbard Street Dance Chicago.

The Loop Entertainment

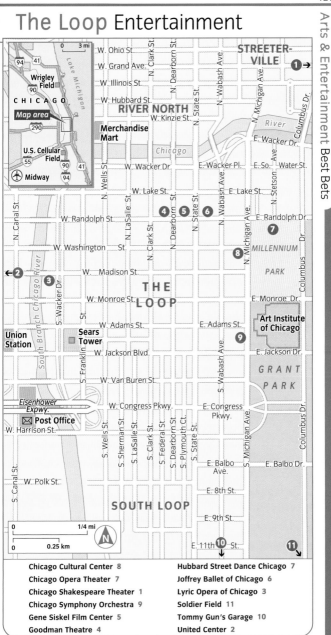

Chicago Cultural Center 8
Chicago Opera Theater 7
Chicago Shakespeare Theater 1
Chicago Symphony Orchestra 9
Gene Siskel Film Center 5
Goodman Theatre 4

Hubbard Street Dance Chicago 7
Joffrey Ballet of Chicago 6
Lyric Opera of Chicago 3
Soldier Field 11
Tommy Gun's Garage 10
United Center 2

Lincoln Park Entertainment

Blue Man Group 4
Emerald City Theater Company 6
Facets Multi-Media 5
ImprovOlympic 3
Late-Night Catechism 10
Music Box Theatre 1
Park West 8
The Second City 11
Steppenwolf Theatre Company 9
Victory Gardens Biograph Theater 7
Wrigley Field 2
Zanies Comedy Club 12

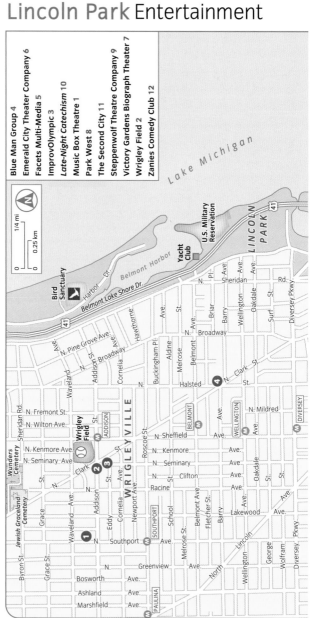

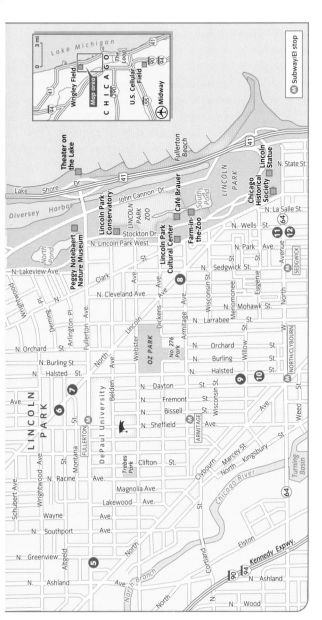

Chicago Arts & Entertainment

Charter One Pavilion 6

Lookingglass Theatre Company 5

North Shore Center for the Performing Arts 1

Ravinia Festival 2

Too Much Light Makes the Baby Go Blind 3

U.S. Cellular Field 7

Uptown Poetry Slam at the Green Mill 4

Arts & Entertainment A to Z

Classical Music & Concerts
★ **Chicago Cultural Center** THE LOOP   Free Dame Myra Hess Memorial classical concerts take place every Wednesday in the Preston Bradley Hall. Other free concerts are often staged here in the afternoons; check the events line for current schedules. *See p 19, ❶. 78 E. Washington St. ☎ 312/744-6630, or 312/FINE-ART for weekly events. El: Brown Line to Randolph, or Red Line to Washington/State. Map p 121.*

★★ **Chicago Symphony Orchestra** THE LOOP   One of the best and oldest symphony orchestras in the world performs a varied repertoire of classical works at Orchestra Hall from September to June. The "Symphony Center Presents" series features top jazz, world beat, Latin, and cabaret artists. *Symphony Center, 220 S. Michigan Ave. (at Jackson St.). ☎ 312/294-3000. www.cso.org. Tickets $25–$135. El: Red Line to Jackson/State. Map p 121.*

★ **North Shore Center for the Performing Arts** SUBURBAN SKOKIE   Opened in 1996, this state-of-the-art complex has earned comparisons to Washington, D.C.'s Kennedy Center. It's currently the home of the respected Northlight Theater, the Skokie Valley Symphony Orchestra, and a series of touring acts, including comics, dance troupes, and children's programs. *9501 Skokie Blvd. (at Golf Rd.). ☎ 847/673-6300. www.north shorecenter.org. Tickets $25–$50. Take I-90 to Old Orchard Rd. exit; turn right on Old Orchard Rd., and drive past Old Orchard Mall. Turn right on Skokie Blvd. Map p 124.*

★★ **Park West** LINCOLN PARK   Performers love this venue's excellent sound system and cabaret-style

The Chicago Symphony Orchestra, under the direction of Daniel Barenboim, is one of the finest in the world.

seating. You can hear artists such as Sarah McLachlan and Tori Amos to their best advantage here. *322 W. Armitage Ave. ☎ 773/929-5959. www.parkwestchicago.com. Tickets $25 and up, depending on the act. Subway/El: Brown Line to Armitage. Map p 122.*

★★★ **Ravinia Festival** SUBURBAN HIGHLAND PARK   Locals flock to this do-not-miss outdoor festival from mid-June through Labor Day. The park is the unofficial summer home of the Chicago Symphony Orchestra. Performances by dance troupes and jazz and pop performers round out the calendar. *418 Sheridan Rd., Highland Park. ☎ 847/266-5100. www.ravinia.org. Tickets $10 for lawn seating, $25–$50 for the pavilion. Map p 124.*

Comedy Clubs
★★★ **ImprovOlympic** WRIGLEYVILLE   See some of Chicago's top comedic talent stretch their wings. Performances here engage the audience as the talented cast solicits suggestions and

The Best Arts & Entertainment

creates original sketches. *3541 N. Clark St. (at Addison St.).* ☎ *773/880-0199. Cover $5–$14. El: Red Line to Addison. Map p 122.*

★★★ The Second City OLD
TOWN Comedians ranging from Mike Nichols to Dan Ackroyd have studied and performed at this Chicago institution. Two sketch-comedy productions run on the main stage and at ETC (et cetera), a smaller venue. If you just want a quick sampling, free improv sessions take place every night except Friday after the main show. *1616 N. Wells St. (at North Ave.).* ☎ *312/337-3992. www.secondcity.com. Cover $8–$19. El: Brown Line to Sedgwick. Map p 122.*

Zanies Comedy Nite Club OLD TOWN High-caliber comedians treat sold-out houses to the best in traditional stand-up. *1548 N. Wells St. (at North Ave.).* ☎ *312/337-4027. www.chicago.zanies.com. Cover $19–$20, with a 2-item food/drink minimum. Guests must be age 21 or older to enter. El: Brown Line to Sedgwick. Map p 122.*

A Chicago institution, The Second City stages performances by some of the finest comedians in the country.

Dance
★★ Hubbard Street Dance
Chicago THE LOOP This 22-member troupe, Chicago's best-known dance company, incorporates elements of jazz, ballet, theater, and modern dance into its exhilarating performances. *At the Joan W. and Irving B. Harris Theater for Music and Dance, 205 E. Randolph St. (Millennium Park).* ☎ *312/334-7777. www.hubbardstreetdance.com. Tickets about $35. El: Red Line to Lake or Brown Line to Randolph. Map p 121.*

★★ Joffrey Ballet of Chicago
SOUTH LOOP Founded in 1956 in New York, the Joffrey moved into the Joffrey Tower, its new home, in 2008. Each December, Joffrey stages a popular rendition of the holiday favorite, *The Nutcracker.* Other performances focus on classic works of the 20th century. *10 E. Randolph St.* ☎ *312/386-8907. www.joffrey.com. Tickets about $75. Map p 121.*

Film
kids Facets Multi-Media LAKEVIEW This nonprofit group screens independent and experimental films from around the world at its Cinematheque Theatre. Its collection of children's films is the most extensive in the U.S., and it also hosts the Chicago International Children's Film Festival (Oct–Nov), the largest such festival in the country. *1517 W. Fullerton Ave.* ☎ *773/281-9075; 773/281-4114 for program information and showtimes. www.facets.org. Tickets $9. El: Red or Brown line to Fullerton. Map p 122.*

★ Gene Siskel Film Center THE
LOOP Named after the late *Chicago Tribune* film critic, this theater for serious film buffs is part of the School of the Art Institute of Chicago. It offers an array of foreign, art, and experimental films, as well as lectures and discussions with

Scoring Discounted Tickets

Bargain hunters rejoice: The **League of Chicago Theatres** (☎ 312/554-9800; www.chicagoplays.com) operates a telephone hotline that features a daily listing of discounted shows. The call costs $1 per minute, with calls lasting an average of 3 minutes.

Hot Tix (☎ 312/554-9800; www.hottix.org), operated by the League of Chicago Theatres, sells same-day, half-price tickets, online and in person. On Friday, you can buy tickets for weekend productions. Tickets are available at two locations (they must be bought in person), off of Michigan Avenue at the Water Works Visitor Center, 163 E. Pearson St., and in the Loop at 78 W. Randolph St., just east of Clark Street. Hot Tix now accepts major credits cards.

The Steppenwolf Theatre Company's box office usually sells a limited number of half-price, same-day seats. The "Tix at Six" program at the Goodman Theatre offers half-price, day-of-show tickets at the box office at 6pm for evening performances, noon for matinees.

filmmakers. *164 N. State St. ☎ 312/846-2600. www.siskelfilmcenter.org. Tickets $4–$9. El: Red Line to Washington or Brown Line to Randolph. Map p 121.*

★★★ **Music Box Theatre** LAKEVIEW This atmospheric movie house, designed to re-create the open-air feeling of an Italian courtyard, opened in 1929. The now-restored theater screens cult, independent, classic, and foreign films. *3733 W. Southport Ave. ☎ 773/871-6604. www.musicbox theatre.com. Tickets $9. El: Brown Line to Southport. Map p 122.*

Opera
Chicago Opera Theater THE LOOP English-language productions and relatively low ticket prices appeal to this opera company's broad audience. The season runs from February to May and usually focuses on the works of American composers. *At the Joan W. and Irving B. Harris Theater for Music and Dance, 205 E. Randolph Dr. (Millennium Park). ☎ 312/*

704-8414. *www.chicagooperatheater.org. Tickets $35–$115. El: Red Line to Randolph. Map p 121.*

★★★ **Lyric Opera of Chicago** THE LOOP One of the country's premier opera companies stages lavish productions headlined by the world's top talent. It sells out its season (Sept–Mar) far in advance, but you can usually get turn-back tickets just before a performance. *Civic Opera House, 20 N. Wacker Dr. ☎ 312/332-2244. www.lyricopera.org. Tickets $40–$600. El: Brown Line to Washington. Map p 121.*

Theater
★★★ **Blue Man Group** LINCOLN PARK Originally an off-Broadway show that ripped early 1990s performance art (all in good fun), the Blue Man Group's mix of percussion, mime, and music has taken on a life of its own. The troupe has been so successful that they bought their own theater—so expect them to be in Chicago a good long while. *At Briar Street Theatre, 3133 N. Halsted*

St. (at Briar St.). ☎ 773/348-4000. Tickets $49–$59. El: Brown Line to Wellington. Map p 122.

★★★ Chicago Shakespeare Theater

NAVY PIER A stunning 525-seat theater—patterned loosely after the Swan Theatre in Stratford-Upon-Avon—is the backdrop for top-notch performances of Shakespeare's works. Avoid the upper balcony seats if you're not fond of heights. *800 E. Grand Ave. (at the tip of Navy Pier).* ☎ 312/595-5600. www.chicagoshakes.com. Tickets $48–$65. El: Red Line to State/ Grand then free trolley to Navy Pier. Map p 121.

★★ Emerald City Theatre Company

LAKEVIEW This relative newcomer to the kids' theater scene, named for *The Wizard of Oz*, stages four shows a year for kids age 2 and up. Productions range from Tarzan and Jane to Dr. Seuss classics. *At the Apollo Theater, 2540 N. Lincoln Ave.* ☎ 773/935-6100. www.emerald citytheatre.com. Tickets $15 for

The Emerald City Theatre Company stages productions aimed at the young set.

adults; $12 for kids. El: Red or Brown line to Fullerton. Map p 122.

★★★ Goodman Theatre

THE LOOP Dean of the legitimate theaters in Chicago, the Goodman produces both original works and familiar standards in a custom-designed home (p 31, ⓓ). Production values are top-notch and the acting first-rate (Denzel Washington,

Finding Out What's Playing

Getting connected to the Chicago fine-arts scene requires only a phone call to **The Chicago Dance and Music Alliance information line** (☎ 312/987-1123; www.chicagoperformances.org), which features listings of upcoming events.

Other useful tools are the *Chicago Tribune* (www.chicagotribune. com) and its dining/entertainment/nightlife website, www.metromix. com; *Chicago Sun-Times* (www.suntimes.com); and *Daily Herald* (www. dailyherald.com) newspapers, which offer comprehensive weekly listings in their Friday entertainment sections. The papers also run reviews of larger shows around town; for older reviews, check their websites.

Other reliable sources of reviews and commentary are *Chicago* (www.chicagomag.com) and *North Shore* (www.northshoremag.com) magazines. To find out about out-of-the-mainstream performances, pick up the *Chicago Reader* (www.chicagoreader.com) and *New City* (www.newcitychicago.com), the leading free alternative newspapers.

William Hurt, and Brian Dennehy have all performed here). *170 N. Dearborn St. (at Randolph St.).* ☎ *312/443-3800. www.goodman theatre.org. Tickets $30–$50 main stage, $10–$40 studio. El: Red Line to Washington/State, Brown or Orange line to Clark/Lake. Map p 121.*

Late-Nite Catechism LINCOLN PARK Catechism class is in session nightly at this long-running, humorous show. Audience participation is part of the experience, so be prepared to make your own true confessions to the nuns. *At the Royal George Theater Center, 1641 N. Halsted St.* ☎ *312/988-9000. www.late nitecatechism.info. Tickets $30. El: Red Line to North/Clybourn. Map p 122.*

★★★ Lookingglass Theatre Company MAGNIFICENT MILE This up-and-comer, founded by Northwestern theater grads more than a decade ago, stages several surprising and original productions each year. *In The Water Tower Pumping Station, 821 N. Michigan Ave.* ☎ *312/337-0665. www.lookingglass theatre.org. Tickets $30–$60. El: Red Line to Chicago/State. Map p 124.*

★ Steppenwolf Theatre Company LINCOLN PARK Focusing on original, edgy drama, this veteran company has launched the careers of many well-respected actors, including Joan Allen, John Malkovich, and Gary Sinise. A number of the original works and classic revivals staged at the company's state-of-the-art complex go on to Broadway. *1650 N. Halsted St. (at North Ave.).* ☎ *312/335-1650. www.steppenwolf. org. Tickets $20–$55. El: Red Line to North/Clybourn. Map p 122.*

Tommy Gun's Garage SOUTH LOOP A cut above the usual tourist fare, this dinner theater puts on a vaudeville show filled with 1920s-era gangsters, flappers, and

The Lookingglass Theatre Company is renowned for its innovative productions.

gigolos. The food's not bad, either: choose from five entrees (ranging from prime rib to lasagna), and finish your meal off with tiramisu or carrot cake. *2114 S. Wabash Ave. (at E. 21st St.).* ☎ *312/225-0273. Shows run Thurs–Sun nights. 3-course dinner and show $50–$60. Subway/El: Red Line to Cermak/Chinatown. Map p 121.*

Too Much Light Makes the Baby Go Blind NORTH SIDE The longest-running show in town offers 30 "plays" (sketches ranging in tone from humorous to touching) in 60 minutes—a bargain at any price. Seats are first-come, first-served, so arrive at least an hour before the curtain goes up. *At the Neo-Futurarium, 5153 N. Ashland Ave.* ☎ *773/ 275-5255. Shows run Fri–Sun 11:30pm; Sun 7pm. Tickets $7, plus an amount determined by the number on a roll of a die. El: Red Line to Berwyn. Map p 124.*

★★ Uptown Poetry Slam at The Green Mill UPTOWN Poets vie for an open mic to roast and ridicule each other's work every Sunday night at a former speak-easy that's a real Chicago treasure. *At The Green Mill. 4802 N. Broadway (at Lawrence Ave.).* ☎ *773/878-5552. Cover $6. Subway/El: Red Line to Lawrence. Map p 124.*

★★★ Victory Gardens Theater at the Biograph LINCOLN PARK

The third Chicago theater (after the Steppenwolf and the Goodman) to win a Tony Award for sustained excellence by a regional theater. All the shows staged here, on the main stage in the historic Biograph Theater, are world premieres (usually by developing playwrights), and they're always provocative and well acted. *2433 N. Lincoln Ave. (at Belden Ave.).* ☎ *773/871-3000. www.victorygardens.org. Tickets $15–$40. El: Brown Line to Diversey. Map p 122.*

Spectator Sports

Soldier Field SOUTH LOOP

Renovations have vastly improved the amenities at the formerly shabby home of the NFL's Chicago Bears (and Major League Soccer's Chicago Fire). It's a Chicago tradition to brave the often-brutal weather conditions as the wind blows in off Lake Michigan to cheer on the Bears as they battle their archenemy, the Green Bay Packers. *1600 S. Lake Shore Dr.* ☎ *847/295-6600. www. chicagobears.com. Tickets $45–$300. El: Red or Orange line to Roosevelt. Map p 121.*

United Center WEST LOOP

Home of the Chicago Bulls (who won six NBA titles in the 1990s), this massive stadium is alive and kicking again now that the team is back in

Chicago practically worships its beloved Bears, and the best place to see that NFL team is Soldier Field.

contention. The NHL's Chicago Blackhawks also call the United Center home. Outside of sports, you can also catch concerts (U2 and Springsteen, among others), circuses, and ice shows here. *1901 W. Madison St.* ☎ *312/455-4500. www. unitedcenter.com. Tickets start at $10 and climb, depending on the event. Bus: 20, 50, or 19. Map p 121.*

U.S. Cellular Field BRIDGEPORT

Home of the Chicago White Sox and their blue-collar, Cubs-loathing Southside fans. The ballpark features excellent sightlines and amenities, and tickets are easier to come by here than at Wrigley. *333 W. 35th St.* ☎ *312/674-1000. Tickets $14–$41. www.whitesox.mlb.com. El: Red Line to Sox/35th St. Map p 124.*

★★★ Wrigley Field WRIGLEYVILLE

Whether the Cubs win or lose, a visit to their home field is a don't-miss Chicago experience (and tickets tend to sell out accordingly). This baseball mecca is pure magic, from its ivy-covered walls to the hand-operated scoreboard and views of shimmering Lake Michigan from the upper deck. *1060 W. Addison St.* ☎ *773/404-CUBS. www.cubs.mlb.com. Tickets $13 and up. El: Red Line to Addison. Map p 122.* ●

U.S. Cellular Field, home of the 2005 World Series Champion White Sox.

Hotel Best Bets

Most Luxurious
★★★ **Ritz-Carlton Chicago** $$$$
160 E. Pearson St. (p 141)

Best Business Hotel
★★★ **Swissotel** $$$$ *323 E.
Wacker Dr. (p 142)*

Best Views
★★ **Trump International Hotel and
Tower** $$$$ *401 N. Wabash Ave.
(p 143)*

Most Historic Hotel
★★ **The Drake Hotel** $$$$ *140 E.
Walton Place (p 137)*

Hippest Hotel
★★ **Sofitel Chicago Water Tower**
$$$–$$$$ *20 E. Chestnut St. (p 141)*

Best Bed & Breakfast
★ **Windy City Urban Inn** $$–$$$
607 W. Deming Place (p 144)

Best Hotel Away from the
Magnificent Mile
★★★ **Westin Chicago River North**
$$$–$$$$ *320 N. Dearborn St. (p 143)*

Best Moderately Priced Hotel
★ **Best Western Hawthorne Ter-
race** $–$$ *3434 N. Broadway (p 136)*

Best Family Hotel
★★ **Embassy Suites Chicago
Lakeshore** $$–$$$ *511 N. Columbus
Dr. (p 137)*

Best Bathrooms
★★★ **Park Hyatt** $$$$ *800 N. Michigan Ave. (p 140)*

Best Cheap Bed
★ **Red Roof Inn** $ *162 E. Ontario St.
(p 141)*

Best Swimming Pool
★ **InterContinental Chicago** $$$
505 N. Michigan Ave. (p 140)

*The luxurious but unpretentious Park
Hyatt features the city's best bathrooms.*

Most Romantic
★★ **Whitehall Hotel** $$$ *105 E.
Delaware Place (p 144)*

Most Comfortable
★★★ **Talbott Hotel** $$$ *20 E.
Delaware Place (p 142)*

Best Lobby
★ **Chicago Hilton and Towers**
$–$$$$ *720 S. Michigan Ave. (p 138)*

Best Boutique Hotel
★★★ **Hotel Burnham** $$$ *1 W.
Washington St. (p 139)*

Best Rock 'n' Roll Hotel
★ **Hard Rock Hotel** $$$ *230 N.
Michigan Ave. (p 138)*

Best Hotel for Music Fans
★★ **Hotel Sax** $$–$$$ *333 N. Dear-
born St. (p 139)*

Best Spa
★★★ **The Peninsula Chicago** $$$$
108 E. Superior St. (p 140)

Best Neighborhood Hotel
★ **Ambassador East** $$$ *1301 N.
State Pkwy. (p 136)*

Best Hidden Gem
★★ **The Belden–Stratford Apart-
ments** $$$ *2300 N. Lincoln Park
West (p 136)*

Previous page: The House of Blues Hotel.

Magnificent Mile Hotels

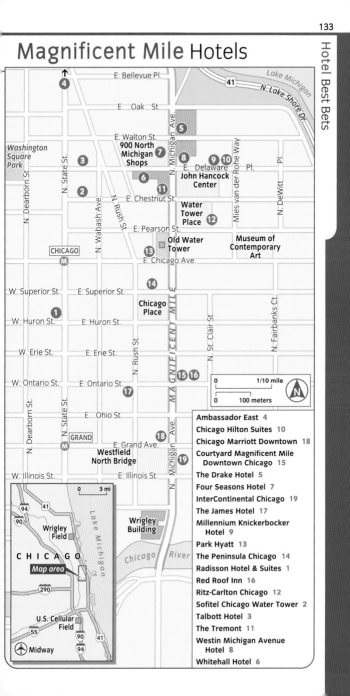

Ambassador East 4
Chicago Hilton Suites 10
Chicago Marriott Downtown 18
Courtyard Magnificent Mile
   Downtown Chicago 15
The Drake Hotel 5
Four Seasons Hotel 7
InterContinental Chicago 19
The James Hotel 17
Millennium Knickerbocker
   Hotel 9
Park Hyatt 13
The Peninsula Chicago 14
Radisson Hotel & Suites 1
Red Roof Inn 16
Ritz-Carlton Chicago 12
Sofitel Chicago Water Tower 2
Talbott Hotel 3
The Tremont 11
Westin Michigan Avenue
   Hotel 8
Whitehall Hotel 6

The Best Hotels

The Loop & River North Hotels

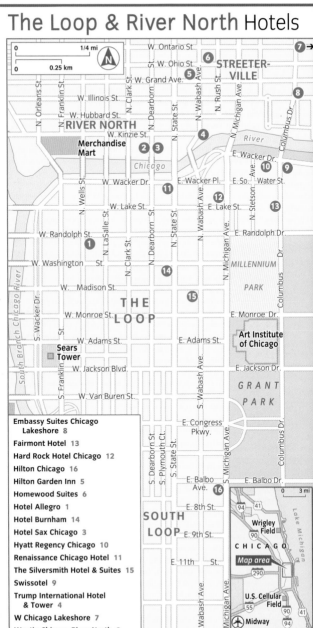

Embassy Suites Chicago
  Lakeshore 8
Fairmont Hotel 13
Hard Rock Hotel Chicago 12
Hilton Chicago 16
Hilton Garden Inn 5
Homewood Suites 6
Hotel Allegro 1
Hotel Burnham 14
Hotel Sax Chicago 3
Hyatt Regency Chicago 10
Renaissance Chicago Hotel 11
The Silversmith Hotel & Suites 15
Swissotel 9
Trump International Hotel
  & Tower 4
W Chicago Lakeshore 7
Westin Chicago River North 2

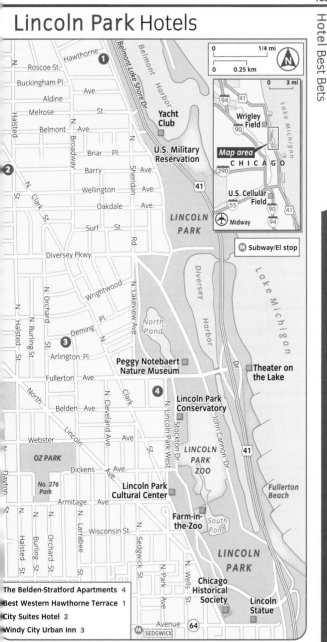

Lincoln Park Hotels

The Belden-Stratford Apartments 4
Best Western Hawthorne Terrace 1
City Suites Hotel 2
Windy City Urban Inn 3

Hotels A to Z

★ **Ambassador East** GOLD COAST   Opened in a leafy residential neighborhood in 1926, this historic hotel welcomed many a celebrity in its heyday (the celebs have moved on, but the elegance remains). The tidy guest rooms feature custom furnishings and marble bathrooms. *1301 N. State Pkwy.* ☎ *888/506-3471 or 312/787-7200. www.theambassadoreasthotel.com. 285 units. Doubles $160–$200. AE, DC, DISC, MC, V. El: Red Line to Clark/Division. Map p 133.*

★★ **The Belden–Stratford Apartments** LINCOLN PARK   This North Side hotel is one of Chicago's best-kept secrets and has a wonderful neighborhood atmosphere. It's set in a gracious apartment building that offers 25 large hotel rooms (ask for one with a view of Lincoln Park). *2300 N. Lincoln Park West (just north of Fullerton Ave.).* ☎ *800/800-6261 or 773/281-2900. www.beldenstratford.com. 25 units. Doubles $209–$299. AE, DC, DISC, MC, V. Bus: 151 to Fullerton. Map p 135.*

★ kids **Best Western Hawthorne Terrace** LAKEVIEW   A fantastic bargain for families who

The Belden–Stratford Apartments are one of the city's best kept secrets.

The historic Ambassador East still sports a high glamour quotient.

don't mind staying a bit north of the beaten track, this hotel offers lots of space and amenities at a great price. If you're driving to Chicago, parking here is a bargain at $20 a day. *3434 N. Broadway.* ☎ *888/401-8781 or 773/244-3434. www.hawthorneterrace.com. 59 units. $149–229 double and suites w/breakfast. AE, DC, DISC, MC, V. El: Red Line to Belmont. Map p 135.*

★★★ **Chicago Hilton Suites** MAGNIFICENT MILE   A step above Chicago's other all-suite hotels in the elegance department. Rooms are warm and inviting. The glass-enclosed pool deck on the 30th floor is a great place to watch the fireworks at Navy Pier. *198 E. Delaware Place (at Mies van der Rohe St.).* ☎ *800/222-TREE or 312/664-1100. www.hilton.com. 345 units. Doubles $109–$309. AE, DC, DISC, MC, V. El: Red Line to Chicago/State. Map p 133.*

★★★ **Chicago Marriott Downtown** MAGNIFICENT MILE   You'll feel at home in the comfortable and large guest rooms, but this hotel's location in the heart of the Magnificent Mile is its biggest asset. Fitness enthusiasts will appreciate the above-average health club facilities, which even include a basketball court on the deck of the ninth floor, where the indoor pool is also located. *540 N. Michigan Ave. (at Grand Ave.).* ☎ *312/836-0100. www. marriott.com. 1,192 units. Doubles $220. AE, DC, DISC, MC, V. El: Red Line to Grand/State. Map p 133.*

City Suites Hotel LINCOLN PARK This affordable Art Deco hotel offers homey suites with sleeper sofas in the living area and lots of amenities. The drawback: Rooms can be fairly noisy, as some face busy Belmont Avenue, and some face the El tracks. *933 W. Belmont Ave. (at Sheffield Ave.).* ☎ *800/248-9108 or 773/404-3400. www.cityinns.com. 45 units. Doubles $149–$249 w/breakfast. AE, DC, DISC, MC, V. El: Red Line to Belmont. Map p 135.*

★★ Courtyard Magnificent Mile Downtown Chicago MAGNIFICENT MILE This hotel occupies a prime downtown location and caters primarily to business travelers, though its clean and comfy rooms work just as well for families. Amenities include a lovely swimming pool (much better than most) and a fitness room featuring great views of the city. *165 E. Ontario St. (just east of Michigan Ave.).* ☎ *312/573-0800. www.courtyardchicago. com. 306 units. Doubles $249. AE, DC, DISC, MC, V. El: Red Line to Grand/State. Map p 133.*

★★ The Drake Hotel MAGNIFICENT MILE This quietly elegant grande dame (the landmark opened in 1920) still features gracious style and boundless charm. Rooms offer high ceilings, polished woodwork, and marble bathrooms. Don't miss out on afternoon tea in the Palm Court during your stay; it's slightly pricey at $29 per person, but worth it. *140 E. Walton Place (at Michigan Ave.).* ☎ *800/55-DRAKE or 312/787-2200. www.thedrakehotel.com. 537 units. Doubles $199–$425. AE, DC, DISC, MC, V. El: Red Line to Chicago/State. Map p 133.*

★★ Embassy Suites Chicago Lakeshore STREETERVILLE Conveniently located between Navy Pier and Michigan Avenue, this all-suite hotel is popular with families and features spacious units with well-equipped kitchenettes. *511 N. Columbus Dr.* ☎ *312/836-5900. www.embassysuites.com. 455 units. Doubles $199–$299 w/breakfast and happy hour. AE, DC, DISC, MC, V. El: Red Line to Grand/State. Map p 134.*

A Vista Suite at The Drake Hotel, one of the city's most elegant hotels.

★★★ **Fairmont Hotel** RIVER EAST
A few blocks north of the Loop, this chic luxury hotel is popular with politicos and the business set. The exceptionally large guest rooms feature dressing rooms; walk-in closets; and marble bathrooms with huge tubs, separate showers, and TVs. *200 N. Columbus Dr. (at Lake St.).* ☎ *800/526-2008 or 312/565-8000. www.fairmont.com. 692 units. Doubles $129–$389. AE, DC, DISC, MC, V. El: Brown, Orange, or Green line to Randolph. Map p 134.*

The lobby of the chic and luxurious Fairmont Hotel.

★★★ **Four Seasons Hotel** MAGNIFICENT MILE   Consistently ranked among the best hotels in the world, the Four Seasons offers luxe decor and stellar service. The spacious guest rooms are packed with extras (L'Occitane toiletries, for one), and the windows actually open to let in fresh air. *120 E. Delaware Place (at Michigan Ave.).* ☎ *800/332-3442 or 312/280-8800. www.fourseasons. com. 343 units. Doubles $495–$695. AE, DC, DISC, MC, V. El: Red Line to Chicago/State. Map p 133.*

★ **Hard Rock Hotel Chicago** THE LOOP   This hip hotel occupies

The Four Seasons Hotel, one of the finest in the world, towers above the city.

a rehabbed historic skyscraper, the 40-story Carbide and Carbon Building, though the rooms are fashionably modern. As expected, the theme here is music: Pop tunes echo through the lobby, TV monitors show videos, and glass cases display pop-star memorabilia. *230 N. Michigan Ave. (at Lake St.).* ☎ *866/ 966-5166 or 312/345-1000. www. hardrockhotelchicago.com. 387 units. Doubles $169–$349. AE, DC, DISC, MC, V. El: Red or Blue line to Lake. Map p 134.*

★ **kids** **Hilton Chicago** SOUTH LOOP   Sprawling over several blocks, this virtual city features well-appointed rooms (many with two bathrooms) and a great location. Public areas abound with shops, bars, restaurants, and artwork. *720 S. Michigan Ave. (at Balbo Dr.).* ☎ *800-HILTONS or 312/922-4400. www.hilton.com. 1,554 units. Doubles $129–$399. AE, DC, DISC, MC, V. El: Red Line to Harrison/State. Map p 134.*

Hilton Garden Inn RIVER NORTH
This bland business hotel also pleases families because of its ample rooms; the great vistas from its top-level floors; and an enviable location near the ESPN Zone, Oysy sushi bar, and the Nordstrom mall. *10 E. Grand Ave. (at State St.).* ☎ *800/HILTONS or*

312/595-0000. 348 units. Doubles $189–$329. AE, DC, DISC, MC, V. El: Red Line to State/Grand. Map p 134.

Homewood Suites RIVER NORTH An excellent choice for families, this simple-yet-comfy hotel offers one-bedroom suites, each with a full kitchen. 40 E. Grand Ave. (at Wabash St.). ☎ 800/CALL-HOME or 312/644-2222. www.homewoodsuiteschicago. com. 233 units. Doubles $109–$449 w/breakfast. AE, DC, DISC, MC, V. El: Red Line to State/Grand. Map p 134.

★ Hotel Allegro THE LOOP Adjoining the historic Palace Theatre, this colorful boutique hotel appeals to the young and hip. It's warmly (if boldly) decorated, features a fun vibe, and offers great value. 171 W. Randolph St. (at LaSalle St.). ☎ 312/236-0123. www.allegrochicago.com. 483 units. Doubles $169–$329. AE, DC, DISC, MC, V. El: All lines to Washington. Map p 134.

★★★ Hotel Burnham THE LOOP One of the world's first skyscrapers, D. H. Burnham's Reliance Building (p 10, ❺) is now home to this stylish boutique hotel, Chicago's most distinctive and a must for architecture buffs. You'll marvel at

The stylish Hotel Burnham is a must for architecture buffs.

the huge guest-room windows that stretch from floor to ceiling. Ask for a high, corner room overlooking Macy's. 1 W. Washington St. (at State St.). ☎ 866/690-1986 or 312/782-1111. www.burnhamhotel.com. 122 units. Doubles $299. AE, DISC, MC, V. El: Red Line to Washington/State. Map p 134.

★★ Hotel Sax Chicago RIVER NORTH   Located in the entertainment-packed Marina Towers complex, this bohemian boutique hotel is a remodel of the former House of Blues Hotel. A constant stream of performers from the House of Blues club next door ensures that this hotel is for those who want an experience as much as a place to lay their heads. 333 N. Dearborn St. ☎ 877/569-3742 or 312/245-0333. www.hotelsax chicago.com. 353 units. Doubles $269–$449. AE, DC, DISC, MC, V. El: Red Line to Grand/State. Map p 134.

kids **Hyatt Regency Chicago** RIVER EAST   This sprawling and busy convention hotel (Hyatt's flagship in the U.S.) is as impersonal as Union Station, but the modern rooms feature all the amenities you'd expect of this high-end chain. It's surprisingly good for families—with all the hustle and bustle, kids

The Crowne Plaza Chicago/The Silversmith offers some of the most distinctive accommodations in Chicago. See p 141.

The Best Hotels

blend right in. *151 E. Wacker Dr. ☎ 312/565-1234. www.hyatt.com. 2,019 units. Doubles $180–$330. AE, DC, DISC, MC, V. El: Red Line to State/Lake. Map p 134.*

★ InterContinental Chicago

MAGNIFICENT MILE   A sentimental favorite of locals, this hotel is both eccentric (its decor spans numerous architectural styles ranging from medieval English to Mesopotamian) and comfortable. The south tower's Roman-style pool—the best in the city—was originally part of the 1929-built Medinah Athletic Club. *505 N. Michigan Ave. (at Grand Ave.). ☎ 800/ 327-0200 or 312/944-4100. http:// chicago.intercontinental.com. 790 units. Doubles $239–$350. AE, DC, DISC, MC, V. El: Red Line to Grand/State. Map p 133.*

★★ The James Hotel RIVER

NORTH   One of the city's newer hotels, The James blurs the line between upscale luxury and stylish boutique. Proximity to Michigan Avenue shopping, River North nightlife, and the Loop theater district make this sleek, modern hotel a great choice for grown-up travelers in search of a modern hotel experience. *55 E. Ontario St. (at Rush St.). ☎ 877/526-3755 or 312/337-1000. www.jameshotels.com. 297 units.*

The luxurious pool at The Peninsula Chicago offers exceptional views of the city.

A double room at the Hilton Chicago.

Doubles $189–$529. AE, DC, DISC, MC, V. El: Red Line to State/Grand. Map p 133.

Millennium Knickerbocker

Hotel MAGNIFICENT MILE   Built in 1927, this historic hotel exudes vintage charm. Today, it offers spruced-up rooms, good value, and a superb location. *163 E. Walton St. (just east of Michigan Ave.). ☎ 800/621-8140 or 312/751-8100. www.millennium hotels.com. 305 units. Doubles $169– $299. AE, DC, DISC, MC, V. El: Red Line to Chicago/State. Map p 133.*

★★★ Park Hyatt Chicago

MAGNIFICENT MILE   Part hotel, part condominium building, this sleek, contemporary property is the coolest in town. Luxurious but unstuffy, the guest rooms feature plush furnishings and artwork; the full windows in the bathrooms take best advantage of the marvelous views. *800 N. Michigan Ave. (at Chicago Ave.). ☎ 800/233-1234 or 312/335-1234. 198 units. Doubles $385–$525. AE, DC, DISC, MC, V. El: Red Line to Chicago/State. Map p 133.*

★★★ The Peninsula Chicago

MAGNIFICENT MILE   Service at this Art Deco bastion of luxury is practically a religion. The in-room technology—a small silver "command station" allows guests to control the lights, curtains, and room temperature—is also worthy of worship.

108 E. Superior St. (at Michigan Ave.). ☎ 866/288-8889 or 312/337-2888. http://chicago.peninsula.com. 339 units. Doubles $525–$650. AE, DC, MC, V. El: Red Line to Chicago/State. Map p 133.

★ **Red Roof Inn** MAGNIFICENT MILE This is your best bet for low-priced lodgings near pricey Michigan Avenue. The rooms and amenities match the budget prices, but who cares when you're spending most of your time out on the town? 162 E. Ontario St. (at St. Clair). ☎ 800/733-7663 or 312/787-3580. 195 units. Doubles $96–$159. AE, DC, DISC, MC, V. El: Red Line to Grand/State. Map p 133.

Renaissance Chicago Hotel THE LOOP This upscale business hotel features bay windows that offer priceless views of the river and city. Comfortable guest rooms are decorated in dark woods, with plush carpeting and rich draperies and fabrics. 1 W. Wacker Dr. (at State St.). ☎ 800/HOTELS-1 or 312/372-7200. www.marriott.com. 553 units. Doubles $199–$399. AE, DC, DISC, MC, V. El: Brown Line to State/Lake or Red Line to Washington/State. Map p 134.

★★★ **Ritz-Carlton Chicago** MAGNIFICENT MILE Set above the Water Tower Place mall (p 83), this superluxurious celebrity magnet is known for its tiptop service and open and airy setting. The hotel's atrium is the perfect spot for afternoon tea or an evening aperitif. 160 E. Pearson St. (just east of N. Michigan Ave.). ☎ 800/621-6906 or 312/266-1000. www.fourseasons.com/chicagorc. 435 units. Doubles $495–$635. AE, DC, DISC, MC, V. El: Red Line to Chicago/State. Map p 133.

★★ **The Silversmith Hotel & Suites** THE LOOP This distinctive landmark building was built in 1897 to house silversmiths and jewelers, and has plenty of personality. Rooms, exquisitely decorated in the Arts and Crafts style, offer oversize bathrooms and fabulous views. 10 S. Wabash Ave. (at Madison St.). ☎ 800/2 CROWNE or 312/372-7696. www.silversmithchicagohotel.com. 143 units. Doubles $179–$359. AE, DC, DISC, MC, V. El: Orange, Brown, or Green line to Madison/Wabash, or Red Line to Washington/State. Map p 134.

★★ **Sofitel Chicago Water Tower** MAGNIFICENT MILE Sofitel, drawing on the city's tradition of great architecture, built this soaring, triangular tower with a glass-and-aluminum facade that sparkles in

The Trump Hotel offers fantastic views of the city.

One of the charming Talbott Hotel's first-rate bathrooms.

the sun. The interior has a European, modern feel. The fairly compact guest rooms feature contemporary decor, sleek bathrooms, and good views of the city. *20 E. Chestnut St. (at Wabash St.).* ☎ *800/SOFITEL or 312/324-4000. www.sofitel.com. 415 units. Doubles $249–$555. AE, DC, DISC, MC, V. El: Red Line to Chicago/State. Map p 133.*

★★★ **Swissotel Chicago** THE LOOP This sleek, modern hotel is all business and may therefore feel a bit icy to some. Still, its ingenious triangular design gives every room a panoramic vista of Lake Michigan, Grant Park, and/or the Chicago River, and exercising in the Penthouse Health Club and Spa, perched on the 42nd floor, will give you a true birds eye-view of the city. *323 E. Wacker Dr.* ☎ *888/737-9477 or 312/565-0565. www.swissotelchicago.com. 632 units. Doubles $159–$409. AE, DC, DISC, MC, V. El: Red, Brown, Orange, or Green line to Randolph. Map p 134.*

★★★ **Talbott Hotel** MAGNIFICENT MILE This hidden gem combines the charm of an English inn with a location that's hard to beat, just west of the Magnificent Mile. Many of the exceptionally large rooms have kitchens and sitting rooms. The cozy bar and restaurant offer first-rate people-watching opportunities. *20 E. Delaware Place (between Rush and State sts.).* ☎ *800-TALBOTT or 312/944-4970. www.talbotthotel.com. 149 units. Doubles $169–$449. AE, DC, DISC, MC, V. El: Red Line to Chicago/State. Map p 133.*

★★ **The Tremont** MAGNIFICENT MILE A small, European-style hotel with great appeal and good amenities, but be ready for small (though tastefully furnished) rooms. *100 E. Chestnut St. (just west of Michigan Ave.).* ☎ *800/621-8133 or 312/751-1900. www.tremontchicago.com. 130 units. Doubles $149–$329. AE, DC, DISC, MC, V. El: Red Line to Chicago/State. Map p 133.*

When Is the Off Season?

Chicago is becoming a year-round, 7-days-a-week destination. That said, you can usually find a few good buys from January through March—unless a mega-convention is swallowing up huge numbers of hotel rooms. In the winter months, the **Chicago Office of Tourism** website (www.877chicago.com) advertises hotel specials, some as low as $69 per night (though these rates often come with blackout dates and minimum-stay requirements). Most of the more centrally located hotels are priced from $99 to $139 per night before taxes. Late fall, when the weather is often mild and pleasant, is also a time to snare lower room rates, particularly on weekends when all the business travelers have left town.

★★★ Trump International Hotel and Tower Chicago

RIVER NORTH Chicago's newest entry onto the hotel scene, this Trump hotel perches on the river and offers fantastic city views (book a suite ending in "00" for an east-facing room, the best view). Creams and grays make this place more subtle than gilded, and don't miss dinner at the 16th-floor restaurant, Sixteen. *401 N. Wabash Ave. (at the river).* ☎ *877/458-7867 or 312/588-8000. www.trumpchicago.com. 339 units. Doubles $329–$529. AE, DC, DISC, MC, V. El: Red Line to State/Harrison. Map p 134.*

★★ W Chicago Lakeshore

STREETERVILLE The only hotel situated on the lakefront, this swanky boutique property tries hard to achieve hipness and caters to singles and couples. The trendy guest rooms are a bit gloomy, but if you need a pick-me-up you can relax in the hotel's branch of New York's famed Bliss Spa. *644 N. Lake Shore Dr. (at Ontario St.).* ☎ *877/W-HOTELS or 312/943-9200. www.whotels.com. 520 units. Doubles $219–$429. AE,*

European in style, The Tremont is a great spot for a weekend getaway.

DC, DISC, MC, V. El: Red Line to Grand/State. Map p 134.

★★★ Westin Chicago River North

RIVER NORTH Though this handsome hotel caters mostly to the business set, its furniture and artwork give it a residential feel. Request a room facing south for a fantastic view overlooking the Chicago River. *320 N. Dearborn St.* ☎ *800/WESTIN1 or 312/744-1900. www.westinchicago.com. 424 units. Doubles $199–$350. AE, DC, DISC, MC, V. El: Brown, Orange, or Green line to State/Lake. Map p 134.*

★ Westin Michigan Avenue Hotel

MAGNIFICENT MILE An ideal location (especially for shoppers—Bloomingdale's and the John Hancock Center are right across the street) makes this hotel a winner. Ask for a tower lake-view room, which is larger than a standard and features an upgraded bathroom and turndown service. *909 N. Michigan Ave. (at Delaware Place).* ☎ *800/WESTIN-1 or 312/943-7200. www.westin.com. 743 units. Doubles $189–$389. AE, DC, DISC, MC, V. El: Red Line to Chicago/State. Map p 133.*

Shoppers especially appreciate the Westin Michigan Avenue Hotel's super location.

The comfy Windy City Urban Inn offers charming rooms in quiet surroundings.

Chippendale desks, and high-end toiletries. Expect narrow hallways and small bathrooms. *105 E. Delaware Place (just west of Michigan Ave.).* ☎ *800/948-4255 or 312/944-6300. www.thewhitehallhotel.com. 222 units. Doubles $199–$379. AE, DC, DISC, MC, V. El: Red Line to Chicago/State. Map p 133.*

★ **Windy City Urban Inn** LINCOLN PARK   This grand 1886 B&B, located on a tranquil side street, offers charming rooms and apartments (the best bet for families). The owners—a well-known political reporter and his wife—are excellent resources for visitors who want to get beyond the usual tourist sights. Blues and jazz play during the excellent buffet breakfast, which features many local food favorites. *607 W. Deming Place.* ☎ *877/897-7091 or 773/248-7091. www.windycityinn.com. 8 units. Doubles $125–$255 w/breakfast. Kids over age 10 welcome. AE, DC, DISC, MC, V. El: Red Line to Fullerton. Map p 135.* ●

★★ **Whitehall Hotel** MAGNIFICENT MILE   European style and ambience abound at this landmark hideaway. The classically stylish and comfortable accommodations include mahogany furnishings,

Finding Your Way to a B&B

One of the best ways to locate a bed-and-breakfast in Chicago is through a reservation service. I recommend **At Home Inn Chicago, Inc.** (☎ 800/375-7084 or 312/640-1050; www.athomeinnchicago.com). This service represents about 50 establishments, all located within the city, in areas ranging from the South Loop to the Lakeview neighborhood (with a few farther north). Offerings include a mix of hosted guest rooms in houses and apartments, and unhosted accommodations in self-contained apartments.

Prices vary according to the type of accommodations you select and the location of the property. For example, $250 a night will get you a two-bedroom, two-bath condo in a Gold Coast high-rise. For about $225 a night, you can unpack in a studio apartment in the Printers Row neighborhood of the South Loop.

Oak Park

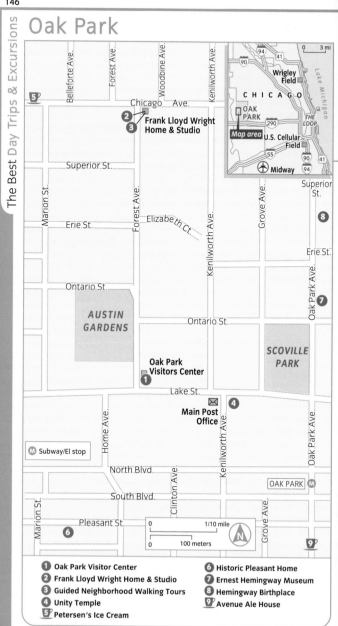

Frank Lloyd Wright Home & Studio

Chicago Ave.

Superior St.

Erie St.

Elizabeth Ct.

Ontario St.

AUSTIN GARDENS

Ontario St.

Oak Park Visitors Center

Lake St.

Main Post Office

SCOVILLE PARK

Ⓜ Subway/El stop

North Blvd.

South Blvd.

OAK PARK Ⓜ

Pleasant St.

0   1/10 mile

0   100 meters

N

- ❶ Oak Park Visitor Center
- ❷ Frank Lloyd Wright Home & Studio
- ❸ Guided Neighborhood Walking Tours
- ❹ Unity Temple
- ☕5 Petersen's Ice Cream
- ❻ Historic Pleasant Home
- ❼ Ernest Hemingway Museum
- ❽ Hemingway Birthplace
- 🍺9 Avenue Ale House

Previous page: The Grosse Pointe Lighthouse and Maritime Museum.

This historic and scenic suburb on the western fringe of Chicago was Ernest Hemingway's birthplace and boyhood home, as well as the location of Frank Lloyd Wright's first home and studio. It's home to the country's largest concentration of houses and buildings designed and built by Wright, and features architecture that's functional, appropriate to its natural setting, and stimulating to the imagination. START: **Take the El (Green Line) to Harlem Avenue, about a 25-minute ride from downtown. Get off the train at Harlem and walk 2 blocks north to the Oak Park Visitor Center at Lake Street.**

❶ **Oak Park Visitor Center.** Pick up useful maps of the area before tackling the historic district, located just a few blocks away. You can also purchase special event tickets, souvenirs, and themed audio tours. *158 N. Forest Ave.* ☎ *888/OAK-PARK or 708/524-7800. www.visitoakpark. com. Apr–Oct daily 10am–5pm; Nov–Mar daily 10am–4pm.*

❷ ★★★ **Frank Lloyd Wright Home & Studio.** For the first 20 years of Wright's career, this remarkable complex served first and foremost as the sanctuary from which

Nathan Moore House, one of several homes designed by Frank Lloyd Wright in Oak Park's historic district.

the famous architect designed and executed more than 130 of his 430 completed buildings. The home began life as a simple shingled cottage that Wright (1867–1959) built for his bride in 1889 at the age of 22, but it became a work in progress, as Wright remodeled it constantly until 1911 (though he left the house in 1909 after separating from his wife). The home was Wright's showcase and laboratory for his famous Prairie style, but it also embraces many idiosyncratic features, including a barrel-vaulted children's playroom and a studio with an octagonal balcony suspended by chains. It has been restored to its 1909 appearance. 🕐 *1–2 hr. 951 Chicago Ave.* ☎ *708/848-1976. www.wrightplus. org. Admission $12 adults, $10 seniors and kids 7–18, free for kids under 7. Combined admission for Home & Studio tour and guided or self-guided historic district tour (see*

The studio from which Frank Lloyd Wright executed more than 130 of his 430 completed buildings.

below) *$20 adults, $16 seniors and kids 7–18. Admission to Home & Studio is by guided tour only; tours depart from the Ginkgo Tree Bookshop Mon–Fri 11am, 1pm, and 3pm; Sat–Sun every 20 min. 11am–3:30pm. Facilities for people with disabilities are limited; call in advance.*

The Arthur B. Heurtly House, one of several Wright homes visitors will see on tours of the historic district.

③ ★★★ **Guided Neighborhood Walking Tours.** On these weekend-only detailed tours, you can check out the exteriors of the houses designed by Wright, as well as the charming Victorian homes that he hated so intensely. If you prefer to tour on your own (or you come during the week), you can rent an audiocassette for a self-guided tour of the district, available at the Gingko Tree Bookshop daily from 10am to 3:30pm ($12 adults; $10 seniors and kids). ⏱ *1 hr. Tours depart from the Ginkgo Tree Bookshop in the Frank Lloyd Wright Home & Studio, 951 Chicago Ave.* ☎ *708/ 848-1976. www.wrightplus.org. Guided tours $12 adults, $10 seniors and children 7–18, free for children under 7. Sat–Sun 10:30am–4pm (tour times more limited Nov–Feb).*

④ ★★ **Unity Temple.** This National Historic Landmark's reinforced concrete exterior is as forbidding as a mausoleum. Built between 1905 and 1908 for the Unitarian Universalist Congregation, the cubist-style church is one of Wright's greatest masterpieces and the only public building from his "Golden" period that still stands. The detailing

Unity Temple, one of Frank Lloyd Wright's greatest architectural achievements.

in the considerably cheerier interior contains the entire architectural alphabet of the Prairie School of architectural design, from the skylight to the prominent use of wood trim. ⏱ *45 min. for a guided tour. 875 Lake St.* ☎ *708/383-8873. www.unitytemple-utrf.org. Admission $8 adults, $6 seniors, students, and kids. Sat–Sun on the hour, 1–4pm.*

☕ ⑤ ★★★ **Petersen's Ice Cream Parlour & Sweet Shoppe** has been serving up classic American favorites since 1919. There's wonderfully rich ice cream (the specialty is the Merry-Go-Round, a chocolate sundae topped with animal cookies and a parasol), soup and sandwiches, and kiddie treats such as dinosaur-shaped chicken nuggets. *1100 W. Chicago Ave.* ☎ *708/386-6131. $.*

⑥ ★ **Historic Pleasant Home.** Named for its location at Pleasant and Home streets, this opulent, 30-room mansion is a must-see for fans of architecture and historic homes. It was built in 1897 by prominent Prairie School architect George W. Maher (1864–1926) for investment banker and philanthropist John W. Farson. Of some 300 structures that Maher designed, it's the only one open to the public and was designated a National Historic Landmark in 1996. You'll see colorful art glass,

custom furniture and light fixtures, and Maher's unique use of his "motif-rhythm" theory, where repeated decorative motifs are incorporated into every facet of the home. ⏱ *1 hr. for a guided tour. 217 Home St.* ☎ *708/383-2654. www. pleasanthome.org. Admission $5 adults, $3 seniors, students, and kids; free Thurs. Tours Thurs–Sat 12:30, 1:30, and 2:30pm.*

❼ Ernest Hemingway Museum. Frank Lloyd Wright may be Oak Park's favorite son, but the town's most famous native son is Ernest Hemingway (1899–1961), who resided here for the first 18 years of his life. Operated by the Ernest Hemingway Foundation, this museum, a former church, traces the author's life from his first job out of high school as a young reporter with the *Kansas City Star* to his work as a war correspondent in Europe during World War II. Videos of 15 films made from his works, from *A Farewell to Arms* (1921) to *Islands in the Stream* (1977), are shown. ⏱ *1–2 hr. 200 N. Oak Park Ave.* ☎ *708/524-5383. www.ehfop.org. Admission $8 adults, $6 seniors and students, free for kids under 5. Admission covers both the museum and the Hemingway Birthplace (see below). Sun–Fri 1–5pm; Sat 10am–5pm.*

❽ Hemingway Birthplace. Also operated by the Ernest Hemingway Foundation, this lovely Queen Anne home, with a wrap-around porch and turrets, has been

The Ernest B. Hemingway Museum examines the life of Oak Park's most famous native son.

restored to replicate its appearance at the end of the 19th century. The home was built in 1890 for Hemingway's grandfather, Ernest Hall. Hemingway was born here on July 21, 1899, though the author actually spent most of his youth at 600 N. Kenilworth Ave., a few blocks away (that house is privately owned). This is an appealing stop for fans of historic houses, whether you're a Hemingway fan or not. *339 N. Oak Park Ave.* ☎ *708/524-5383. www. ehfop.org. Admission $8 adults, $6 seniors and students, free for kids under 5. Admission covers both the Birthplace and the Hemingway Museum (see above). Sun–Fri 1–5pm; Sat 10am–5pm.*

Near Unity Temple, **❾ Avenue Ale House** is a local sports bar that specializes in generous steaks, chops, hearty sandwiches, homemade French onion soup, and giant salads. Don't miss the juicy Vidalia Burger, topped with Swiss cheese and caramelized onions. Eight beers are on tap, and 50 more are available in the bottle. When the weather's good, opt for the outdoor dining area on the rooftop. *825 S. Oak Park Ave.* ☎ *708/848-2801. $$.*

The Hemingway Birthplace, where Papa was born in 1899, is worth visiting even if you're not a fan of the novelist.

Evanston

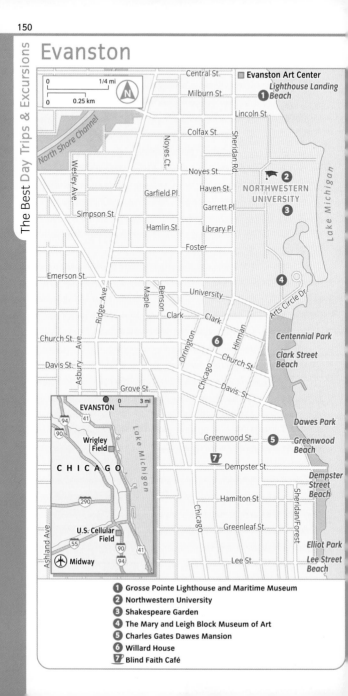

1 Grosse Pointe Lighthouse and Maritime Museum
2 Northwestern University
3 Shakespeare Garden
4 The Mary and Leigh Block Museum of Art
5 Charles Gates Dawes Mansion
6 Willard House
7 Blind Faith Café

The oldest suburb of Chicago, Evanston is home to a bustling downtown, grand old homes, and the Northwestern University campus. It combines the peaceful feeling and green space of suburban life with the culture and lively atmosphere that you'd expect of an urban center, including sophisticated dining and boutique shopping. START: **Catch the Metra North train line from Northwestern Station in the Loop for the 20-minute ride to the Davis Street station. Walk east on Davis Street into the heart of downtown Evanston.**

❶ Grosse Point Lighthouse and Maritime Museum.

This lighthouse, a National Historic Landmark built by the U.S. government in 1873, served as a beacon when Lake Michigan still teemed with cargo-laden ships and shipwrecks were a very real threat. Be sure to stroll the scenic grounds. If you're here during the summer, it's worth taking a tour of the lighthouse's interior—you get to climb the 141 steps to the top of the tower and are rewarded with a wonderful view. ⏱ *45 min. 2601 Sheridan Rd.* ☎ *847/ 328-6961. www.grossepointelighthouse.net. Admission $5 adults, $3 children 8–12, children under 8 not admitted for safety reasons. Tours of the interior conducted at 2, 3, and 4pm weekends June–Sept only; grounds open year-round daily.*

❷ Northwestern University.

This world-class university makes its home on a beautiful lakefront campus, and many of its architecturally significant buildings make the campus worthy of several hours of exploration. Don't miss the sublime stained-glass facade of the **Alice Millar Chapel.** Other standouts include the Norman Gothic **Deering Library,** patterned after Cambridge University's King's College Chapel; and the Romanesque **Revival Fisk Hall,** designed by Daniel Burnham and home to the university's prestigious Medill School of Journalism. ⏱ *1–2 hr. Sheridan Rd. (at Chicago Ave.).* ☎ *847/491-3741. www.northwestern.edu. Free admission.*

❸ Shakespeare Garden.

In 1915, the Drama League of America asked its members to come up with ways to commemorate the 300th anniversary of Shakespeare's death. Noted Chicago landscape architect Jens J. Jensen responded with this gem: A National Historic Landmark that features several memorials to the Bard and more than 50 plants that were either mentioned in Shakespeare's plays or common in Tudor England. Boxed in by hawthorn trees and perfectly manicured hedgerows, the garden's a lovely spot for strolling. ⏱ *10 min. At Northwestern University, east of Sheridan Rd., entrance off Garrett Place.* ☎ *847/491-3741. www.northwestern.edu. Free admission.*

❹ The Mary and Leigh Block Museum of Art.

This fine-arts

Northwestern University is renowned for both its academics and architecture.

The Best Day Trips & Excursions

haven offers a top-notch collection of prints, photographs, and drawings, as well as always-intriguing temporary exhibitions. Don't miss the outdoor sculpture garden. 🕐 *30 min. At Northwestern University, 40 Arts Circle Dr.* ☎ *847/491-4000. www.blockmuseum. northwestern.edu. Free admission. Tues 10am–5pm; Wed–Fri 10am–8pm; Sat–Sun noon–5pm.*

Dürer Print from the Mary and Leigh Block Museum of Art.

⑥ **Willard House.** Frances Willard (1839–98), social reformer and founder of the Women's Christian Temperance Union (WCTU), spent most of her adult life in Evanston. Nine of the 17 rooms in this old Victorian "Rest Cottage" (as Willard called it) have been converted into a museum of period furnishings and temperance memorabilia. Among the personal effects on display is the bicycle Willard affectionately called "Gladys" and learned to ride late in life—spurring women across the country to do the same. The headquarters of the WCTU is still located on-site. 🕐 *1 hr. 1730 Chicago Ave.* ☎ *847/328-7500. www.franceswillardhouse.org. Admission $5 adults, $3 kids 12 and under. Open 1st and 3rd Sun of every month from 1–4pm.*

The Charles Gates Dawes Mansion, home of the Evanston Historical Society.

⑤ **Charles Gates Dawes Mansion.** Dawes was a wealthy financier who served as vice president under Calvin Coolidge and won the 1925 Nobel Peace Prize for his smooth handling of German reparations after World War I on behalf of the League of Nations. Dawes's former home—completed in 1896—now houses the Evanston History Center, which offers tours of this restored landmark. The 25-room home was designed in the manner of a French château and features a collection of historic costumes, decorative arts, and antiques. 🕐 *1 hr. 225 Greenwood St.* ☎ *847/475-3410. www.evanstonhistorical.org. Admission $5 adults, $3 seniors and kids 18 and under. Thurs–Sun 1–5pm.*

Experience Evanston's bohemian side with a cup of coffee or light snack at the ⑦ **Blind Faith Café,** where the organic and vegetarian specialties include scrambled tofu, huevos rancheros, granola, tempting baked goods, and whole-grain pancakes. *525 Dempster St.* ☎ *847/ 328-6875. $$.* ●

Historic Willard House is the headquarters of the Women's Christian Temperance Union.

The
Savvy Traveler

Before You Go

Government Tourist Offices

The **Chicago Office of Tourism,** Chicago Cultural Center, 78 E. Washington St., Chicago, IL 60602 (☎ **877/CHICAGO** or TTY 866/710-0294; www.choosechicago.com), dispenses information to both domestic and international visitors.

You can also contact the **Illinois Bureau of Tourism** (☎ **800/2CONNECT** or TTY 800/406-6418; www.enjoyillinois.com).

The Best Times to Go

The ideal time to visit Chicago is in summer or fall. Summer offers a nonstop selection of special events and outdoor activities, though you will face crowds and the occasional period of hot, muggy weather. In autumn, days are generally sunny and crowds at major tourist attractions grow thinner. Snow generally doesn't start falling until November.

Spring is extremely unpredictable, with dramatic fluctuations between cold and warm weather, and usually lots of rain. Winter, though not any worse than in many other northern cities, is generally cold and snowy. That said, museum-lovers and those on a tight budget might find winter a good time to visit: You'll find no lines at museums, lots of sales in the stores, and the cheapest rates at hotels.

Festivals & Special Events

Ask the **Chicago Office of Tourism** (☎ **877/CHICAGO**; www.choosechicago.com) to mail you a copy of the *Chicago Visitor's Guide.* Also ask for the latest materials produced by the **Mayor's Office of Special Events** (☎ **312/744-3315**; www.cityofchicago.org/specialevents), or call the **Special Events Hot Line** at ☎ **312/744-3370** (TTY 312/744-

2964), which keeps current with citywide and neighborhood festivals.

JAN. All the latest boats and recreational vehicles are put on display at the **Chicago Boat, RV & Outdoor Show** (☎ 312/946-6200; www.chicagoboatshow.com), which also features trout fishing, a climbing wall, boating safety seminars, and big-time entertainment. The action takes place in mid-January.

FEB. More than a million car buffs flock to the **Chicago Auto Show** (☎ **630/495-2282**) in mid-February. More than a thousand cars and trucks, domestic and foreign, current and futuristic, are on display. Look for special weekend packages at area hotels that include show tickets.

MAR. The Chicago River is dyed green for the **St. Patrick's Day Parade,** a Chicago tradition since the 1840s that's held on the Saturday before March 17. The parade route is Columbus Drive from Balbo Drive to Monroe Street. Visit www.chiagostpatsparade.com for more information.

APR. Join the ever-hopeful fans of the Cubs (☎ **773/404-CUBS** or visit www.cubs.mlb.com) or the White Sox (☎ **312/674-1000** or visit www.whitesox.mlb.com) on **Opening Day.** Be sure to get your tickets early for this eagerly awaited day, and go prepared with warm gear, because it's usually freezing cold. Early April.

MAY. On the third Saturday in May, you can take the annual **Wright Plus Tour** (☎ **708/848-1976**; www.wrightplus.org), a rare look at the interiors of 10 notable buildings in Oak Park. Tickets go on sale March 1 and can sell out within 6 weeks.

Previous page: Steps at an El station.

JUNE. One of the largest free outdoor book fairs in the country, **Printers Row Book Fair** (☎ 312/222-3986) features more than 150 booksellers displaying new, used, and antiquarian books for sale. It takes place the first weekend in June.

Dozens of acts perform over the 4 days of the **Chicago Blues Festival** (☎ 312/744-3315). Blues Fest is free and takes place the second weekend in June in Millennium Park.

Highland Park's **Ravinia Festival** (☎ 847/266-5100; www.ravinia. com) is the open-air summer home of the Chicago Symphony Orchestra and many first-rate visiting orchestras, chamber ensembles, pop artists, dance companies, and so forth. It runs from June through September.

The Grant Park Music Festival (☎ 312/742-7638; www.grantparkmusicfestival.com) at Pritzker Pavilion in Millennium Park offers free outdoor musical concerts from the last week in June through August.

The city claims that **Taste of Chicago** (☎ 312/744-3315) is the largest free outdoor food fest in the nation. The 3.5-million rib and pizza lovers who feed at this colossal alfresco trough say they're right. The festival runs from late June through early July; admission is free, though you pay for the sampling.

The floats and marching units at the **Gay and Lesbian Pride Parade** (☎ 773/348-8243; www. chicagopridecalendar.org) have to be seen to be believed. It's held the last Sunday in June.

JULY. The **Independence Day Celebration** (☎ 312/744-3315) takes places in Chicago on July 3. Concerts and fireworks are the highlights of the festivities in Grant Park. Expect huge crowds.

The annual **Old St. Patrick's World's Largest Block Party** (☎ 312/648-1021; www.oldstpats. org) is a hugely popular blowout that's hosted by the city's oldest church in mid-July. Six bands—the party always lands some major acts—perform over 2 nights.

AUG. The U.S. Air Force Thunderbirds and Navy Seals usually put in an appearance at the **Chicago Air & Water Show** (☎ 312/744-3315), which is held the third weekend in August. Admission is free to this hugely popular aquatic and aerial spectacular.

The **Viva! Chicago Latin Music Festival** (☎ 312/744-3315), held on the last weekend in August, runs the gamut from salsa to mambo to the hottest Latin rock outfits. Admission is free.

SEPT. Several national headliners are always on hand at the **Chicago Jazz Festival** (☎ 312/744-3315). The free event takes place the first weekend in September.

Held at various music venues around the city in late September, the **World Music Festival Chicago** (☎ 312/742-1938; www.cityof chicago.org/worldmusic) features top performers from around the globe, performing traditional, contemporary, and fusion music. Shows are a mix of free and ticketed ($10 or less) events.

OCT. The oldest U.S. festival of its kind, the **Chicago International Film Festival** (☎ 312/683-0121; www.chicagofilmfestival.org) screens films from around the world at various theaters over 2 weeks beginning the first Thursday in October.

NOV. All the city's best-known dance troupes (Hubbard Street, Joffrey Ballet, and so on) and many smaller companies participate in the month-long **Dance Chicago** festival (☎ 773/989-0698; www.dance chicago.com).

DEC. The esteemed Joffrey Ballet of Chicago performs its Victorian-American twist on *The Nutcracker* from late Thanksgiving to mid-December. For tickets, call ☎ 312/559-1212 (Ticketmaster), or contact the Joffrey office at ☎ 312/739-0120; www.joffrey.com.

The Weather

Chicagoans like to joke that if you don't like the weather, just wait an hour—it will change. The key is to be prepared for a wide range of weather with clothing that can take you from a sunny morning to a chilly, drizzly evening.

The city has a reputation for being extremely cold in the winter, though it doesn't really get much colder than any comparable northern city. (Though blustery winds do blow in from Lake Michigan, Chicago's nickname, the Windy City, is due to the hot air generated by its politicos, not its weather.) Still, days of subzero temperatures, snowstorms, and freezing wind chills are not unheard of. If you arrive in winter, a hat and a good pair of boots are musts.

Summer in Chicago can be tough to take as well: Temperatures can soar past 90°F (32°C) for several days at a stretch, and the humidity can rise to stifling proportions. That said, breezes coming off Lake Michigan usually help to cool things off.

As close to your departure as possible, check the local weather forecast at the websites of the *Chicago Tribune* newspaper (www.chicagotribune.com) or The Weather Channel (www.weather.com).

Useful Websites

- **www.enjoyillinois.com**: If you plan to travel beyond city limits, this site, run by the Illinois Bureau of Tourism, can give you the scoop on the suburbs and beyond.

- **www.metromix.com**: Comprehensive entertainment and nightlife listings from the *Chicago Tribune*.

- **www.cityofchicago.org/exploringchicago**: The official site of the Chicago Office of Tourism gives a good overview of what's happening in town.

- **http://chicago.citysearch.com**: This local edition of the national Citysearch sites offers reviews of bars, restaurants, shows, and shops.

- **www.ticketweb.org**: Many of the city's performing arts groups sell tickets online through this site.

- **www.hotrooms.com**: This excellent local service is the best site for hotel deals in Chicago.

- **www.chicagoist.com**: Want to see what issues have Chicagoans riled up? Check out this sounding board for local news.

Cellphones

It's a good bet that your cellphone will work in Chicago, but the U.S. has a very fragmented **GSM (Global System for Mobiles) wireless network,** so take a look at your wireless company's coverage map before heading out. (To see where GSM phones work in the U.S., check out **www.t-mobile.com/coverage**).

You can always rent a phone from **InTouch USA** (☎ 800/872-7626; www.intouchglobal.com) or a rental-car location, but be aware that you'll pay $1 a minute or more for airtime.

Car Rentals

Unless you plan on taking a day trip to Indiana Dunes (p 86), I recommend that you don't rent a car. And even if you do plan on leaving the city limits during your stay, rent a car only for the day you'll need one. You're far better off sticking to public transportation, taxis, and your own two feet. Parking in Chicago is scarce and expensive, and gasoline (petrol) isn't cheap.

CHICAGO'S AVERAGE TEMPERATURES & PRECIPITATION

	JAN	FEB	MAR	APR	MAY	JUNE
High °F	20	34	44	59	70	79
Low °F	14	18	28	39	48	58
High °C	−7	1	7	15	21	26
Low °C	−10	−8	−2	4	9	14
Rainfall (in.)	1.60	1.31	2.59	3.66	3.15	4.08
Rainfall (cm)	4.06	3.33	6.58	9.30	8	10.36

	JULY	AUG	SEPT	OCT	NOV	DEC
High °F	85	82	76	64	48	35
Low °F	63	62	54	42	31	20
High °C	29	28	24	18	9	2
Low °C	17	17	12	6	−1	−7
Rainfall (in.)	3.63	3.53	3.35	2.28	2.06	2.10
Rainfall (cm)	9.22	8.94	8.51	5.79	5.23	5.33

If you still want to rent a car, the best deals are usually found at rental-car company websites, although all the major online travel agencies also offer rental-car reservations services.

Getting There

By Plane

Chicago is served by two major airports. **O'Hare International Airport** (☎ 773/686-2200; www.ohare.com) has long battled with Atlanta's Hartsfield for the title of the world's busiest airport. It's located about 15 miles (24km) northwest of the Loop. Though taxis are plentiful (a cab ride into town averages $35), traffic can be horrendous (the ride can last an hour or more). If you arrive around rush hour and aren't carting around lots of luggage, I highly recommend taking the El (see "Getting Around," below) as it's both cheaper and faster. The 45-minute trip on the El's Blue Line from O'Hare to downtown costs $2.

Midway International Airport (☎ 773/838-0600; www.flychicago. com; online airport code MDW) is located 10 miles (16km) southwest of downtown Chicago. Although

fewer airlines operate routes here, Midway is closer to the Loop and attracts more discount airlines, so you may be able to get a cheaper fare if you fly here. Taxis are available, and a cab ride (about $30) from Midway to the Loop usually takes about 20 minutes (though in bad traffic, the journey can take considerably longer). Again, I recommend taking public transportation. The 20- to 30-minute trip on the El's Orange Line from Midway to the downtown area costs $2. **Note:** The train station at Midway is a significant walk from the terminal—without the benefit of O'Hare's moving sidewalks—so be prepared if you've got heavy bags.

Another transportation option at both airports is **Continental Airport Express** (☎ 888/2-THEVAN; www.airportexpress.com). This shuttle's blue-and-white vans service most first-class hotels in Chicago;

ticket counters are located at both airports near the baggage claim. For transportation to the airport, reserve a spot at your hotel (check with the bell captain). The cost is $25 one-way ($45 round-trip) to or from O'Hare and $20 one-way ($36 round-trip) to or from Midway. Less expensive "group rates" are available for two or more people traveling together. The shuttles operate from 4am to 11:30pm.

By Car

Interstate highways from all major points in the U.S. either run through or terminate in Chicago. **I-80** and **I-90** approach from the east, crossing the northern sector of Illinois, with I-90 splitting off and emptying into Chicago via the **Skyway** and the **Dan Ryan Expressway.** From Chicago, I-90 runs through Wisconsin, following a northern route to Seattle.

I-55 snakes up the Mississippi Valley from the vicinity of New Orleans and enters Chicago from the west along **the Stevenson Expressway.** In the opposite direction it provides an outlet to the southwest. **I-57** originates in southern Illinois and forms part of the interstate linkage to Florida and the South, connecting within Chicago on the west leg of the Dan Ryan. **I-94**

links Detroit with Chicago, arriving in Chicago as the **Calumet Expressway** and leaving the city as the **Kennedy Expressway** en route to the Northwest.

By Train

A national rail hub, Chicago is served by a plethora of Amtrak trains. Contact **Amtrak** (☎ 800/USA-RAIL; www.amtrak.com) for tickets or to get the company's useful travel planner, which includes information on train accommodations and package tours.

Trains pull into **Union Station,** 210 S. Canal St. (between Adams and Jackson streets; ☎ 312/655-2385). Bus nos. 1, 60, 125, 151, and 156 all stop at the station, which is just west across the river from the Loop. The nearest El stop is at Clinton Street and Congress Parkway (on the Blue Line), which is 3 blocks away.

By Bus

Greyhound (☎ 800/231-2222; www.greyhound.com), the sole nationwide bus line, has a downtown Chicago terminal at 630 W. Harrison St. (☎ 312/408-5800). The location is not within walking distance of the major hotel zones, so you'll need to take a cab or public transportation to get to your accommodations.

Getting Around

By Public Transportation

The **Chicago Transit Authority** (CTA; ☎ 312/836-7000; www.transitchicago.com) operates an extensive system of trains and buses throughout the city. Aside from walking, using public transportation is the quickest and most economical way to move about Chicago.

Subways and elevated trains (known as the El) are generally safe and reliable, although it's advisable to avoid long rides through unfamiliar neighborhoods late at night. Most lines run 24 hours a day, though some do have limited hours, and some stations close down during the evening. The rush hour crush occurs roughly 6 to 9:30am and 3 to 7pm.

Other than on foot or bicycle, the best way to get around Chicago's warren of neighborhoods—the best way to actually see what's around you—is by riding a public bus, especially if you're staying near the lakefront, where the trains don't run. Virtually every place in the city is within close walking distance of a bus stop. Look for the *blue-and-white signs to locate bus stops,* which are spaced about 2 blocks apart.

A few buses that are particularly handy for many visitors are the **no. 146 Marine/Michigan,** an express bus from Belmont Avenue on the North Side that cruises down North Lake Shore Drive (and through Lincoln Park during nonpeak times) to North Michigan Avenue, State Street, and the Grant Park museum campus; the **no. 151 Sheridan,** which passes through Lincoln Park en route to inner Lake Shore Drive and then travels along Michigan Avenue as far south as Adams Street, where it turns west into the Loop (and stops at Union Station); and the **no. 156 LaSalle,** which goes through Lincoln Park and then into the Loop's financial district on LaSalle Street. Note that many bus routes shut down late at night (when you're probably better off taking a cab anyway).

Cash fares for the bus, subway, and El are $2 (kids 7–11 are $1, and under age 7 ride free), and they won't sell you a transfer when you use cash. I recommend buying a **Chicago Card,** which is a credit-card sized card that automatically deducts the exact fare each time you ride. Riders can obtain cards at vending machines located at all CTA train stations (but not on buses, so if you don't have a card be sure you have exact change before boarding). You pay only $1.75 per ride with a card, and 25¢ for a transfer that allows CTA riders to make two transfers on the bus or El within 2

hours of receipt. With a Chicago Card, kids under 7 ride free, and those between the ages of 7 and 11 pay 85¢ (15¢ for transfers).

The CTA operates a useful information line that will help you find the bus or El train that will get you to your destination: ☎ **836-7000** (from any area code in the city or suburbs) or TTY ☎ 836-4949. The line is staffed from 5am to 1am. You can also check out the CTA's website at www.transitchicago.com. Excellent CTA comprehensive maps, which include both El and bus routes, are usually available at subway or El stations, or by calling the CTA.

Visitors may consider buying a **Visitor Pass,** which works like a fare card and allows individual users unlimited rides on the El and CTA buses over a 24-hour period. The cards come in 1-, 2-, 3-, and 5-day varieties and cost $5 to $18. They're sold at airports, hotels, museums, Hot Tix outlets, transportation hubs, and Chicago Office of Tourism visitor information centers (☎ **877/ CHICAGO [244-2246]**). You can also buy them in advance online at www. transitchicago.com or by calling ☎ **888/YOUR-CTA.** Though the passes save you the trouble of feeding the fare machines yourself, they're economical only if you plan to make at least three distinct trips at least 2 or more hours apart.

If you plan to head to Evanston (p 150), you'll need to take the Union Pacific line of the **Metra** commuter railroad (☎ **312/322-6777** or TTY ☎ 312/322-6774, Mon–Fri 8am– 5pm; at other times, call the Transit Information Center at ☎ **312/836- 7000** or TTY ☎ 312/836-4949; www.metrarail.com), out of **North- Western Station** at Madison and Canal streets (☎ **312/496-4777**).

By Taxi
Taxis are a convenient way to get around the Loop and to get to the

dining, shopping, and entertainment options found beyond downtown. They are easy to hail in the Loop, on the Magnificent Mile and the Gold Coast, in River North, and in Lincoln Park, but if you go much beyond these key areas, you might need to call. Cab companies include **Flash Cab** (☎ 773/561-1444), **Yellow Cab** (☎ 312/TAXI-CAB), and **Checker Cab** (☎ 312/CHECKER).

The meter in Chicago cabs currently starts at $2.25 for the first mile and costs 20¢ for each ⅕ of a mile; each 36 seconds of time elapsed is 20¢ with a $1 surcharge for the first additional rider and 50¢ for each person after that.

By Car

Try to avoid driving in Chicago if possible; it's easier and cheaper to get around by hopping public transportation or a taxi. If you must drive, you'll find that Chicago is laid out in a grid pattern so logical that it's relatively easy to get around by car.

For information on parking in the city, see "Parking," below.

Fast Facts

APARTMENT RENTALS **DeWitt Place,** 900 N. DeWitt Place (at Delaware Street; ☎ 312/642-7020), rents studios and one-bedroom condos on a daily or monthly basis, in a near-perfect location under the shadow of the John Hancock Center. For a complete listing of apartment rentals, contact the Chicago Convention and Tourism Bureau at ☎ 877-CHICAGO.

AREA CODES The 312 area code applies to the Loop and the neighborhoods closest to it, including River North, North Michigan Avenue, and the Gold Coast. The code for the rest of the city is 773. *Note:* You must dial "1" plus the area code for all telephone numbers, even if you are making a call within the same area code.

ATMS & CASH POINTS The **Cirrus** (☎ 800/424-7787; www.mastercard.com) and **PLUS** (☎ 800/843-7587; www.visa.com) networks span the globe; look at the back of your bank card to see which network you're on, then call or check online for automated teller machine (ATM) locations in Chicago (they're found all over the city, so you shouldn't have trouble finding one).

Be sure you know your personal identification number (PIN) before you leave home, and be sure to find out your daily withdrawal limit before you depart. Also keep in mind that many banks impose a fee every time a card is used at a different bank's ATM, and that fee can be higher for international transactions (up to $5 or more) than for domestic ones (where they're rarely more than $1.50).

Note: Some small establishments in Chicago won't take credit cards, so it's always wise to carry a small amount of cash on you.

BABYSITTING Check first with the concierge or desk staff at your hotel; many hotels maintain lists of reliable sitters and babysitting services. Many top hotels work with **American ChildCare Service** (☎ 312/644-7300; www.americanchildcare.com), a state-licensed and insured babysitting service that can match you with a sitter. All of its sitters are required to pass background checks, provide multiple child-care references, and are trained in infant and child CPR. It's best to make a reservation 24 hours in advance; the office is open from 9am to 5pm. Rates are

$19 per hour, with a 4-hour minimum, and a $20 fee for the agency.

B&Bs **At Home Inn Chicago,** P.O. Box 14088, Chicago, IL 60614 (☎ 800/375-7084 or 312/640-1050; www.athomeinnchicago.com), offers a centralized reservations service for more than 70 accommodations, from high-rise and loft apartments to guest rooms in private homes. Alternately, the **Chicago Bed and Breakfast Association** (www.chicago-bed-breakfast.com) runs a website that links to various properties around the city.

BANKING HOURS   Banking hours in Chicago normally run from 9am (8am, in some cases) to 5pm Monday through Friday, with select banks remaining open later on specified afternoons and evenings.

CONSULATES & EMBASSIES   All embassies are located in the nation's capital, Washington, D.C. Some consulates are located in major U.S. cities, and most nations have a mission to the United Nations in New York City. If your country isn't listed below, call for directory information in Washington, D.C. (☎ 202/555-1212), or log on to **www.embassy.org/embassies**.

The embassy of **Australia** is at 1601 Massachusetts Ave. NW, Washington, DC 20036 (☎ 202/797-3000; www.austemb.org). There are consulates in New York, Honolulu, Los Angeles, and San Francisco.

The embassy of **Canada** is at 501 Pennsylvania Ave. NW, Washington, DC 20001 (☎ 202/682-1740; www.canadianembassy.org). Canadian consulates are in Buffalo (New York State), Detroit, Los Angeles, New York, and Seattle.

The embassy of Ireland is at 2234 Massachusetts Ave. NW, Washington, DC 20008 (☎ 202/462-3939; www.irelandemb.org). Consulates are in Boston, Chicago, New York, San Francisco, and other cities.

The embassy of **New Zealand** is at 37 Observatory Circle NW, Washington, DC 20008 (☎ 202/328-4800; www.nzemb.org). Consulates are in Los Angeles, Salt Lake City, San Francisco, and Seattle.

The embassy of the **United Kingdom** is at 3100 Massachusetts Ave. NW, Washington, DC 20008 (☎ 202/462-1340; www.britainusa.com). Consulates are in Atlanta, Boston, Chicago, Cleveland, Houston, Los Angeles, New York, San Francisco, and Seattle.

CUSTOMS   **What You Can Bring into the United States** Every visitor more than 21 years of age may bring in, free of duty, the following: 1 liter of wine or hard liquor; 200 cigarettes, 100 cigars (but not from Cuba), or 3 pounds of smoking tobacco; and $100 worth of gifts. These exemptions are offered to travelers who spend at least 72 hours in the United States and who have not claimed them within the preceding 6 months. It is altogether forbidden to bring into the country foodstuffs (particularly fruit, cooked meats, and canned goods) and plants (vegetables, seeds, tropical plants, and the like). Foreign tourists may carry in or out up to $10,000 in U.S. or foreign currency with no formalities; larger sums must be declared to U.S. Customs on entering or leaving, which includes filing form CM 4790. For details regarding U.S. Customs and Border Protection, consult your nearest U.S. embassy or consulate, or **U.S. Customs** (☎ 202/927-1770; www.customs.ustreas.gov).

What You Can Take Home from the United States:

Canadian Citizens: For a clear summary of Canadian rules, write for the booklet *I Declare,* issued by the **Canada Border Services Agency** (☎ 800/461-9999 in

Canada, or 204/983-3500; www.
cbsa-asfc.gc.ca).

U.K. Citizens: For information,
contact **HM Customs & Excise** at
☎ **0845/010-9000** (from outside
the U.K., 020/8929-0152), or consult
their website at **www.hmce.gov.uk**.

Australian Citizens: A helpful
brochure available from Australian
consulates or Customs offices is
Know Before You Go. For more information, call the **Australian Customs Service** at ☎ **1300/363-263**,
or log on to **www.customs.gov.au.**

New Zealand Citizens: Most ques-
tions are answered in a free pam-
phlet available at New Zealand
consulates and Customs offices:
*New Zealand Customs Guide for
Travellers, Notice no. 4.* For more
information, contact **New Zealand
Customs,** The Customhouse, 17–21
Whitmore St., Box 2218, Wellington
(☎ **04/473-6099** or 0800/428-786;
www.customs.govt.nz).

DENTISTS   The referral service of
the **Chicago Dental Society**
(☎ **312/836-7300**; www.cds.org)
can refer you to an area dentist.
Your hotel concierge may also keep
a list of dentists.

DINING   You'll save money on often-
expensive room service by going
out for breakfast. Most restaurants
begin serving lunch by 11:30am,
some as early as 11am. Dinner service usually starts at 5:30pm, with
the last seating at 9:30pm, as many
kitchens close around 10pm.

The dress code in most Chicago
restaurants is usually quite relaxed.
For men, an open-collared shirt and
khakis should be just fine, even in
the nicer restaurants. A few places
still maintain a coat-and-tie dress
code (The Pump Room, p 117, is
one of those).

If you're planning on doing some
fine dining at an in-demand restaurant, such as Everest (p 101), you
may need to book up to 3 months in
advance. Otherwise, most restaurant reservations can be made by
calling the restaurant directly during
the week that you're visiting; you
can always walk in, but waits may be
long. Another option is to make a
reservation through **www.open
table.com**, a free online reservations service.

DOCTORS   In the event of a medical
emergency, your best bet—unless
you have friends who can recommend a doctor—is to rely on your
hotel physician or go to the nearest
hospital emergency room. **Northwestern Memorial Hospital** also
has a **Physician Referral Service**
(☎ **877/926-4664**). Also see "Hospitals" below.

DRINKING LAWS   The legal age for
the purchase and consumption of
alcoholic beverages is 21; proof of
age is required and often requested
at bars, nightclubs, and restaurants,
so it's always a good idea to bring ID
when you go out. In Chicago, beer,
wine, and other alcoholic beverages
are sold at liquor stores and super-
markets. Bars may sell alcohol until
2am, although some nightclubs have
special licenses that allow alcohol
sales until 4am. Do not carry open
containers of alcohol in your car or
any public area that isn't zoned for
alcohol consumption. The police can
fine you on the spot. And nothing
will ruin your trip faster than getting
a citation for DUI (driving under the
influence), so don't even think about
driving while intoxicated.

ELECTRICITY   Like Canada, the
United States uses 110–120 volts
AC (60 cycles), compared to 220–
240 volts AC (50 cycles) in most of
Europe, Australia, and New Zealand.
If your small appliances use 220–240
volts, you'll need a 110-volt trans-
former and a plug adapter with two
flat parallel pins to operate them
here. Downward converters that
change 220–240 volts to 110–120

volts are difficult to find in the United States, so bring one with you.

EMERGENCIES For fire and police emergencies, call ☎ 911. This is a free call. If it is a medical emergency, a city ambulance will take the patient to the nearest hospital emergency room. The nonemergency phone number for the Chicago Police Department is ☎ 311. If you desire a specific, nonpublic ambulance, call **Vandenberg Ambulance** (☎ 773/521-7777). A centrally located emergency room in Chicago is **Northwestern Memorial Hospital,** 251 E. Huron St. (☎ 312/926-2000; www.nmh.org), a state-of-the-art medical center right off North Michigan Avenue. The emergency department (☎ 312/926-5188, or 312/944-2358 for TDD access) is located at 251 E. Erie St. near Fairbanks Court.

EVENT LISTINGS Every Thursday, the *Chicago Reader* (☎ 312/828-0350; www.chireader.com), a free weekly, publishes current entertainment and cultural listings. The Friday and "Weekend Plus" sections of the *Chicago Tribune* (☎ 312/222-3232; www.chicagotribune.com) and the *Chicago Sun-Times* (☎ 312/321-3000; www.suntimes.com) also feature extensive event listings.

Also, see "Useful Websites," above.

FAMILY TRAVEL Look for items tagged with a "kids" icon in this book. You can pick up a free copy of *Chicago Parent* magazine at any local bookstore, public library, or park district building. The magazine includes a calendar of events geared to families with kids. For more extensive recommendations, you might want to purchase a copy of *Frommer's Chicago with Kids* (Wiley Publishing, Inc.).

GAY & LESBIAN TRAVELERS Chicago is a very gay-friendly city. The neighborhood commonly referred to as "Boys Town" (roughly from Belmont Ave. north to Irving Park Ave., and from Halsted St. east to the lakefront) is the center of gay nightlife (and plenty of daytime action, too). **Gay and Lesbian Pride Week** (☎ 773/348-8243), highlighted by a lively parade on the North Side, is a major event on the Chicago calendar each June. You also might want to stop by **Unabridged Books,** 3251 N. Broadway (☎ 773/883-9119), an excellent independent bookseller with a large lesbian and gay selection. Here and elsewhere in the Lakeview neighborhood, you can pick up several gay publications, including the weekly *Chicago Free Press* (www.chicagofreepress.com) and *Windy City Times* (www.windycitymediagroup.com/index.html), which both cover local news and entertainment.

The **International Gay and Lesbian Travel Association (IGLTA;** ☎ 800/448-8550 or 954/776-2626; www.iglta.org) is the trade association for the gay and lesbian travel industry. Its website offers an online directory of gay- and lesbian-friendly travel businesses.

HOLIDAYS Banks, government offices, and post offices are closed on the following legal national holidays: January 1 (New Year's Day), the third Monday in January (Martin Luther King, Jr., Day), the third Monday in February (Presidents' Day), the last Monday in May (Memorial Day), July 4 (Independence Day), the first Monday in September (Labor Day), the second Monday in October (Columbus Day), November 11 (Veterans' Day), the fourth Thursday in November (Thanksgiving Day), and December 25 (Christmas). Also, the Tuesday following the first Monday in November is Election Day and is a federal government holiday in presidential-election years (held every 4 years, and next in 2012). Stores, museums, and restaurants are open most holidays, except for Thanksgiving, Christmas, and New Year's Day.

INSURANCE **For Domestic Visitors:** Trip-cancellation insurance helps you get your money back if you have to back out of a trip, if you have to go home early, or if your travel supplier goes bankrupt. Allowed reasons for cancellation can range from sickness to natural disasters to the State Department declaring your destination unsafe for travel. (Insurers usually won't cover vague fears, though.) In this unstable world, trip-cancellation insurance is a good buy if you're getting tickets well in advance. Insurance policy details vary, so read the fine print—and especially make sure that your airline is on the list of carriers covered in case of bankruptcy. For information, contact one of the following insurers: **Access America** (☎ 866/807-3982; www.accessamerica.com), **Travel Guard International** (☎ 800/826-4919; www.travelguard.com), **Travel Insured International** (☎ 800/243-3174; www.travelinsured.com), or **Travelex Insurance Services** (☎ 888/457-4602; www.travelex-insurance.com).

Medical Insurance: Although it's not required of travelers, health insurance is highly recommended. Unlike many European countries, the United States does not usually offer free or low-cost medical care to its citizens or visitors. Doctors and hospitals are expensive, and in most cases will require advance payment or proof of coverage before they render their services. Though lack of health insurance may prevent you from being admitted to a hospital in nonemergencies, don't worry about being left on a street corner to die: The American way is to fix you now and bill the living daylights out of you later.

Insurance for British Travelers: Most big travel agents offer their own insurance and will probably try to sell you their package when you book a holiday. Think before you sign. **The Association of British Insurers** (☎ 020/7600-3333; www.abi.org.uk) gives advice by phone and publishes *Holiday Insurance,* a free guide to policy provisions and prices. You might also shop around for better deals: Try **Columbus Direct** (☎ 020/7375-0011; www.columbusdirect.net).

Insurance for Canadian Travelers: Canadians should check with their provincial health plan offices, or call **Health Canada** (☎ 613/957-2991; www.hc-sc.gc.ca) to find out the extent of your coverage and what documentation and receipts you must take home in case you are treated in the United States.

Lost-Luggage Insurance: On domestic flights, checked baggage is covered up to $3,000 per ticketed passenger. On international flights (including U.S. portions of international trips), baggage is limited to approximately $9 per pound (1.1kg), up to approximately $635 per checked bag. If you plan to check items more valuable than the standard liability, see if your valuables are covered by your homeowner's policy, or get baggage insurance as part of your comprehensive travel-insurance package. Don't buy insurance at the airport, as it's usually overpriced. Be sure to take any valuables or irreplaceable items with you in your carry-on luggage, since many valuables (including books, money, and electronics) aren't covered by airline policies.

If your luggage is lost, immediately file a lost-luggage claim at the airport, detailing the luggage contents. For most airlines, you must report delayed, damaged, or lost baggage within 4 hours of arrival. The airlines are required to deliver luggage, once found, directly to your house or destination free of charge.

INTERNET ACCESS   Many Chicago hotels have business centers equipped with computers available for guests' use. Internet access is available to the public at the Harold Washington Library Center, 400 S. State St. (☎ 312/747-4300), and at the Internet cafe inside the Apple computer store at 679 N. Michigan Ave. (☎ 312/981-4104). Most Starbucks coffee shops and McDonald's restaurants in downtown Chicago offer wireless Internet access.

LIMOS   For limo service from either O'Hare or Midway, call **Carey Limousine of Chicago** (☎ 773/763-0009) or **Chicago Limousine Services** (☎ 312/726-1035).

LOST & FOUND   Be sure to notify all your credit card companies the minute you discover your wallet has been lost or stolen, and file a report at the nearest police precinct (☎ 311). Your insurance company may require a police report before covering any claims. Most credit card companies have an emergency toll-free number to call if your card is lost or stolen; they may be able to wire you a cash advance immediately or deliver an emergency credit card in a day or two. Visa's U.S. emergency number is ☎ **800/847-2911** or 410/581-9994. American Express cardholders and traveler's check holders should call ☎ **800/221-7282.** MasterCard holders should call ☎ **800/307-7309** or 636/722-7111. For other credit cards, call the toll-free number directory at ☎ **800/555-1212.** If you need emergency cash over the weekend, when all banks and American Express offices are closed, you can have money wired to you via **Western Union** (☎ 800/325-6000; www.westernunion.com).

MAIL & POSTAGE   The main post office is located at 433 W. Harrison St. (☎ 312/983-8182); free parking is available. You can pick up mail at the main post office that is addressed to you and marked "General Delivery" (Poste Restante); you'll need to show photo ID.

Other branches can be found by calling ☎ 800/275-8700 or logging onto www.usps.com.

At press time, domestic postage rates were 27¢ for a postcard and 42¢ for a letter. For international mail, a first-class letter of up to 1 ounce costs 94¢ (72¢ to Canada and Mexico); a first-class postcard costs the same as a letter. For more information, go to www.usps.com and click on "calculate postage."

PARKING   Parking can be a nightmare, and regulations are vigorously enforced throughout the city. The streets around Michigan Avenue have no-parking restrictions during rush hour—believe me, your car will be towed immediately. Many neighborhoods have adopted resident-only parking that prohibits others from parking on their streets, usually after 6pm each day (even all day in a few areas, such as Old Town). The neighborhood around Wrigley Field is off-limits during Cubs night games, so look for yellow sidewalk signs alerting drivers about the dozen-and-a-half times the Cubs play under lights. The very best parking deal in the Loop is the city-run **East Monroe Garage** (www.grantparkparking.com), which charges $13 for 12 hours or fewer (enter on Columbus St., just east of Michigan Ave., and just south of E. Randolph St.).

PASSES   The Chicago **CityPass** gets you into the city's biggest attractions (The Art Institute, Field Museum of Natural History, Shedd Aquarium, Adler Planetarium, Museum of Science and Industry, and Hancock Observatory) at a 50% discount over the museums' individual admission fees. The cost at press time was $59 for adults and $49 for kids. You can buy a CityPass (valid for 9 days from its first use) at any of the museums listed above, or purchase one online before you get to town (www.city pass.com).

PASSPORTS **For Residents of Australia:** You can pick up an application from your local post office or any branch of Passports Australia, but you must schedule an interview at the passport office to present your application materials. Call the **Australian Passport Information Service** at ☎ 131-232, or visit the government website at **www. passports.gov.au**.

For Residents of Canada: Passport applications are available at travel agencies throughout Canada or from the central **Passport Office,** Department of Foreign Affairs and International Trade, Ottawa, ON K1A 0G3 (☎ 800/567-6868; www.ppt. gc.ca). *Note:* Canadian children who travel must have their own passport. However, if you hold a valid Canadian passport issued before December 11, 2001, that bears the name of your child, the passport remains valid for you and your child until it expires.

For Residents of Ireland: You can apply for a 10-year passport at the **Passport Office,** Setanta Centre, Molesworth Street, Dublin 2 (☎ 01/671-1633; www.irlgov.ie/iveagh). Those under age 18 and over 65 must apply for a 3-year passport. You can also apply at 1A South Mall, Cork (☎ 021/272-525), or at most main post offices.

For Residents of New Zealand: You can pick up a passport application at any New Zealand Passports Office or download it from their website. Contact the **Passports Office** at ☎ 0800/225-050 in New Zealand or 04/474-8100, or log on to **www.passports.govt.nz**.

For Residents of the United Kingdom: To pick up an application for a standard 10-year passport (5-yr. passport for children under 16), visit your nearest passport office, major post office, or travel agency, or contact the **United Kingdom Passport Service** at ☎ 0870/521-0410, or search its website at **www.ukpa.gov.uk**.

International visitors should always keep a photocopy of their passport with them when traveling. If your passport is lost or stolen, having a copy significantly facilitates the reissuing process at a local consulate or embassy. Keep your passport and other valuables in your room's safe or in the hotel safe.

PHARMACIES Located on the Magnificent Mile just south of the Water Tower, **Walgreens,** 757 N. Michigan Ave. at Chicago Avenue (☎ 312/664-4000; www.walgreens.com), is open 24 hours.

SAFETY Chicago has all the crime problems of any urban center, so use your common sense and stay cautious and alert. After dark, try to stick to well-lighted streets along the Magnificent Mile, River North, Gold Coast, and Lincoln Park, which are all high-traffic areas, even late into the night. Avoid such neighborhoods as Hyde Park, Wicker Park (beyond the busy intersection of Milwaukee, Damen, and North aves.), and Pilsen, which border more troublesome areas. Don't walk on empty streets alone at night, even those that seem perfectly safe. Muggings can—and do—happen anywhere. When in doubt, ask your hotel's concierge.

The El is generally quite safe, even at night, although some of the downtown stations can feel eerily deserted late in the evening. Buses are a safe option, too, especially nos. 146 and 151, which pick up along North Michigan Avenue and State Street and connect to the North Side via Lincoln Park.

SHOPPING   Shops generally keep normal business hours, 10am to 6pm Monday through Saturday. Most stores stay open late at least 1 evening a week, usually on Thursday. Certain shops, such as bookstores, stay open during the evening hours all week. Most shops and malls (other than those in the Loop) open on Sunday, usually from noon to 5pm. Malls generally stay open to 7pm the rest of the week. Note that the local sales tax, a steep 10.25%, is the highest of all major cities in the United States.

SPECTATOR SPORTS   Chicago fans are nothing if not loyal, and, for that reason, attending a home game in any sport is an uplifting experience. The **Chicago Bears** (☎ 847/295-6600; www.chicagobears.com) are not the celebrated NFL team of the past, but that doesn't stop locals from partying out at Soldier Field in freezing "Bear Weather."

The **Chicago Bulls** (☎ 312/455-4000) aren't the NBA team of Michael Jordan's heyday, but on the plus side, it's a lot easier to get tickets. The NHL's **Chicago Blackhawks** (☎ 312/455-7000; www.chicago blackhawks.com) have a devoted, impassioned following of fans who work themselves into a frenzy despite the lack of on-ice heroics.

Baseball and Chicago share a checkered past (the city's best known for the 1919 "Black Sox" scandal and the perennially losing Cubs). Still, no matter how poorly the **Chicago Cubs** (☎ 773/404-CUBS; www.cubs.mlb.com) are doing in the standings, a trip out to Wrigley Field is a special Chicago experience and tickets go fast; most weekend and night games are sold out by Memorial Day. The **Chicago White Sox** (☎ 312/674-1000; www.whitesox.mlb.com) don't command the kind of loyalty the Cubs do, but do offer a brand-new stadium and obtainable tickets.

TAXES   The local sales tax is 10.25%. Restaurants in the central part of the city, roughly the 312 area code, are taxed an additional 1%, for a total of 11.25%. The hotel room tax is a steep 15.4%.

TAXIS   See "By Taxi" in "Getting Around," above.

TELEPHONES   For **directory assistance** ("information"), dial 411. Hotel surcharges on long-distance and local calls are astronomical, so you're usually better off using a **cell** or **public pay telephone,** which you'll find clearly marked in most public buildings and private establishments as well as on the street. **Local calls** made from public pay phones in Chicago usually cost 50¢. Pay phones do not accept pennies, and none will take anything larger than a quarter.

TICKETS   Theater tickets should always be obtained as far in advance as possible; if you're set on seeing the latest touring Broadway production, you might need to book up to 3 months in advance. Tickets for most major Chicago events are sold through **Ticketmaster** (☎ 312/559-1212; www.ticketmaster.com). **Hot Tix** (☎ 312/554-9800; www.hottix.org), operated by the League of Chicago Theatres, sells same-day, half-price tickets. For more information on buying discount tickets in advance, see p 127.

TIPPING   In hotels, tip **bellhops** at least $1 per bag and tip the **chamber staff** $1 to $2 per day (more if you've left a disaster area). Tip the **doorman** or **concierge** only if he or she has provided you with some specific service (for example, calling a cab for you or obtaining difficult-to-get theater tickets). Tip the **valet-parking attendant** $1 every time you get your car.

In restaurants, bars, and nightclubs, tip **service staff** 15% to 20% of the check, tip **bartenders** 10% to 15%, tip **checkroom attendants** $1 per garment, and tip **valet-parking attendants** $1 per vehicle.

As for other service personnel, tip **cab drivers** 15% of the fare; tip **skycaps** at airports at least $1 per bag; and tip **hairdressers** and **barbers** 15% to 20%.

TOILETS   You won't find public toilets or restrooms on the streets. Your best bet for good, clean facilities are hotel lobbies, bars, fast-food restaurants, museums, and department stores. If possible, avoid toilets at parks and beaches, which tend to be dirty.

TOURIST OFFICES   The main **Chicago Office of Tourism Visitor Center** (☎ 877/CHICAGO or TTY 866/710-0294; www.877chicago.com) is on the first floor of the Chicago Cultural Center, 77 E. Randolph St. (at Michigan Ave.).

The smaller **Chicago Water Works Visitor Center** is in the heart of the city's shopping district, in the old pumping station at Michigan and Chicago avenues.

The **Illinois Bureau of Tourism** operates an information desk in the lobby of the James R. Thompson Center (☎ 312/814-9600), 100 W. Randolph St.

TOURIST TRAPS & SCAMS   If you're planning on attending sporting or concert events, beware of ticket scalpers. Buy your tickets in advance from a legitimate source, as many of the tickets sold by scalpers are counterfeit.

TOURS   **Gray Line** (☎ 800/621-4153 or 312/251-3107; www.grayline.com) offers several orientation and neighborhood tours of the city in well-appointed buses. Tours run $25 to $40.

The **Chicago Greeter** (☎ 312/744-8000; www.chicagogreeter.com) program matches tourists with local Chicagoans who serve as volunteer guides. Visitors may request a specific neighborhood or theme (everything from Polish heritage sites to Chicago movie locations), and a greeter gives them a free, 2- to 4-hour tour. (Greeters won't escort groups of more than six people.) Specific requests should be made at least a week in advance.

Chicago Trolley Company (☎ 773/648-5000; www.chicagotrolley.com) offers guided tours on a fleet of rubber-wheeled "San Francisco–style" trolleys that stop at a number of popular spots around the city. You can stay on for the full 1½-hour ride or get on and off at each stop. An all-day hop-on, hop-off pass costs $29 adults, $21 seniors, and $19 kids 3 to 11.

Started in 1935, **Wendella Sightseeing Boats** (☎ 312/337-1446; www.wendellaboats.com) operates a 1-hour tour along the Chicago River and a 1½-hour tour along the river and out onto Lake Michigan. Tours run April to October. Tickets cost $23 adults, $21 seniors, $12 kids under 12.

TRAVELERS WITH DISABILITIES   Most of Chicago's sidewalks, as well as major museums and tourist attractions, are fitted with wheelchair ramps. Many hotels provide special accommodations for visitors in wheelchairs, such as ramps and large bathrooms, as well as telecommunications devices for visitors with hearing impairments; enquire when you make your reservation.

Pace Bus offers door-to-door lift services to and from O'Hare International Airport for travelers with disabilities. One week's notice is required, and visitors must be registered with a similar program in their home city. For information, call ☎ 800/606-1282, or visit www.pacebus.com.

Several of the **Chicago Transit Authority's (CTA's)** El stations on each line are fitted with elevators. Call the CTA at ☎ 312/836-7000 for a list of those that are accessible. All city buses are equipped to accommodate wheelchairs.

Horizons for the Blind, 2 N. Williams St., Crystal Lake, IL 60014 (☎ **815/444-8800**), is a social-service agency that can provide information about local hotels equipped with Braille signage and cultural attractions that offer Braille signage and special tours. The **Illinois Relay Center** enables hearing- and speech-impaired TTY callers to call individuals or businesses without TTYs 24 hours a day. Calls are confidential and billed at regular phone rates. Call TTY at ☎ **800/526-0844** or voice 800/526-0857. The city of Chicago operates a 24-hour information service for hearing-impaired callers with TTY equipment; call ☎ **312/744-8599**.

For specific information on facilities for people with disabilities, call or write the **Mayor's Office for People with Disabilities,** 121 N. LaSalle St., Room 1104, Chicago, IL 60602 (☎ **312/744-7050** for voice; 312/744-4964 for TTY).

WEATHER For current weather conditions and the National Weather Service's forecast, dial ☎ **312/976-1212** (for a fee), or check the weather online at www.chicago tribune.com or www.weather.com.

Chicago: A Brief History

1673 French explorers Marquette and Joliet discover portage at Chicago linking the Great Lakes region with the Mississippi River valley.

1779 Afro-French-Canadian trapper Jean Baptiste Point du Sable establishes a trading post on the north bank of the Chicago River. A settlement follows 2 years later.

1818 Illinois is admitted to the Union as the 21st state.

1833 Town of Chicago is officially incorporated, with little more than 300 residents.

1837 Chicago is incorporated as a city, with about 4,000 residents.

1847 *Chicago Tribune* begins publishing.

1848 The 96-mile (154km) Illinois and Michigan Canal is opened, linking the Great Lakes with the Mississippi River.

1865 Chicago stockyards are founded.

1871 Great Chicago Fire burns large sections of the city; rebuilding begins while the ashes are still warm.

1882 The 10-story Montauk Building, the world's first skyscraper, is erected.

1885 William Le Baron Jenney's nine-story Home Insurance Building, the world's first steel-frame skyscraper, is built.

1886 Dynamite bomb explodes during a political rally near Haymarket Square, causing a riot in which eight policemen and four civilians are killed, and almost 100 are wounded.

1892 The city's first elevated train goes into operation.

1893 Chicago hosts its first World's Fair, the World's Columbian Exposition.

1900 The flow of the Chicago River is reversed to end the dumping of sewage into Lake Michigan.

1919 "Black Sox" bribery scandal perpetrated by eight Chicago White Sox players stuns baseball.

1920–33 During Prohibition, Chicago becomes a "wide-open town"; rival mobs battle violently throughout the city for control of distribution and sale of illegal alcohol.

1924 University of Chicago students Nathan Leopold and Richard Loeb murder 14-year-old Bobby Franks. They are defended by famed attorney Clarence Darrow in the "Trial of the Century."

1929 On St. Valentine's Day, Al Capone's gang murders seven members of rival George "Bugs" Moran's crew in a Clark Street garage.

1931 Al Capone finally goes to jail for tax evasion.

1933 Chicago Mayor Anton Cermak, on a political trip to Miami, is shot and killed during an attempt on president-elect FDR's life.

1933–34 Chicago hosts its second World's Fair, "A Century of Progress."

1934 Bank robber and "Public Enemy Number One" John Dillinger is gunned down by police outside the Biograph Theater.

1942 Scientists, led by Enrico Fermi, create the world's first nuclear chain reaction under Stagg Field at the University of Chicago.

1953 Chicago native Hugh Hefner starts publishing *Playboy* (the original Playboy Mansion was located in Chicago's Gold Coast neighborhood).

1955 Richard J. Daley begins term as mayor; he is widely regarded as the "last of the big-city bosses."

1966 Civil rights leader Martin Luther King, Jr., moves to Chicago to lead a fair housing campaign.

1968 Anti–Vietnam War protests in conjunction with the Democratic National Convention end in police riot and a "shoot to kill" order by Mayor Richard J. Daley.

1974 The 1,454-foot Sears Tower is completed, becoming the tallest building in the world.

1979 Jane Byrne becomes the first woman elected mayor of Chicago.

1983 Harold Washington becomes the first African-American mayor of Chicago.

1986 The Chicago Bears win their only Super Bowl.

1989 Richard M. Daley, the son of the long-serving mayor, is elected mayor.

1996 The city patches up its turbulent political history by hosting the Democratic National Convention, its first national political gathering in 3 decades.

2001 Chicago's second airport, Midway, opens a new $800-million terminal.

2004 Millennium Park, Chicago's largest public works project in decades, opens at the north end of Grant Park.

2007 Spertus Museum, 610 S. Michigan Ave. (☎ 312/322-1747), added another example of eye-catching architecture to Michigan Avenue with the opening of its new building dedicated to Jewish history, art and culture in fall 2007.

2008 Trump International Hotel and Tower opens at 401 N. Wabash Ave. The 92-story building becomes the second-tallest in Chicago, after the Sears Tower.

Chicago's Architecture

Although the Great Chicago Fire leveled almost 3 square miles (2.6 sq. km) of the downtown area in 1871, it did clear the stage for Chicago's emergence as the country's pre-eminent city for architecture.

To learn more about Chicago's architecture, take a tour by foot, boat, or bus with the Chicago Architecture Foundation. (See p 14, ❶.)

Richardsonian Romanesque (1870–1900)

Boston-based architect Henry Hobson Richardson (1838–86) explored designs and forms based on the Romanesque (a style distinguished by rounded arches, thick walls, and small windows). His structures, ranging from university and civic buildings to railroad stations and homes, were marked by a simplification of form and the elimination of extraneous ornament and historical detail—features that set his buildings apart from others of the period.

The overall effect depended on mass, volume, and scale.

Richardsonian Romanesque buildings share the following characteristics:

- A massive quality

- Arched entrances

- Squat towers

- Deeply recessed porches and doorways

- Heavy masonry exteriors

- Use of rough-hewn stone

Richardson's **John J. Glessner House,** 1800 S. Prairie Ave. (1885–87), an elegant urban residence, still stands on Chicago's near South Side. It had a strong influence on Chicago architects, notably Louis Sullivan. The most celebrated example of Richardson's influence is the **Auditorium Building,** 430 S. Michigan Ave. (1887–89), an important early example of the emerging Chicago skyscraper.

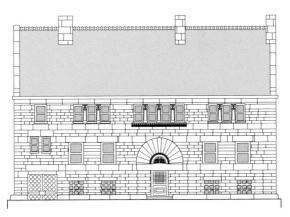

John J. Glessner House

Early Skyscrapers (1880–1920)

Experimentation with cast and wrought iron in the construction of interior skeletons in the 1840s eventually allowed buildings to rise to previously unattainable heights. Following the Great Chicago Fire of 1871, important technical innovations—involving safety elevators, electricity, fireproofing, foundations, plumbing, and telecommunications—combined with advances in skeletal construction to create a new building type, the skyscraper. These buildings were spacious, cost-effective, efficient, and quickly erected—in short, the perfect architectural solution for Chicago's growing downtown.

Solving the technical problems of the skyscraper did not resolve how the building should look. Most solutions relied on historical precedents, including decoration reminiscent of the Romanesque, with its rounded arches; Gothic, with its spires, pointy arches, and even buttresses; or Beaux Arts, with its exuberant classical details. Louis Sullivan (1865–1924) was the first to formalize a vision of a tall building based on the parts of a classical column. His theories inspired the **Chicago school of architecture,** examples of which still fill the city's downtown.

Features of the Chicago school include:

- A rectangular shape with a flat roof
- Tripartite divisions of the facade similar to that of a classical column with a base (usually of two stories), shaft (midsection with a repetitive window pattern), and capital (typically an elaborate, terra cotta cornice)
- Exterior expression of the building's interior skeleton through an emphasis on horizontal and vertical elements

- Large windows made possible by the development of load-bearing interior skeletons; particularly popular are Chicago windows (large windows flanked by two narrow ones with double-hung sashes)
- Use of terra cotta, a light and fireproof material that could be cast in any shape and attached to the exterior, often for decoration

A good example of the development of the skyscraper is the **Monadnock Building,** 53 W. Jackson Blvd. (1889–93). Built in two parts, the northern section has masonry load-bearing walls, while the southern half has a steel frame clad in terra cotta. To support its 17 stories, the northern section has 6-foot-thick (1.8m) walls at its base. The entire building is notable for its clean, contemporary lines.

An excellent example of the Chicago school is the recently restored **Reliance Building** (p 10, ⑤), now Hotel Burnham (p 139), 1 W. Washington St. (1891–95), outstanding for its use of glass and decorative spandrels (the horizontal panel below a window).

A good later example (taller and more technically sophisticated than its earlier incarnations) that most visitors will pass at some point during their visit is the **Tribune Tower,** 435 N. Michigan Ave. (1923–25).

Second Renaissance Revival (1890–1920)

Buildings in this style show a definite studied formalism. A relative faithfulness to Renaissance precedents of window and doorway treatments distinguish it from the much looser adaptations of the Italianate, a mid-19th-century style that took its inspiration from Italian architecture. Scale and size, in turn, set the Second Renaissance Revival apart from the first, which occurred from about 1840 to 1890. The grand buildings of the Second Renaissance Revival, with their textural richness, well suited the tastes of the wealthy Gilded Age. The style was used primarily on the East Coast but also in Chicago for swank town houses, government buildings, and private clubs.

Typical features include:

- A cubelike structure with a massive, imposing quality

- Symmetrical arrangement of the facade, including distinct horizontal divisions

- A different stylistic treatment for each floor, with different column capitals, finishes, and window treatments on each level

- Use of rustification (masonry cut in massive blocks and separated from each other by deep joints) on the lowest floor

- The mixing of Greek and Roman styles on the same facade (Roman arches and arcades may appear with Greek-style windows with straight-heads or pediments, a low-pitched triangular feature above a window, door, or pavilion)

- A cornice (a projecting feature along the roofline) supported by large brackets

- A balustrade (a railing supported by a series of short posts) above the cornice

A fine example of this style is the **Chicago Cultural Center** (p 19, ❶), 78 E. Washington St. (1897), originally built as a public library. This tasteful edifice, with its sumptuous decor, was constructed in part to help secure Chicago's reputation as a culture-conscious city.

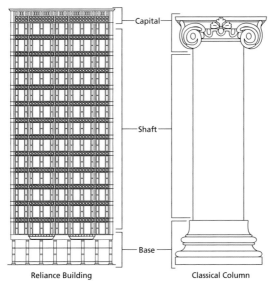

Capital

Shaft

Base

Reliance Building   Classical Column

Reliance Building and Classical Column

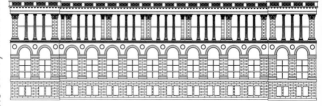

Chicago Cultural Center

Beaux Arts (1890–1920)

This style takes its name from the Ecole des Beaux-Arts in Paris, where a number of prominent American architects (including H. H. Richardson and Louis Sullivan) received their training, beginning around the mid–19th century. These architects adopted the academic principles of the Ecole, which emphasized the study of Greek and Roman structures, composition, and symmetry, and the creation of elaborate presentation drawings. Because of the idealized origins and grandiose use of classical forms, the Beaux Arts in America was seen as the ideal style for expressing civic pride.

Grandiose compositions, an exuberance of detail, and a variety of stone finishes typify most Beaux Arts structures. Particular features include:

- A pronounced cornice topped by a parapet (a low wall), balustrade, or attic story
- Projecting pavilions, often with colossal columns grouped in pairs
- Windows framed by free-standing columns, a sill with a balustrade, and pediments or decorative keystones (the central stone of an arch)
- Grand staircases
- Grand arched openings
- Classical decoration: free-standing statuary, ornamental panels, swags, and medallions

Chicago has several Beaux Arts buildings, exhibiting the style's main features. Examples include the oldest part of the **Art Institute of Chicago,** Michigan Avenue at Adams Street, which was built for the World's Columbian Exposition in 1893; and the gleaming white **Wrigley Building,** 400–410 N. Michigan Ave. (1919–24), which serves as a gateway to North Michigan Avenue.

Art Deco (1925–33)

Art Deco is a decorative style that took its name from the Exposition Internationale des Arts Décoratif, held in Paris in 1925. One of the first widely accepted styles not based on historic precedents (the jazzy style embodied the idea of modernity), it influenced all areas of design, from jewelry and household goods to cars, trains, and ocean liners.

Art Deco buildings are characterized by a linear, hard edge or angular composition, often with a vertical emphasis and highlighted with stylized decoration. The Chicago zoning ordinance of 1923, which required setbacks in buildings above a certain height to ensure that light and air could reach the street, gave Art Deco skyscrapers their distinctive profile. Other important features include:

- An emphasis on geometric form
- Strips of windows with decorated spandrels, adding to the sense of verticality

- Use of hard-edged, low-relief ornamentation around doors and windows

- Frequent use of marble and black and silver tones

- Decorative motifs of parallel straight lines, zigzags, chevrons (see illustration at left), and stylized florals

Prime examples of this period include the **Chicago Board of Trade,** 141 W. Jackson Blvd. (1930), with its dramatic facade and pyramidal roof; and **135 S. LaSalle St.** (1934), which has a magnificent Art Deco lobby.

International Style (1932–45)

The International Style was popularized in the United States after 1932 through the teachings and designs of Ludwig Mies van der Rohe (1886–1969), a German émigré who taught and practiced architecture in Chicago after leaving the progressive Bauhaus school of design. Structures all shared a stark simplicity and vigorous functionalism, a definite break from historically based, decorative styles. Interpretations of the "Miesian" International Style were built in most U.S. cities as late as 1980. In the 1950s, erecting an office building in this mode made companies appear progressive. In later decades, after the International Style was a corporate mainstay, the style took on conservative connotations.

Features of the International Style as popularized by Mies van der Rohe include:

- A rectangular shape

- Frequent use of glass

- Balance and regularity, but not symmetry

- Horizontal bands of windows

- Windows meeting at corners

- Absence of ornamentation

- Clear expression of the building's form and function (the interior structure of stacked office floors is clearly visible, as are the locations of mechanical systems, such as elevator shafts and air-conditioning units)

- Placement, or cantilevering, of building on tall piers

Some famous Mies van der Rohe designs are the **Chicago Federal Center,** Dearborn Street between Adams Street and Jackson Boulevard (1959–74), and **860–880 N. Lake Shore Dr.** (1949–51). Interesting interpretations of the style by Skidmore, Owings & Merrill, a Chicago firm that helped make the International Style a corporate staple, are the **Sears Tower** (1968–74), and the **John Hancock Center** (1969; p 34, **5**)—two impressive engineering feats rising to 110 and 100 stories, respectively.

Postmodern (1975–90)

Postmodernism burst on the scene in the 1970s with the reintroduction of historical precedents in architecture. With many feeling that the office towers of the previous

CHICAGO BOARD OF TRADE

Chicago Board of Trade

style were too cold, postmodernists began to incorporate classical details and recognizable forms into their designs—often applied in outrageous proportions.

Postmodern skyscrapers tend to include:

- An overall shape (or incorporation) of a recognizable object not necessarily associated with architecture

- Classical details, such as columns, domes, or vaults, often oversize and used in inventive ways

- A distinctive profile in the skyline

- Use of stone rather than glass

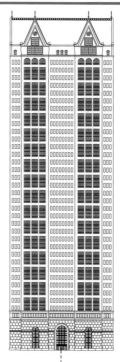

190 S. LaSalle Street (1987) brings the shape of a famous Chicago building back to the skyline. The overall design is that of the 1892 Masonic Temple (now razed), complete with the tripartite divisions of the Chicago school. An extremely modern interpretation of a three-part skyscraper—but you have to look for the divisions to find them—is **333 W. Wacker Drive** (1979–83; p 28, ❸), an elegant, green-glass structure that curves along a bend in the Chicago River.

190 S. LaSalle Street

Toll-Free Numbers & Websites

Airlines

AER LINGUS
☎ 800/474-7424 in the U.S.
☎ 01/886-8888 in Ireland
www.aerlingus.com

AIR CANADA
☎ 888/247-2262
www.aircanada.ca

AIR NEW ZEALAND
☎ 0800/737-767 in New Zealand
www.airnewzealand.com

AIRTRAN AIRLINES
☎ 800/247-8726
www.airtran.com

AMERICAN AIRLINES
☎ 800/433-7300
www.aa.com

ATA AIRLINES
☎ 800/1-FLY-ATA
www.ata.com

BRITISH AIRWAYS
☎ 800/247-9297
☎ 0345/222-111 or 0845/77-333-77 in Britain
www.british-airways.com

CONTINENTAL AIRLINES
☎ 800/525-0280
www.continental.com

DELTA AIR LINES
☎ 800/221-1212
www.delta.com

FRONTIER AIRLINES
☎ 800/432-1359
www.frontierairlines.com

NORTHWEST AIRLINES
☎ 800/225-2525
www.nwa.com

QANTAS
☎ 800/227-4500 in the U.S.
☎ 13 13 13 in Australia
www.qantas.com

SOUTHWEST AIRLINES
☎ 800/435-9792
www.southwest.com

UNITED AIRLINES
☎ 800/241-6522
www.united.com

US AIRWAYS
☎ 800/428-4322
www.usairways.com

Car-Rental Agencies

ALAMO
☎ 800/327-9633
www.goalamo.com

AVIS
☎ 800/331-1212 in the
continental U.S.
☎ 800/TRY-AVIS in Canada
www.avis.com

BUDGET
☎ 800/527-0700
www.budget.com

DOLLAR
☎ 800/800-4000
www.dollar.com

ENTERPRISE
☎ 800/325-8007
www.enterprise.com

HERTZ
☎ 800/654-3131
www.hertz.com

NATIONAL
☎ 800/CAR-RENT
www.nationalcar.com

THRIFTY
☎ 800/367-2277
www.thrifty.com

Major Hotel & Motel Chains

BEST WESTERN INTERNATIONAL
☎ 800/528-1234
www.bestwestern.com

COMFORT INNS
☎ 800/228-5150
www.hotelchoice.com

CROWNE PLAZA HOTELS
☎ 888/303-1746
www.crowneplaza.com

EMBASSY SUITES
☎ 800/EMBASSY
www.embassysuites.com

FOUR SEASONS
☎ 800/819-5053
www.fourseasons.com

HILTON HOTELS
☎ 800/HILTONS
www.hilton.com

HOLIDAY INN
☎ 800/HOLIDAY
www.ichotelsgroup.com

HOWARD JOHNSON
☎ 800/654-2000
www.hojo.com

HYATT HOTELS & RESORTS
☎ 800/228-9000
www.hyatt.com

INTER-CONTINENTAL HOTELS &
RESORTS
☎ 888/567-8725
www.ichotelsgroup.com

LOEWS HOTELS
☎ 800/23LOEWS
www.loewshotels.com

MARRIOTT HOTELS
☎ 800/228-9290
www.marriott.com

OMNI
☎ 800/THEOMNI
www.omnihotels.com

RADISSON HOTELS INTERNATIONAL
☎ 800/333-3333
www.radisson.com

RITZ-CARLTON
☎ 800/241-3333
www.ritzcarlton.com

SHERATON HOTELS & RESORTS
☎ 800/325-3535
www.sheraton.com

WESTIN HOTELS & RESORTS
☎ 800/937-8461
www.westin.com

Index

See also Accommodations and Restaurant indexes, below.